LAW AND PHILOSOPHY IN THE LATE ROMAN REPUBLIC

The middle of the second until the middle of the first century BCE is one of the most creative periods in the history of human thought, and an important part of this was the interaction between Roman jurists and Hellenistic philosophers. In this highly original book, René Brouwer shows how jurists transformed the study of law into a science with the help of philosophical methods and concepts, such as division, rules and persons, and also how philosophers came to share the jurists' preoccupations with cases and private property. The relevance of this cross-fertilization for present-day law and philosophy cannot be overestimated: in law, its legacy includes the academic study of law and the Western models of dispute resolution, while in philosophy, the method of casuistry and the concept of just property.

RENÉ BROUWER teaches philosophy and law at the University of Utrecht. He has published on a variety of subjects in the philosophy and history of law as well as in ancient philosophy, including *The Stoic Sage* (Cambridge, 2014).

Bust of Carneades(?). Rome, Museo Torlonia, inv. 63. Photo: DAI Rom (C. Faraglia), neg. D-DAI-Rome 34.177.

LAW AND PHILOSOPHY IN THE LATE ROMAN REPUBLIC

RENÉ BROUWER

University of Utrecht, The Netherlands

CAMBRIDGE
UNIVERSITY PRESS

CAMBRIDGE
UNIVERSITY PRESS

University Printing House, Cambridge CB2 8BS, United Kingdom

One Liberty Plaza, 20th Floor, New York, NY 10006, USA

477 Williamstown Road, Port Melbourne, VIC 3207, Australia

314–321, 3rd Floor, Plot 3, Splendor Forum, Jasola District Centre, New Delhi – 110025, India

79 Anson Road, #06–04/06, Singapore 079906

Cambridge University Press is part of the University of Cambridge.

It furthers the University's mission by disseminating knowledge in the pursuit of education, learning, and research at the highest international levels of excellence.

www.cambridge.org
Information on this title: www.cambridge.org/9781108491488
DOI: 10.1017/9781108868907

First published 2021

Printed in the United Kingdom by TJ Books Limited, Padstow Cornwall

A catalogue record for this publication is available from the British Library.

Library of Congress Cataloging-in-Publication Data
NAMES: Brouwer, René, author.
TITLE: Law and philosophy in the late Roman Republic / René Brouwer, Universiteit Utrecht, The Netherlands.
DESCRIPTION: Cambridge, United Kingdom ; New York, NY : Cambridge University Press, 2021. | Includes bibliographical references and index.
IDENTIFIERS: LCCN 2021011678 (print) | LCCN 2021011679 (ebook) | ISBN 9781108491488 (hardback) | ISBN 9781108798341 (paperback) | ISBN 9781108868907 (epub)
SUBJECTS: LCSH: Roman law—Philosophy. | Philosophy, Ancient—Influence. | Rome—History—Republic, 265–30 B.C.
CLASSIFICATION: LCC KJA172 .B76 2021 (print) | LCC KJA172 (ebook) | DDC 340.5/4—dc23
LC record available at https://lccn.loc.gov/2021011678
LC ebook record available at https://lccn.loc.gov/2021011679

ISBN 978-1-108-49148-8 Hardback

Table of contents

Preface

This is a book about how much law and philosophy as emerging disciplines owe to each other. It has been written for jurists and philosophers alike, and indeed all others who are interested in the developments of these disciplines in late Republican Rome, and well beyond. It is thus neither just a book on philosophy for jurists nor – much rarer – a book on law for philosophers. The writing of this book has been something of a balancing act, in finding the right approach for these audiences with their different outlooks and expectations.

In the years that I worked on the book, I was fortunate enough to have been able to try out earlier versions of the chapters with classicists, ancient philosophers, philosophers as well as historians of science, legal historians (including the Romanists of the Société Internationale pour l'Histoire des Droits de l'Antiquité), and jurists. Earlier versions of the chapters were presented in Amsterdam, Brussels, Groningen, Guildford, Istanbul, Moscow, Naples, Nijmegen, Tübingen and Utrecht. It would be impossible to list here all those who by their questions and remarks on these always joyful occasions helped me to develop and clarify my thoughts further, but I am truly grateful to all who did.

For their written comments and encouragements I would like to thank Thomas Finkenauer, Malcolm Schofield, Emmanuele Vimercati and especially Francesco Giglio. I am furthermore grateful for the written exchanges with Dmitry Dozhdev on how to evaluate the 2nd century CE historian Pomponius as a source for the legal developments in the late Roman Republic, and with Antonia Lolordo for making me think again about the notion of person. Earlier versions of sections 5.2–5 of Chapter 5 have been published in 2019 in her volume on persons in Christia Mercer's exciting Oxford Philosophical Concepts series; they are used here in a somewhat modified form with kind permission from Oxford University Press, New York. Further words of thanks should go to Alice van Harten, who helped me with the structure of the book, to Jörn

Mixdorf, who read the different versions of the chapters so carefully and supportively, and to Suzy Masson, who looked into my English. At the Press, Michael Sharp's enthusiasm and efficient dealings with the development of the book is acknowledged with much pleasure. With their constructive comments, the anonymous readers for the Press enabled me to develop my thoughts further: I am tremendously grateful to them.

Unfortunately, no portraits explicitly attributed to the protagonists responsible for the interaction between law and philosophy in the late Roman Republic have survived. The portrait on the frontispiece is traditionally ascribed to the Academic philosopher Carneades of Cyrene, one of the three philosophers sent by the Athenians as ambassadors to Rome in 155 BCE. This attribution cannot be correct, however: it does not resemble the other busts that are extant with his name inscribed on them (Schefold 1943, 140–1). With three copies surviving in Rome, he must have been a popular figure among the Roman elite. Two copies can be found in the Vatican museums; the third and 'best' (Dillon 2006, 152) copy belongs to the Torlonia collection (Visconti 1884–1885, no. 63, pl. 16; not in Settis and Gasparri 2020) and is shown here in C. Faraglia's picture (Neg. 34.1777) from the archives of the German Archeological Institute in Rome. According to Zanker (1995, 185), this portrait represents a Stoic from the late second century BCE, possibly Panaetius of Rhodes, the most famous of all the Stoics who visited Rome in late Republican times, and who – unlike Carneades – was one of the protagonists responsible for the interaction between law and philosophy: his closely shorn beard resembles that of Chrysippus, the second head of the Stoic school, but his unusual large eyes give him a more straightforward and pragmatic appearance. Whereas the uncertainties about the attribution are already a fitting expression of the difficulties that go with the study of law and philosophy in the late Roman Republic (the portrait could just as well be that of another famous Roman Stoic, such as Carneades' colleague-ambassador Diogenes of Babylon or Panaetius' pupil Hecato of Rhodes), the portrait itself can be taken to represent the cross-fertilisation between the striving for wisdom of the Hellenistic thinkers on the one hand and the pragmatism of the Roman jurists on the other.

CHAPTER 1

Introduction

1.1 Interaction

The subject of this book is the interaction between Roman jurists and Hellenistic philosophers from the middle of the second century until the middle of the 1st century BCE, an interaction which is perhaps one of the most creative in the history of human thought and which had a lasting influence both in law and in philosophy.[1] As a result, modes of thinking in both law and philosophy were developed that are now often taken for granted. This study therefore has a twofold aim: first, to offer an account of the interaction as such, and second, to rethink the present and bring about an awareness of the choices that have been made, relating not only to the methods of resolving legal disputes and of doing philosophy but also to the subjects considered worthy of attention in both disciplines.

Whereas the influence of the Romans on the Greeks started in the second century, the influence of the Greeks on the Romans is part of a longer tradition. Already prior to Alexander the Great (356–323 BCE[2]) conquering the Eastern part of the Mediterranean world, the Romans showed a keen interest in the Greeks. Here, the Romans differed from most Mediterranean people, with the exception of the Etruscans.[3] This influence can be discerned in religion and literature, but also to an extent in law and in philosophy. As for religion and literature, the Romans were clearly fascinated by Greek mythology: the beginnings of Roman literature, from 240 BCE onwards, has even been characterised as a translation of the Greek myths into Latin.[4]

[1] Rawson 1985, 214, Bryen 2014, 359.
[2] Dates of historical figures (as well as the ancient authors) will be given where they are first mentioned in the text.
[3] Momigliano 1971, 12–22, Humm 2018, 200–2.
[4] Feeney 2016, cf. Suerbaum 2002, 25–29, Manuwald 2011, 15–20, Bettini 2012, McElduff 2013.

In law, even though modern scholars tend to question the historicity of the (later) accounts of a Roman embassy to Athens in 452 BCE,[5] Greek influence (via the Greek colonies in Southern Italy) on the statute of the Twelve Tables is generally accepted. This statute, inspired by Greek example, is best regarded as a solution to the social tensions that existed between the patrician and plebeian classes.[6]

With regard to philosophy, a later Roman tradition has it that Pythagoras was a particular influence on Rome's second king, Numa.[7] This is impossible for chronological reasons: Numa, as Romulus' successor, must have died around 725 BCE, whereas Pythagoras was born around 570 BCE. As with the Twelve Tables, it seems more likely that this tradition came into being in the 4th century BCE, as a result of the contact between Romans and Pythagoreans in Southern Italy – here notable thinkers such as Archytas of Tarentum (*c.*427–348 BCE) spring to mind. The Romans would have been particularly interested in the Pythagorean notion of harmony: *homonoia* in Greek, or *concordia* in Latin. Towards the end of the 4th century, they put up a statue of Pythagoras,[8] and built a shrine to Concordia.[9] The story of Numa's Pythagorean philosophy is thought to originate within Rome itself: families that had risen to importance, such as the Aemilii and the Pinarii, justified their social position by claiming King Numa as their distinguished ancestor and at same time presenting him as an early follower of Pythagoras' doctrine of social harmony.[10]

In the 3rd century BCE, the influence of the Greeks on the Romans would become part of a broader pattern of what (after the 19th-century German historian Droysen) is referred to as the 'Hellenistic' age, in which Greek language and culture spread outwards and fused with other cultures in the Mediterranean world.[11] Although Droysen himself never clearly

[5] Livy (59 BCE–17 CE) 3.31.8, Pomponius (2nd century CE), *Handbook* in *Digest* 1.2.2.3–4; the sources are conveniently assembled in Düll 1995. For sceptical assessments of the influence of the Greeks, see e.g. Ruschenbusch 1963 and Wieacker 1971.

[6] Berger 1932,1940, Toher 1986, Cornell 1995, 275, Wolf 2015, Cascione 2018, Humm 2018, 96.

[7] Among the accounts, see e.g. Cicero, *Tusculan Disputations* 4.2 (Garbarino fr. 6), cf. Guibal 1937, 31.

[8] Pliny the Elder (23/4–79 CE), *Natural History* 34.26.

[9] Livy (59 BCE–17 CE) 9.46.6–7, Pliny the Elder, *Natural History* 33.19–20.

[10] The Aemilii changed their *cognomen* Mamercini into Mamerci, after Mamercus, the son of Numa, who would have been named after Marmakos, the son (or the father) of Pythagoras. See Plutarch (later first to early second century CE), *Life of Numa* 8.18–19, *Life of Aemilius Paullus* 2.1–2, cf. Humm 2005, 541–600, Russo 2005, Humm 2014, Humm 2017.

[11] Droysen 1836, 4–5: 'Osten und Westen waren zur Verschmelzung reif, schnell erfolgte von beiden Seiten Durchgährung und Umgestaltung. [. . .] Mag es uns erlaubt sein, dies neue

delineated the period, it is now usually understood as the period following the death of Alexander the Great in 323 BCE until Augustus' victory in the battle of Actium in 31 BCE, which marks the end of a century of civil war and the beginning of Imperial rule in Rome.

From the 2nd century BCE onwards the Romans started to exercise their own influence on the Greeks, at first militarily.[12] In the battle of Pydna in July 168 BCE, Lucius Aemilius Paullus (the father of Publius Cornelius Scipio Aemilianus Africanus, who we will encounter throughout this book) defeated Perseus, the last king of Macedonia, and the Greek city-states came under Rome's control.[13] Contact between Greeks and Romans intensified. Rome had not only become the political capital of the Mediterranean world; with the arrival of Hellenistic thinkers, it would also develop into an intellectual centre.

The interaction between Roman jurists and Hellenistic philosophers proved to be especially fertile. Under the influence of the Roman jurists, Hellenistic, especially Stoic, philosophers – among whom Diogenes of Babylon, Antipater of Tarsus, Panaetius of Rhodes and Hecaton of Rhodes should be mentioned – changed their outlook. They not only developed an interest in casuistry, but also devoted their attention to more mundane topics such as respect for private property. Under the influence of Hellenistic philosophers, Roman jurists started to rethink their own practice: with the help of the method of logic, and with abstract notions like rules and persons, the jurists started to study law on an abstract, 'scientific' level, getting to grasp with their legal output in a more systematic manner.

These developments in both philosophy and law were influential too. In law, under the influence of the philosophers, Republican jurists laid the foundations for the manner in which disputes are resolved on the European continent and beyond. In the first centuries of the Roman Empire, these Republican foundations were developed by what historians of Roman law refer to as the classical lawyers, who – yet again for teaching purposes – systematised the legal material further. In the 6th century CE, on the orders of the Byzantine Emperor Justinian (482–565), one of these systematisations of law was itself proclaimed to be law. In this Byzantine

weltgeschichtliche Prinzip mit dem Namen des Hellenistischen zu bezeichnen.' Cf. Schulz 1961, 7, Bichlin 1991, Scholz 2015, 13–14, Thonemann 2016, 6.

12 The reasons behind this expansion are much debated: did the Romans actively strive for an empire or had they simply become too important not to be drawn into an ever-expanding range of conflicts? For studies on Roman imperialism, see Garnsey and Whitaker 1978, Baronowski 2011, Erskine 2010, Griffin 2008, Schofield 2013, Atkins 2018, 166–91.

13 For a recent account see Waterfield 2014.

form, it would become the model for the codes in continental jurisdictions: in the early modern period, the Byzantine version of a teaching manual with its origins in the late Republican era would be adapted to time and place and thus become the basis for the different national codifications on the European continent.

As for the influence of Roman law on philosophy, the introduction of casuistry in philosophy would be lasting. In ethics, the focus of the Roman Stoics shifted from virtue as a perfect disposition to action and to the possible conflict between different courses of action. This shift would result in more modern forms of ethics, in which the main focus is, after all, on the evaluation of actions. Such an evaluation can be performed by considering the action in itself (particularism) or by applying an overall theory, with the help of which either the starting point of an action (as in Kant's deontology) or its result (as in Bentham's utilitarianism) can be used as the point of assessment. Also Roman socio-legal notions, such as dignity and property, were given the attention that they still have in philosophy.

In the second half of the first century, interaction between upper-class Roman jurists and Hellenistic philosophers appears to have come to a halt. Perhaps this can be explained as a result of the civil war. Already during the later decades of the civil war the Roman Republic had in fact ceased to function.[14] Moreover, after the war ended with the battle of Actium in 31 BCE and Octavian effectively became the sole ruler in Rome, the scene changed dramatically. As Ronald Syme put it,[15] of the members of the Roman upper class, who had hitherto been responsible for the resolution of legal disputes in Rome, 'few [. . .] survived and they mattered not at all'. Many of the 'new men', who had made a career in Republican Rome, had lost their lives, including Cicero (106–43 BCE), who was murdered on 7 December 43 BCE on the orders of Marc Antony and Octavian (or Augustus, as Octavian would be called later), after he had obtained absolute control over the Roman *res publica*.[16] Of course, in these circumstances there would be little need for advice from philosophers or little to pick up from the Romans.

[14] Flower 2010, 32; cf. her helpful division of Rome's 'archaic' history into thirteen periods, including six republics, at 33.

[15] Syme 1939, 490, referring to Juvenal (first half of the 2nd century CE), *Satire* 8.1: *stemmata quid faciunt?*: 'What good are family trees?' As Green 1974, 187 commented: 'In this satire J. brings in the name of almost every distinguished Roman family.'

[16] On how Augustus appropriated the notion *res publica* for his absolute rule see Moatti 2018, 251–69.

At any rate, after the civil war, in the Imperial period, interaction between jurists and philosophers would become more eclectic. Among jurists an interest can be discerned in Aristotle's notion of corrective justice, which would be applied with regard to the law of obligations, and in the Stoic notion of the common law, or natural law as it came to be called. Philosophers developed an interest in the Roman understanding of freedom as 'doing what one pleases'. In Chapter 8, section 8.1, I will briefly come back to these later developments.

For the remainder of this Introduction, I will elaborate on my approach to the topic of the interaction between law and philosophy. In section 1.3, I will make clear that this study is above all a reconstruction of the interaction based on the extant ancient sources. In section 1.4, I will suggest that such a reconstruction best originates in the practices of philosophy and law as they were conducted at the time. In section 1.5, I will touch upon the role of rhetoric in the interaction between jurists and philosophers. I will end with an overview of the structure of this study (section 1.6). I will start, however, with an overview of earlier approaches to this subject.

1.2 Earlier approaches

As for earlier studies of the interaction between law and philosophy, despite its profound importance for developments in both areas, modern scholarship has (perhaps understandably) rather neglected this period.

For historians of Roman law ('Romanists'), the 2nd century BCE is still firmly within what is referred to as the archaic period of Roman law.[17] Romanists usually focus on the classical period, from 50 until 250 CE, when Roman jurists, such as Salvius Julianus (*c.*110–*c.*170 CE), Ulpian (*c.*170–223 CE), and Paulus (*fl.*222–235 CE), offered their sophisticated solutions to legal problems, which ever since have guided how such problems are resolved today.

For historians of philosophy in antiquity ('ancient philosophers'), the 2nd century BCE falls within the period they refer to as – following Droysen – the Hellenistic period. Whereas in modern scholarship most attention was previously paid to the classical period of Greek thought, with Plato (*c.*429–347 BCE) and Aristotle (384–322 BCE) as the pivotal figures, this has changed since the 1980s, with the publication of studies that

[17] For archaic or 'altrömisch', see e.g. Kaser 1971. For a discussion of periodisation in Roman law, Wieacker 1988, 19–25 can be consulted.

showed the philosophical relevance of discussions among Hellenistic philosophers, such as the edited volume *Doubt and Dogmatism*,[18] and – perhaps even more important – the collection of fragments and commentary by Tony Long and David Sedley, which made the thinking of Hellenistic philosophers both accessible and pertinent.[19] Even with this rise of interest in Hellenistic philosophy, the focus remains above all on the beginnings of the Hellenistic period, with the 2nd and 1st centuries BCE somewhat overlooked.

Among Romanists, the influence of Hellenistic philosophy on Roman law has been discussed and assessed differently.[20] Within the range of options, on the one extreme we find Alan Watson, who maintains that Roman law developed as an autonomous discipline, with little or no influence from philosophy.[21] The catch phrase here is 'legal isolationism'. On the other extreme, some have even gone as far as to proclaim that Roman law would have been the product of the Greeks.[22] Others, like Franz Wieacker, have taken up an intermediate position, accepting some influence from Hellenistic thinkers.[23] In this study I will follow suit, defending a moderate position: whereas law in Rome had developed as a largely autonomous discipline, it was nevertheless influenced by Hellenistic philosophers in different and influential ways.

However, in these earlier, more moderate studies usually little nuance is used, as the legal historian Fritz Schulz already remarked: there the Hellenisation of Roman law is often presented from a generalised point of view of what is usually referred to as 'Greek philosophy'.[24] In the Hellenistic period Greek thinkers organised themselves in groups or schools, e.g. by declaring themselves to be followers of a particular philosopher, by agreeing about a particular method of investigating and/or by a shared set of doctrines.[25] A discussion of the influence of Hellenistic philosophy on Roman law thus needs to take these differences into account.[26] In two excellent recent studies, the influence of Hellenistic

[18] Schofield, Burnyeat and Barnes 1980. [19] Long and Sedley 1987.

[20] See Senn 1927, Guibal 1937, Schulz 1961, 100, Wieacker 1988, 618–39, Schiavone 2017, part three, Mantovani 2018b, 79–128.

[21] Watson 1974, 186–95, Watson 1995b, 158–63. [22] Barta 2010; cf. Finkenauer 2012.

[23] Wieacker 1969. See further Chapter 3, section 3.1.

[24] Schulz 1961, 100 (cf. 1946, 84): 'Immer wieder hat man sich mit dem Problem des Einflusses [. . .] beschäftigt, aber man verfuhr zu wenig kritisch und hielt die verschiedenen Zeiten zu wenig auseinander.'

[25] See further Chapter 2, section 2.2.

[26] Behrends 1978 (cf. his 1980a, 1980b, 2008) stressed the difference between the dogmatic Stoics on the one hand and the sceptical Academics on the other hand (see Chapter 2, section 2.1), unfortunately without clear recourse to the sources. In Behrends' interpretation the Academics

philosophy on Roman law is already discussed in a more nuanced manner. Moatti 1997 (English translation 2015) discusses the influence of Hellenistic philosophy on law as part of a broader account of the arrival of philosophy in Republican Rome. Schiavone 2017 (second edition; the English translation of the first edition was published in 2012) deals with the influence of philosophy on law within a broadly set up, overall history of Roman law – from its beginnings until late antiquity. In this study, in contrast to Moatti, I will focus on the influence of philosophy on law only; in contrast to Schiavone, I will focus on the crucial period of the late Republic.[27]

Among ancient philosophers, in comparison with the Romanists dealing with the influence of philosophy on law, far fewer scholars have dealt with the influence of law on philosophy. Only more recently has the influence of Roman law on philosophy in the late Republic attracted some attention.[28] While scholarly work on Roman thought moves at a fast pace these days,[29] the study of the influence of Roman law on Hellenistic thought has remained an underdeveloped topic.

1.3 Sources

Neglect of the study of the late Republican period among Romanists and ancient philosophers alike has clearly much to do with a lack of evidence for both law and philosophy: neither in the domain of law or philosophy are we well served with sources.[30]

Above all, almost all evidence about, let alone by, the main protagonists in both law and philosophy is of a later date. The account of interactions

are the 'empiricists', offering an understanding of law in terms of human made 'institutions', whereas the Stoics are the 'rationalists', allowing an understanding of law in terms of 'principles'. Unfortunately, Behrend's distinction is misleading for a number of reasons. Not only does the contrast between institutional Academics and principled Stoics lack a basis in the sources, but also in their epistemology the Stoics are 'empiricists'. Moreover, Behrends turns the sceptical Academics into dogmatists of a sort, while he disregards the fact that the Stoics presented a mitigated version of their doctrines to the Romans.

27 In his as of yet unpublished inaugural lecture (2018) Giglio also brings up the topic of the ancient origins of the 'mind'(-set) of what he refers to as 'the modern jurist'. He emphasises both the importance of Aristotle (see Chapter 2, section 2.2) and of rhetoric (see this chapter, section 1.5) for the development of law.

28 See Griffin 2013a. Among the exceptions are Jonsen and Toulmin 1988, 75–88 and Schofield 1999a (with regard to casuistry, see Chapter 6 below) and Schiesaro 2007 (in the didactic poem *On the Nature of Things* by the Epicurean Lucretius, *c.*99–55 BCE).

29 Barnes and Griffin 1989, Griffin and Barnes 1997, Morford 2002, Maso 2012, Woolf 2015, Boys-Stones 2017, Atkins 2018.

30 For a brief assessment of the state of the sources on late Republican 'Roman' Stoicism, see Wildberger 2018, 169.

offered here will thus necessarily have to be a cautious reconstruction based on later ancient sources.[31] The authors of these later accounts not only have their own preoccupations,[32] but in comparison with modern historians of law or philosophy they are also usually less inclined to provide evidence for their claims.[33] The sources that we do have can thus not be taken at face value: their accounts will have to be checked for reliability and, as much as possible, read in combination with each other.

For law, the most important sources are Cicero's writings from the 1st century BCE, Pomponius' *Handbook*, which survived in Justinian's 6th-century CE *Digest* of Roman law, and Gaius' *Teaching Manual* (or *Institutes*, as it is commonly referred to in what is only a transliteration of the original title), which was rediscovered at the beginning of the 19th century. Both Pomponius' *Handbook* and Gaius' *Teaching Manual* were written in the 2nd century CE.[34]

With regard to Cicero's writings on law, it is important to stress that he was not a jurist, in the sense that he performed the uniquely Roman activity of advising those responsible for the resolution of disputes on how to deal with them (more on this below in Chapter 2, section 1). Cicero considered himself above all to be a politician – someone serving the public good and aiming at enhancing Rome's glory.[35] For 'new men', like Cicero, who coming from the province did not belong to the Roman establishment, knowledge of Rome's law – next to expertise in rhetoric – was a means of making a career as a politician. By showing off in public speeches, especially in highly visible criminal cases, ambitious politicians could make a name for themselves and perhaps achieve the consulship, the highest office in the Roman republic. Cicero indeed managed to become a consul in 63 BCE.[36] His extant speeches and writings, especially on rhetoric and philosophy, thus contain many passages on developments in

31 The dates of the authors of the ancient accounts will usually be given where they appear first in the text.

32 The earliest historians are usually preoccupied with 'great deeds', or with 'founders'. See, e.g. Marincola 2017, xxxii–xxxvii.

33 Pitcher 2009, 1–24 is a helpful discussion.

34 Since this study aims to contribute towards presenting the origins of established traditions to a wider audience, here and in the remainder of the book I will offer the titles of the ancient writings as much as possible in the modern vernacular. For those used to the Latin abbreviations of the standard titles, the bibliography offers a list of the titles as they are translated here, with reference to these standard titles (and the editions consulted).

35 See, especially, Habicht 1990, at ix: 'He was, body and soul, a politician', and 2: 'All his life he wanted nothing more than to be a statesman'. For Cicero's writings on philosophy as a service to the public good, see below n. 49.

36 For oratory as a means to power, see van der Blom 2016.

Roman law. His writings on rhetoric include *On Invention*, *On the Best Kind of Orator*, *On the Divisions of Oratory*, *Topics* (all on rhetorical theory),[37] the *Brutus* (a history of Roman oratory[38]), and two works on the good orator, *On the Orator* and *Orator*, written in 55 and 46 BCE respectively. In *On the Orator*, Cicero offers an account of the good orator in 1st century BCE Rome; in the *Orator*, he moves beyond this earlier contextual account and describes the ideal perfect orator.[39] His writings on philosophy will be briefly introduced below.

Sextus Pomponius was a productive jurist,[40] whose *Handbook* can be found in the second chapter of the first book of Justinian's *Digest*, the Byzantine compilation of Roman law, which contains the bulk of the production of the Roman jurists as we know it today. Pomponius' *Handbook* constitutes the first and most important surviving account of what he presents as the 'origin and development' of Roman law.[41] Among historians, the reliability of the information given by Pomponius has been questioned, for different kinds of reasons. Pomponius' account contains major inaccuracies[42] and omissions;[43] it is furthermore framed as a history of successions which deals with matters that are still relevant in his own 2nd century CE.[44] It thus needs to be treated with even more caution than usual: wherever possible, the particular passages used in this study will therefore be carefully checked against other evidence.[45]

Gaius was another productive jurist about whom we know next to nothing, not even his family name – some have put even his very existence into doubt.[46] His teaching manual or introductory textbook is above all a systematic overview of Roman private law, the first of its kind that has

[37] A useful collection of these treatises with an up-to-date bibliography is Manzoni 2019.

[38] For a discussion of the *Brutus* as a history, see Kaster 2020, 14–15.

[39] The 'idea' of the orator – at *Orator* 10, Cicero explicitly refers to Plato's notion here – can only be imitated, but never fully realized by actual orators.

[40] On Pomponius and his *Handbook* see especially Nörr 1976, cf. Bauman 1983, 15 and Bauman 1989, 288. For Pomponius as an 'excellent' jurist see Ankum 1974.

[41] *Digest* 1.2.2.1: *origo atque processus*; for the importance of Pomponius' account see especially Nörr 1976, 533, for a discussion of the phrase, see Nörr 1976, 563–9.

[42] See, e.g. Jörs 1888, 10–11 and Liebs 1997, 146. For an overview of passages that need to be treated with caution, see Nörr 1976, 533–9.

[43] See, e.g. Krüger 1912, 57: Pomponius only refers to jurists whose opinions are still used in the 2nd century CE and leaves others out.

[44] Harries 2006, 31 speaks of his 'tendency to impose on a more complex past his own narrative of "succession" of jurists, to create a sense of development and continuity'.

[45] For examples in this book, see e.g. the passages on the origin of the praetorship at *Digest* 1.2.2.27, which will be discussed in Chapter 2, section 2.1, and on the founders of the civil law at *Digest* 1.2.2.39, for which see Chapter 3, section 3.1 and Chapter 6, section 6.3.

[46] For Gaius, see Honoré 1962, Stanojević 1989. Pugsley 1994 suggests identifying Gaius with Pomponius; Stanojević 1997 offers a critical reply to Pugsley's suggestion.

survived.[47] In places it also contains accounts of the historical background of specific institutions, especially of the formulary proceedings (see Chapter 2, section 1).

For the developments of philosophy in Rome, Cicero's writings are our most important source.[48] Most of the treatises on philosophy were written in his free time, when his services for the 'public cause' (*res publica*) were not in demand. Cicero presents them as another service to his fellow citizens.[49] The philosophical treatises are in the first place relevant as a source of information on the positions of the different Hellenistic philosophers. Cicero considered himself to be a sceptic of a moderate sort: with regard to each topic, he first set out the positions that the philosophers had taken up on a specific topic, then chose the position he considered to be most probable. The treatises are relevant in another sense, too. Cicero took on the difficult task of translating the abstract terms the Greek-speaking philosophers had invented, making their thought accessible in Latin. In the intellectual autobiography at the beginning of the second book of *On Divination*, Cicero formulates his aim thus: 'opening up [Greek] philosophy and making it accessible in the Latin language' (4), which would be 'a magnificent and glorious contribution to the Romans: to be able to do without the Greek writers in the study of philosophy' (5).[50]

Cicero wrote most of these texts in two short, but remarkably productive periods. Between 55 and 51 BCE, he composed not only *On the Orator* (mentioned above), but also *On Laws* and *On the res publica*. Between 46 and 44 BCE, when he also worked on *Brutus* and the *Topics* already referred to above, the *Varro* and the *Lucullus* (also referred to as *Academic Books*, book 1 and book 2, respectively), *On Ends*, *Tusculan Disputations*, *On the Nature of the Gods*, *On Divination*, *On Fate*, *On Old Age*, *On Friendship*, *On the Paradoxes of the Stoics* and *On Appropriate Actions* (or commonly but less accurately known as *On Duties*) were written.

The reconstruction of the interaction between Hellenistic philosophers and Roman jurists on the basis of later accounts is greatly helped by

47 It only just survived, though: for its rediscovery in 1816, see Varvaro 2014.

48 A renewed interest in Cicero's writings in their own right rather than as a source for earlier thinkers (as they will indeed often be used here) can be discerned among ancient philosophers and legal historians alike: see Atkins 2013, McConnell 2014, Zarecki 2014 Woolf 2015, Du Plessis 2016.

49 See Cicero, *On Divination* 2.1: *quaerenti mihi multumque et diu cogitanti, quanam re possem prodesse quam plurimis, ne quando intermitterem consulere rei publicae, nulla maior occurrebat, quam si optimarum artium vias traderem meis civibus.* See further Baraz 2012.

50 *nisi quae causa gravior obstitisset, nullum philosophiae locum esse pateremur, qui non Latinis litteris inlustratus pateret.* [...] *magnificum illud etiam Romanisque hominibus gloriosum, ut Graecis de philosophia litteris non egeant.*

collections of bits and pieces that modern scholars have been assembled with regard to either a specific topic or (groups of) thinker(s). If only to acknowledge my debt to them, I will refer to these collections of 'fragments' (here conveniently used for the passages that survived from, but also about the ancient authors), wherever possible.[51]

As already mentioned in section 1.3, since students of law are not usually familiar with the sources in philosophy and students of philosophy are not usually familiar with legal sources, the variety of extant sources will thus be offered as much as possible below (if only to make them more easily accessible), both in translation in the main text as well in the original languages in the footnotes.[52] Discussion of the modern, learned, secondary literature from the fields of Roman law and ancient philosophy, however important and relevant, will usually also be relegated to the footnotes.

1.4 Emerging practices

This reconstruction of the interaction will be grounded as much as possible in the ancient practices of law and philosophy as they were understood at the time. It may be helpful to add a few words here on these emerging practices, which, in various ways, differ to modern (multiple) conceptions of law and philosophy.[53]

[51] For the evidence on the interaction between Romans and Greek philosophers until the end of the 2nd century BCE, Garbarino 1973, which will be referred to as Garbarino below, is particularly helpful. (Garbarino 2003 is a collection of the evidence on the writings of a philosophical nature by Romans until Seneca, and has thus a more limited scope.)

For the older Roman jurists, see Riccobono and others 1968–1972 (= *FIRA*), for Quintus Mucius Scaevola, see Ferrary, Schiavone and Stolfi 2018 (= FSS) in the series *Scriptores iuris Romani*. Furthermore, Lenel 1889, a re-arrangement of Justinian's *Digest* according to author, is important.

For the Hellenistic philosophers overall see Long and Sedley 1987, who offer a selection of the evidence, with extensive discussion. For the Academics after Plato, especially Arcesilaus and Carneades, Mette's collections can be consulted; for Arcesilaus, see now also Vezzoli's collection. For the Peripatetics after Aristotle, especially Critolaus of Phaselis, see still the 1969 volume of Wehrli's series *Die Schule der Peripatetiker* (no volume on Critolaus yet in the *Rutgers University Series in Classical Humanities* on the Peripatetics; for a convenient list of both series see Baltussen 2016, 171–3). For the Cynics, see Giannantoni, volume 2. For the Roman Stoics, Diogenes of Babylon and Antipater of Tarsus, see volume 3 of von Arnim's *SVF*, for Panaetius of Rhodes see three (!) collections (by van Straaten, Alesse and Vimercati), for Hecato of Rhodes Gomoll's collection needs to be consulted (to which Christelle Veillard's reworked 2008 dissertation can hopefully soon be added). Brad Inwood is working on a collection of the evidence on the Roman Stoics. For the references to the collections see the list of primary sources.

[52] The translations are my own, unless acknowledged.

[53] For modern conceptions of law, see e.g. Glenn 2014, for philosophy see, e.g. Overgaard, Gilbert and Burwood 2013.

With regard to law, from a historical point of view at least (modern jurists may disagree), a good starting point for describing a legal order is the practice of dispute resolution rather than the subsequent products of this practice.[54] The focus here will thus be on the emerging institutions of dispute resolution and their agents, such as assemblies, respected citizens, priests, politicians and legal advisors, rather than the products of these institutions. Modern jurists somewhat misleadingly refer to these products as the 'sources' of law: in Rome the most important of these sources were 'statute' (*lex*) and 'case law' (*ius*).

As we will see, the Roman practice of dispute resolution was unique in the ancient world, and at any rate rather different from, for example, the practice as it developed in ancient Athens. The Roman practice developed in an elitist manner, especially with regard to disputes among citizens themselves. The Romans came to refer to this part of their practice as 'civil law' (*ius civile*), to be distinguished from dispute resolution in the public domain about how to organize the community and about conduct that goes against the public interest, that is in constitutional and criminal law.[55] The range of disputes to be solved in civil law was broad, and included disputes about conduct that in modern legal orders will usually be regarded as belonging to criminal law, including 'murder' (*parricidium*) and 'theft' (*furtum*). The scope of criminal law was restricted to conduct that went directly against the public good, such as 'treason' (*maiestas*) and 'extortion' by provincial governors (*res repetundae*). Different from trials in civil law, such conduct against the public good was not judged in an elitist manner but rather by the people in an assembly and later also by jury in a *quaestio*. Trials by jury were first specially set up for each case: such trials were referred to as *quaestiones extraordinoriae*. From the second half of the second century onwards such trials were dealt with in a permanent court, the *quaestiones perpetuae*.[56] In this study, the focus is on the emergence of the elitist practice of Roman civil law.

In the Greek world another unique practice developed – philosophy, literally the love of wisdom. The traditional meaning of wisdom is a mastered expertise, as in Homer's *Iliad*, at 5.410–13, which gives the example of a carpenter who has mastered his craft; with a broader scope,

[54] Bryen 2014, 349, Glenn 2014, 135, cf. Kaser, Knütel and Lohsse 2021, vii.

[55] On the different understandings of the notion of 'criminal law' in the Roman and modern world, see Riggsby 2016.

[56] For Roman criminal law see Kunkel 1962, Jones 1972, Bauman 1996, Harries 2007, McKnight 2017.

wisdom was also used with regard to the Seven Sages.[57] Plato, here presumably already following Socrates (469–399 BCE), used the term *philo-sophia* in a specific sense: next to dealing with or exercising wisdom, it came to mean 'striving for' wisdom.[58] In the slipstream of this new meaning of philosophy, in his *Republic* Plato offered a new meaning of wisdom, too, as the all-encompassing knowledge of a higher reality, which the philosopher-king ought to possess in order to rule the ideal city.

In the Hellenistic period (and long thereafter), philosophy continued to be understood as this broad, encompassing discipline. In the Hellenistic period the study of philosophy was typically carried out in schools. 'School' is the imperfect translation of *haeresis*: a group of thinkers, who have accepted a similar outlook, and who usually meet in the same place, not necessarily in a building. School is hence somewhat misleading, but so are the alternatives 'sect' or 'persuasion'. In each school the thinkers offered their own outlook.[59] Rather than referring in a general sense to love of wisdom, the term 'philosophy' hence also acquired the narrow sense of the outlook of a school.[60]

In most of the schools the study of wisdom was divided into parts, usually logic, ethics and physics. This is how the sceptic Sextus Empiricus (second half of the 2nd century CE) describes how the division came into being:

> More complete seems to have been the approach of those who say that of philosophy one part is physics, another ethics, and another logic. Of this group Plato is implicitly the founder, since he discussed many matters in physics, many in ethics, and not a few in logic; explicitly Xenocrates and his followers, the Peripatetics, and the Stoics used the distinction.[61] (tr. Bett)

Among the thinkers mentioned by Sextus Empiricus, above all the Stoics developed this tripartition, which would turn out to be influential not only

57 For evidence and discussion, see Althoff and Zeller 2006.

58 For the origins of the word 'philosophy', in the sources already attributed to Pythagoras, see Burkert 1960 (who considers the attribution a later intervention) and Moore 2020, esp. 21–4 (who carefully reconsiders Burkert's rejection of the evidence).

59 On this outlook based organisation of higher education in the Hellenistic period see Scholz 2015, 297.

60 For the narrow meaning, see e.g. Diogenes Laertius (3rd century CE) 6.103.

61 *Against the Professors* 7.16 (Platonists fr. 101.1 Dörrie and Baltes, Xenocrates fr. 1 Isnardi Parente and Dorandi, *SVF* 2.38): ἐντελέστερον δὲ παρὰ τούτους οἱ εἰπόντες τῆς φιλοσοφίας τὸ μέν τι εἶναι φυσικὸν τὸ δὲ ἠθικὸν τὸ δὲ λογικόν· ὧν δυνάμει μὲν Πλάτων ἐστὶν ἀρχηγός, περὶ πολλῶν μὲν φυσικῶν, [περὶ] πολλῶν δὲ ἠθικῶν, οὐκ ὀλίγων δὲ λογικῶν διαλεχθείς· ῥητότατα δὲ οἱ περὶ τὸν Ξενοκράτη καὶ οἱ ἀπὸ τοῦ Περιπάτου, ἔτι δὲ οἱ ἀπὸ τῆς Στοᾶς ἔχονται τῆσδε τῆς διαιρέσεως.

in the Hellenistic period, but also in later antiquity and beyond.[62] They defined logic as the study of all matters with regard to 'discourse' (*logos*), physics as the study of 'nature' (*phusis*), and ethics (from *ēthos*, 'character') as the study of 'human matters',[63] while stressing the interrelatedness of the parts.[64] They offered further subdivisions. With regard to logic, its simplest subdivision was into rhetoric and dialectic, the study of arguing correctly in the form of long speeches or of short questions and answers respectively,[65] to which epistemology was added, as the science of what is true and what is false.[66] Dialectic was further subdivided into the study of the validity of arguments (or logic in a modern sense) and the study of language (or grammar).[67] Similarly, subdivisions of physics and ethics were developed.[68]

In short – in the Hellenistic period, philosophy or the study of wisdom was considered to be a broad discipline, which encompassed – in a top-down manner – its different parts. Someone interested in wisdom would study these disciplines according to the doctrines that were endorsed within his particular school or learn how to criticise the doctrines held by members of the other schools.

1.5 Rhetoric?

In this book the reconstruction of the interaction between law and philosophy will be restricted to the late Republican practices of law and philosophy. However, in modern scholarship the influence of Greek rhetoric has also been brought up, especially in relation to developments in law.[69] In this section I will set out why rhetoric will not be part of the reconstruction offered here.

[62] The division is still used by Immanuel Kant (1724–1804) in his *Groundwork of the Metaphysics of Morals*, where in the first sentences he states that 'this division suits the nature of the subject perfectly; there is no need to improve upon it'.

[63] See Aëtius, *Placita* 874e (*SVF* 2.35, LS 26A, *FDS* 15), Diogenes Laertius 7.39 (*SVF* 2.37, LS 26B, *FDS* 1).

[64] Diogenes Laertius 7.40 (*SVF* 2.38, LS 31A, *FDS* 33), Sextus Empiricus, *Against the Professors* 7.16 (*SVF* 2.38, LS 31D, *FDS* 33). For a discussion of the three parts of wisdom and their interrelatedness see Brouwer 2014, 8–41.

[65] The harmonious relation between rhetoric and dialectic was illustrated by Zeno of Citium (*c.*334–263 BCE), the founder of Stoicism, with one of his hand similes: a clenched fist represents dialectic, whereas the opening and extension of the fingers represent rhetoric (see Sextus Empiricus, *Against the Professors* 2.7, *SVF* 1.75, LS 31E, and Cicero, *Orator* 113, *SVF* 1.75).

[66] Diogenes Laertius 7.41 (*SVF* 2.48, LS 31A, *FDS* 33). Cf. Long 1978, 114.

[67] Diogenes Laertius 7.43 (not in *SVF*, LS 31A, *FDS* 33).

[68] For their division of ethics see below, Chapter 6, section 6.2.

[69] Stroux 1926 and 1934, reprinted in his 1949, Viehweg 1974, Frier 1985, 157–9, Harries 2006, 126–32, Tellegen-Couperus and Tellegen 2013. For a recent overview, see Kacprzak 2016.

As with law and philosophy, let me start with rhetoric as an emerging practice. Rhetoric developed in the Greek cities, especially in democratic Athens: citizens had to convince each other about future policies in the assembly or judged disputes that had arisen between particular citizens. In these institutional settings, excellent public speakers emerged such as Pericles (*c*.495–429 BCE), Isocrates (436–338 BCE) and Demosthenes (384–322 BCE). Rhetoric developed into a discipline in its own right, in a bottom-up manner, from the practice of public speaking. Rhetoricians set up schools (the first and best known was founded by Iscocrates), teaching manuals were written, for example the *Rhetoric to Alexander*, in modern scholarship usually identified with Anaximenes of Lampsacos (*c*.380–320 BCE).[70] Plato would disagree with this type of education: in the *Gorgias* he formulated arguments against rhetoric, such as that it should not be considered a science or form of expertise,[71] but a 'knack' only, and that it was open to misuse. The 4th centry BCE has thus been characterised as the first period of rivalry between philosophy and rhetoric – in von Arnim's words, of a 'quarrel about their place in the educational system'.[72]

A terminological remark may be helpful here. Rhetoric, derived from the Greek *eiro*, 'to speak', can refer both to the practice of civic speech as well as to the study of this practice. For the latter meaning, metarhetoric or the art of rhetoric is sometimes used; rhetoric is then understood as its practice.[73] If rhetoric is used in its theoretical sense, the practice of giving public speeches is referred to as oratory.[74] Oratory is derived from the Latin *orare*, 'to speak', 'to ask'. In its first occurrences *orator* is used to refer to an 'ambassador', someone conveying a message or asking for something; presumably under Cicero's influence, orator acquired the now standard meaning of 'public speaker'.[75]

This brings us to the Roman Republic, where – as in Athens – speeches were an important aspect of public life.[76] Speeches were used to inform the

[70] See Fuhrmann 1960, 11, Kennedy 1963, 115.
[71] Science should be understood in the broad sense here, rather than in its narrow narrow meaning of natural science. See further Chapter 3, section 3.1.
[72] Von Arnim 1898: 'Kampf um die Jugendbildung.' For the periodisation see e.g. Schenkeveld 1997, 197–202.
[73] See Kennedy 1994, 3. [74] See Habinek 2005.
[75] See Neuhauser 1958, esp. 120 (origin), 156 (an overview of the development towards the meaning of public speaker).
[76] For the evidence see Malcovati 1976, now conveniently translated by Manuwald 2019 (the evidence on Cato the Censor – number 8 in Malcovati – is to be published in a separate volume), for the first history of Roman oratory, see Cicero, *Brutus*.

public (a *contio*), to bring about a decision about the future policies of the community (a *deliberative* speech) or about past conduct of citizens that allegedly went against the interests of the public cause (a *forensic* speech). Speeches were also given at funerals in order to praise the virtues of the deceased and the deceased's ancestors.[77] Cato the Elder (*c.*234–*c.*149 BCE) is the first Roman from whom speeches are extant.[78]

From the beginning of the 2nd century BCE onwards, the Romans came in contact with Greek rhetorical practice and theory.[79] Cato the Elder showed interest in the Greek rhetors, which Plutarch, *Life of Cato the Elder* 2.5 describes in the following manner: 'He was quite well on in years when he took to reading Greek books; then he profited in oratory somewhat from Thucydides [Pericles?], but more from Demosthenes.' In this period, the arrival of actual Greek rhetoricians or teachers of rhetoric in Rome can also be dated.[80] Again, Cato the Elder was interested in their work. This not only shows in his speeches;[81] he also wrote treatises on rhetoric himself, of which bits have been preserved.[82] He characterised the Roman orator as the *vir bonus dicendi peritus*, a 'good man' or a just citizen, who acts according to the law,[83] and who is also 'skilled in speaking'.[84] Later Romans, including Seneca the Elder (54 BCE–39 CE) and Quintilian (*c.*35–*c.*100 CE), expressed their admiration for Cato's characterisation.[85] Cicero can surely be added here – as with other traditional Roman notions, such as 'public task' (*officium*), 'dignity' (*dignitas*), 'rights' (*iura*), or 'faith' (*fides*),[86] he would develop his own more

[77] For the evidence on Roman funeral orations, see Kierdorf 1980, 137–50; for discussion, see Flower 1996, 130–58. On Roman funeral rites, see further Chapter 5, section 5.2.

[78] These include two defence speeches (the first a defence of some of his activities as a consul, frs. 21–40 Malcovati, and the second a justification of the expenses he made as a censor, frs. 173–5 Malcovati), and a deliberative speech from 167, in which he speaks in favour of the Rhodians (frs. 163–71 Malcovati), who had only sympathised, but not actively fought with the Romans at the battle of Pydna. For discussion see Kennedy 1972, 41–7.

[79] For the introduction of Greek rhetoric in Rome, a much discussed topic, see Kroll 1940, 1080–90, Kennedy 1972, 1994, 102–27, Cavarzere 2000, Pernot 2000, 115–69, Dominik 2017, Tornau 2018, 12–17, Riesenweber 2019 can be consulted.

[80] See Suetonius, *On the Teachers of Grammar and Rhetoric* 25.1.

[81] Leeman 1963, 45–9.

[82] For the passages see Cato the Elder, frs. 14–16, Jordan 1840, 80, and, further, the accounts by Cicero, *Brutus* 63, 65 and Quintilian, *Teaching Manual* of *Rhetoric* 3.1.19. For discussion see Neuhauser 1958, 155, Kennedy 1994, 111.

[83] Sinko 1903, Christes 1975, 133–5, Wieacker 1988, 504, Fiori 2011, 108, Fiori 2013, 2014.

[84] See e.g. Seneca the Elder, *Controversies* 1 preface 9, Quintilian, *Teaching Manual of Rhetoric* 12.1.1, cf. the parody by Pliny the Younger (61–113 CE), *Letter* 4.7.5: *vir malus dicendi imperitus*. Cf. Gwynn 1926, 231.

[85] See the references in n. 84.

[86] For *officium* and *dignitas* see Chapter 5, section 5.4, for *iura* see Chapter 8, section 8.1, for Cicero's use of the Roman legal notion of (*bona*) *fides* or (good) faith see *On Appropriate Actions* 1.23.

sophisticated version of the *vir bonus dicendi peritus* by placing it in the context of Greek philosophy and rhetoric.[87]

As with the Hellenistic philosophers (see below Chapter 2, section 2.2), the Greek rhetoricians had a mixed reception in Rome. The Roman establishment considered them to be a threat and tried to ban them.[88] However, these attempts proved to be unsuccessful. To use Cicero's words: 'With the establishment of the rule over all the peoples [. . .] there was hardly a young man, ambitious for fame, who did not think that he should not shine out in the study of speaking in public.'[89] Just like their predecessors in Athens in the 4th century, the success of both philosophers and rhetoricians made them once again compete for their place in an educational system.[90]

Within law, Greek rhetorical theory and practice were surely useful. Among the Greek rhetoricians, Hermagoras of Temnos (second half of the 2nd century) developed the influential theory of the four 'stances' (Greek: *staseis*, Latin: *status*). Hermagoras distinguished four questions under which a case can be considered, especially useful in dealing with criminal cases: What are the facts? How are they to be qualified? Are there any special circumstances? Has the court jurisdiction?[91] In his early work *On Invention*, Cicero would offer a version of Hermagoras' theory in Latin – now our main source on the theory. In the second half of the 1st century BCE, Aristotle's *Topics* were published in Rome, whereupon Cicero almost immediately wrote his own version. In these works the jurists could find 'topics' (Greek: *topoi*), commonplaces, stock descriptions and matters a speaker might want to discuss with regard to a particular subject.[92]

As for the usefulness of rhetoric in law, a distinction needs to be made between civil and criminal law. What made rhetoric more useful in criminal than in civil cases is that in criminal cases the decision had to

[87] See e.g. *On the Orator* 1.23–36.

[88] For the texts of two decrees in which the rhetoricians were banned see Suetonius, *On the Teachers of Grammar and Rhetoric* 25.2: *nova* [. . .] *non placet*. See further Stroup 2007, 25–32.

[89] *On the Orator* 1.14: *imperio omnium gentium constituto* [. . .] *nemo fere laudis cupidus adulescens non sibi ad dicendum studio omni enitendum putavit.*

[90] See the literature referred to above in n. 72, to which Reinhardt 2000 and Brittain 2001, 298–312 can be added.

[91] The theory is still in use in contemporary criminal law, with the difference that Hermagoras' fourth question, in fact a preliminary one, is put upfront. For the extant sources about the theory see Cicero, *On Invention* 1.10–16 (fr. 13a Matthes, test. 29 Woerther), Quintilian, *Teaching Manual of Rhetoric* 3.6.55–60 (fr. 13b Matthes, test. 26 Woerther), [Augustine], *On Rhetoric* 9 (fr. 13c Matthes, test. 28 Woerther), cf. Kennedy 1994, 97–101.

[92] For the characterisation of 'topics' see Kennedy 1994, 61; for their usefulness in law, see Viehweg 1974.

be made by the public, either in one of Rome's assemblies or by the jurors in specially set up courts. These platforms allowed those with political ambitions to act as lawyers to the parties and try to persuade the judges with all possible rhetorical means. As already mentioned above (section 1.3), Cicero is the obvious example here: as a 'new man' (*homo novus*), arriving in Rome from the province, he was able to make a name for himself as a lawyer. The trial speeches that are extant from the late Republican period are hence usually criminal rather than civil.[93]

In the 2nd century BCE, new developments in civil law created new 'rhetorical' opportunities. As we will see in the next chapter, section 2.1, a less rigid type of procedure emerged, and a liberal method of interpretation began to be used. The use of these opportunities is especially notable in two cases often referred to by, above all, Cicero.[94] The Curiana lawsuit (no. 93 in Alexander 1990) is a case on how to interpret a will, according to the letter of the text or according to the intention of the testator.[95] The Caecina lawsuit is yet again an inheritance case that boils down to the question of whether a text (here a phrase in the praetor's edict, see the next chapter, section 2.1), should be interpreted literally or liberally.[96] These cases are exceptional, though: few cases in the civil law attracted the attention of the Roman orators or the Roman public.[97] As Franz Wieacker formulated it, 'the judgment in the civil law would not have offered rhetoric an uneducated audience whose emotions could be easily brought into play'.[98] In the civil law, judges or their expert legal advisors would not primarily be interested in a persuasive speech, but rather in finding the right answer, in accordance with Roman legal tradition.

If the arrival of Greek rhetoricians implied a second phase in the 'quarrel' between rhetoricians and philosophers, to use Von Arnim's phrase from n. 72 again,[99] with regard to law this quarrel took place in the domain of public (including criminal) law rather than that of civil

93 For an overview of the trials that took place between 149 and 150 BCE, see Alexander 1990, who notes that 'most of the trials listed here are criminal' (xii–xiii).

94 Already mentioned by Stroux 1926/1949, 28–33/42–8.

95 For the evidence, see Cicero, *On the Orator* 1.180, 1.242–5, 2.24, 2.140, 2.220–3, *Brutus* 144, 194–9.

96 The main source is the court speech that Cicero delivered for his client Caecina. See further Frier 1985, cf. Tellegen-Couperus 1991, 37–46. According to Stroux 1934/1949, 130/104, the liberal method of interpretation developed by the rhetoricians would have made law into a rhetorical discipline: cases had to be decided on the basis of a persuasive speech.

97 Fantham 1997, 120, Fantham 2004, 130, Steel 2006, 15, Van der Blom 2016.

98 Wieacker 1950, 256: 'Das *iudicium privatum* hätte der Rhetorik kein unsachliches und emotional ansprechbares Publikum geboten.'

99 For this phase, see further von Arnim 1898, Kasulke 2005, 39–48 and Liebersohn 2010.

law.[100] In public law, rhetoric as the art of persuasion was surely more useful and successful. In this book, then, with its focus on developments in civil law, rhetoric will be left aside.[101] Here the main question is thus how philosophy contributed to the development of civil law (and how civil law contributed to philosophy).

1.6 Structure

The structure of the book is as follows. I will start with a discussion of the state of law and philosophy in the first half of the 2nd century, before the interaction between law and philosophy took place (Chapter 2). Thereafter I will first discuss the influence of Hellenistic philosophers on Roman jurists, then the influence of the jurists on the philosophers. In each direction, the innovations are in both method and substance: new methods were developed and new substantive notions were introduced, or already familiar notions acquired new meanings.

As for the influence of philosophy on law in terms of method, Stoic logic in particular allowed for a systematisation of Roman law. The organically grown output of its civil law had become complicated: as I will show in Chapter 3, the Roman jurists, using the Stoic 'dialectical' methods of classifying and defining, could start to systematise it. From Hellenistic epistemology the Roman jurists, like the grammarians, took over the notion of rule: they started to use it as a mnemotechnical device, yet again in order to get to grips with their growing legal output (Chapter 4). As for the influence of philosophy on law in terms of substance, the Roman jurists became interested in the abstract notion of 'person', in the slipstream of the philosophers, who combined the Greek understanding of person with a more indigenous, that is Etruscan, understanding thereof. 'Person' would thus become one of the central notions in Roman law and beyond (Chapter 5).

Just as with law, the influence of law on philosophy can also be discussed in terms of method and substance. As for method, already in

[100] On the quarrel in law, see e.g. Frier 1985, Harries 2006. In his review of Stroux 1949, Wieacker 1950, 256 varies upon von Arnim's 'quarrel' by bringing Kant's formulation of the 'contest of faculties' (*Streit der Fakultäten*) into play.

[101] Another topic that can be left aside in this context is how the philosophers in their respective schools responded to the challenge that the rhetoricians posed, with the Stoics developing a conception of rhetoric as an extension of dialectic (or logic in the modern sense), such that rhetoric is the science of explaining the condensed argument in logic, and the Academics, especially Philo of Larissa in the 1st century BCE, developing a conception of 'rhetoricised' dialectic (which Cicero would find so appealing). See Liebersohn 2010, Brouwer (unpublished).

the early Hellenistic period a shift of focus can be discerned from a virtue-centred to an action-orientated approach: next to the Socratic question 'What is virtue?', in the 3rd century the early Stoics had become interested in questions about the 'appropriate actions' that can be derived from these virtues. In the 2nd century the 'Roman' Stoics dealt with the disputes that could arise in the concrete applications of such actions. As we will see, in doing so, these Stoics were most likely inspired by the Roman jurists (Chapter 6). As for matters of substance, again in the slipstream of the Roman jurists, for whom private property was an important topic, the 'Roman' Stoics followed suit, and awarded property a novel, central place in thinking about justice, a place which would have a decisive influence on modern, Western ethical thought (Chapter 7).

It should be emphasised here that the overview of the interaction between law and philosophy is not meant to be exhaustive. Influential topics left out are the theoretical foundations of Roman law and constitutional thought. As for the theoretical foundation of Roman law, the origins of the natural law tradition can be found in the interaction between Hellenistic philosophy and Roman law. In Chapter 8, section 8.1, I will briefly return to this important topic. However, it deserves a study in its own right and is best left to another occasion.[102] As for constitutional thought, the Greek historian Polybius (*c.*200–*c.* 118 BCE) used the doctrine of the mixed constitution developed by Plato in his *Laws*,[103] in order to explain Rome's rise to superpower status.[104] Among the Romans, Cicero was clearly interested in the doctrine, by means of which he was able to discuss the superiority of Rome's mixed constitution by bringing in the notion of *consensus iuris*, 'agreement about the law'.[105] In the eighteenth century, this analysis would be used by Montesquieu as the basis for his doctrine of the separation of powers, one of the pillars of constitutional law in many modern jurisdictions.[106]

Furthermore, the interaction occurred on a more piecemeal basis in the Imperial period. In the final chapter, I will pay brief attention to these later developments, especially with regard to the law of obligations and the notion of freedom (Chapter 8, section 8.1). In this chapter, I will also deal

102 See e.g. Brouwer 2021.
103 See Plato, *Laws* 692a, further developed by Aristotle, *Politics* 4.11.
104 For recent introductions see McGing 2010, 169–202, Atkins 2018, 13–24. For an attempt to put Polybius' explanation in the context of Stoicism, see Brouwer 2011b.
105 See Cicero, *On the res publica* 1.39, cf. Schofield 1995, Brouwer 2017. Before the rediscovery in 1819 of large chuncks of Cicero's dialogue, Cicero's notion of *consensus iuris* was extant via Augustine (354–430 CE), *On the City of God*, at 19.21.6.
106 See further Straumann 2016, Atkins 2018.

with the impact of the interaction between law and philosophy (section 8.2). Here, I would not only like to make clear that the interaction has been particularly influential, but also – perhaps above all – that the history of this interaction should make us aware of the choices that have somehow been made, out of the alternative approaches that were available.

CHAPTER 2

Law and philosophy around 150 BCE

Before mapping the interaction between Roman law and Hellenistic philosophy in the period between 150 and 50 BCE some context is needed. What did law and philosophy look like in the 2nd century? I start with an account of Roman law in the 2nd century, which legal historians usually sweep over, paying most attention to the 'classical' period of Roman law and thereafter (section 2.1). The arrival of the Hellenistic philosophers in Rome in the 2nd century BCE is the topic of section 2.2; in most modern accounts of the state of philosophy in Rome, the focus falls on the 1st century, about which we are surely better informed.

2.1 Roman law

As already set out above (Chapter 1, section 1.4), the starting point for examining the Roman legal order will be the institutions that resolve disputes among citizens rather than the products thereof, the 'sources' of law – notably 'statute' (*lex*) and 'case law' (*ius*). What did the Roman institutions of dispute resolution look like in the 2nd century BCE, especially in the domain of *ius civile*?

In modern scholarship, three periods in the development of Roman law are usually distinguished: archaic, classical and post-classical. In the classical period, the Roman jurists, from Marcus Antistius Labeo (d. between 5 and 22 CE) to Ulpian (d.223 CE), produced their best work. In the long 'archaic' period, that made this work possible, disputes were resolved by two types of institutions, depending on whether the dispute concerned the community as a whole or whether the dispute occurred between private citizens. Disputes that concerned the community at large (including those against citizens, who were deemed to have acted against the interests of the community: here the origins of Roman criminal law can be found) were judged by the people in an 'assembly' (*comitium*). Disputes between citizens among each other were usually dealt with by a single judge.

With regard to the resolution of public disputes, in the assemblies, women, foreigners and slaves were excluded from the decision-making process. Votes had different weights: some (groups of) citizens were considered to be more important than others. A decision that concerned the public good, whether directed at the community at large or at one or more private citizens (with the exception of decisions that affected those who had acted against the public good), is referred to as a *lex publica*, a public 'law' or – more precisely – a 'statute'.[1]

A statute typically did not cover a broad field: it was usually a solution to an urgent societal problem. Even the statute of the Twelve Tables of 451–450 BCE (unfortunately lost, but the bits and pieces that are quoted or referred to in the ancient texts have been painstakingly reconstructed[2]), often described as an overall codification, is perhaps best understood as an answer to the problem of tension between the upper, patrician class and the lower, plebeian class.[3]

With regard to the resolution of 'private' disputes, that is between citizens themselves, the solution was entrusted to respected members of the upper class, who were by no means specialists in legal matters, let alone professionals.[4] The elitist character of this type of dispute resolution stands in stark contrast with the egalitarian approach in 4th-century BCE Athens. There, the standard manner of deciding disputes was that citizens presented their case before a randomly selected group of, usually, 501 Athenian citizens (that is, excluding foreigners, women and slaves). A simple majority vote would decide the case, with a judgment in favour of one of the parties.[5] According to the ancient historian Dionysius of Halicarnassus (*c.*60 BCE–7 CE), in his *Roman Antiquities*, at 2.9.1, its elitist character had been in place from the very beginning, when Romulus, the founder of the city, would have assigned the task of delivering justice to members of the upper class, the 'patricians' (*eupatridai* in Dionysius' Greek text).

1 'Law' is an ambiguous term in English: it can refer to a legal order as a whole as well as to a specific product made within this legal order. Law will here be used in its general sense only (*ius* in Latin), for law as a product 'statute' will be used. The etymologies of the Latin *lex* and the English 'statute' run more or less parallel: *lex* is derived from *legere*, 'to speak', a text is spoken and subsequently accepted; 'statute' comes from *statuere*, 'to set up', a text is set up and subsequently accepted (cf. the German *Gesetz* from *setzen*, 'to posit').

2 For the modern editions see Crawford 1996 no. 40, Flach 2004. For a recent commentary, see Cursi 2018.

3 For a later ancient account of the societal problems, see Livy 3.31, cf. e.g. Berger 1932–1940.

4 See e.g. Kaser and Hackl 1996, 48, cf. Wieacker 1944, 10.

5 Our most important source is the late 4th century BCE Aristotelian *Constitution of Athens*, at 63–9. For an account of a trial in Athens, see Todd 1993, 77–163, cf. Lanni 2016, 120–49.

Whether we take Dionysius' account at face value or not, by the middle of the 5th century BCE, with the introduction of the statute of the Twelve Tables, the way in which disputes could be brought before a patrician judge became formalized: a citizen could only have a dispute judged if the possibility was stated in a statute. If so, he could 'act on the basis of a statute' (*lege agere*) or start an 'action on the basis of a statute' (*legis actio*).[6] These actions had a formal, ritualised character. A further development was that if the statutory provision, on the basis of which the action had been started, was unclear, the judge could invoke the 'authority of those with practical wisdom':[7] considered to be those who belonged to the 'college of priests' (*collegium pontificum*). These priestly 'interpretations' (*interpretationes*) had no special name of their own, but came to be referred to under the common term *ius civile*, 'Roman law'. *Ius civile* can thus be either used in a general or in a strict sense.[8]

In the 2nd century BCE, this manner of dispute resolution between private citizens in Rome based on the statute of the Twelve Tables had changed in two ways: first, by the secularisation of the interpretation of statute and, second, by the development of what came to be known as the *ius honorarium*.[9] As for secularisation, already in the 3rd century BCE, the priesthood's monopoly of interpreting and applying statute was broken, so that it also became the domain of members of the patrician families. Some of these families, such as the Mucii, whose members we will encounter in the next chapter(s), became specialists in giving advice to their peers who judged the cases.[10]

For the second development we need to take a closer look at the praetor, who together with the consuls fulfilled the highest political position within the Roman community. For this position, individuals had to be elected by the assemblies; they were honorary, and held for one year only.[11] According to Livy and Pomponius, the praetorship had been introduced in 367–366 BCE, in order to oversee justice in the city.[12] In modern scholarship these ancient accounts have been questioned and understood as an attempt to give more recent developments a venerable ancestry. The

6 For the terminology see Pomponius, *Handbook* in *Digest* 1.2.2.6, for the different actions see Gaius, *Teaching Manual* 4.11–31, cf. Kaser and Hackl 1996, 35.
7 Pomponius, *Handbook* in *Digest* 1.2.2.5: *prudentium auctoritatem.*
8 Pomponius, *Handbook* in *Digest* 1.2.2.5: *communi nomine appellatur ius civile.*
9 Cf. Capogrossi Colognesi 2014, 126–38.
10 Brian Frier 1985, 252, Schiavone 2012/2017, 120/120.
11 For a succinct account see Beard and Crawford 1999, 52–5.
12 Livy 6.42.11: *qui ius in urbe diceret*; Pomponius, *Handbook* in *Digest* 1.2.2.27: *in urbe ius redderet.* Cf. Mommsen 1887, 193–238, Waldstein and Rainer 2014, 82.

praetorship would, rather, have been introduced in order to relieve the consuls of some of their tasks within the city, in order to allow the consuls to deal with military matters outside a city that was continuously at war with its neighbours. Only in the 2nd century BCE would the praetor become responsible for resolving disputes for which no statutory actions were available but where he judged that a solution was necessary.[13]

From the 2nd century BCE onwards, if confronted with a dispute between private citizens, the praetor would, first, investigate whether a statutory action was available at all, and if not, second, determine whether he should allow such a dispute to be presented to a judge. It became customary for the praetor – at the beginning of his year in office – to set out in one of his edicts which disputes he was prepared to consider in order for them to be passed on and decided by a judge. If the dispute could indeed be reformulated in terms of the praetor's edict, the *formula*, or the reformulation of the dispute, which also included the names of the parties and the judge, would then be presented to this judge. In these formulary proceedings, two phases can hence be distinguished: first, the phase before the praetor, *in iure*, where the controversial issue would be determined in the form of a *formula*, and second, the phase before the judge, *apud iudicem*, where the issue would be decided.[14]

Just as with regard to the interpretation of statute, in the formula procedure the 'legal expert' (*iuris consultus*), who as we have seen was usually a member of the upper-class families who had specialised in offering this kind of advice in practical legal matters (usually referred to as 'cautelary jurisprudence'),[15] came to play a role too. In difficult cases he offered his services to the different actors in the proceedings: parties, praetor and judge. The advice given by the legal expert to the judge is known as a *responsum* or 'answer'.[16] The law thus developed on the basis of the power of the praetor, and, informed by the knowledge of the legal specialist, is referred to as the *ius honorarium*.

In sum: in the 2nd century the different ways in which disputes were resolved in Rome brought about a range of products – jurists somewhat

[13] See Mitchell 1990, 184–6, Kunkel and Wittmann 1995, 296, Brennan 2000, 30–1.

[14] The formulary proceedings are mentioned (and thus formally recognized) in the *lex Aebutia* (presumably second half of the 2nd century BCE); see Gaius, *Teaching Manual* 4.30, cf. Metzger 2015, 272 (and n. 36), Kaser, Knütel and Lohsse 2021, 56. For the elements of the *formula*, together with examples see Gaius, *Teaching Manual* 4.39–44, cf. e.g. Schulz 1946/1961, 50/59, Jolowicz and Nicholas 1972, 203–8, Kaser and Hackl 1996, 310–22, Waldstein and Rainer 2014, 144–5, Du Plessis 2020, 74–9, Kaser, Knütel and Lohsse 2021, 71–5, and above all Mantovani 1999.

[15] Wieacker 1961, 137, Frier 1985, 252.

[16] See e.g. Mousourakis 2007, 218 n. 56, Ibbetson 2015, 38.

misleadingly speak of 'sources' here – of which a succinct list is offered by Pomponius, at *Digest* 1.2.2.12, including statute, the *ius civile* and the *ius honorarium*.[17]

Much ink has been spilled over the subject of the importance of these sources vis-à-vis each other,[18] both in quantitative and in qualitative terms. In quantitative terms it has been observed that the number of statutes that deal with private law is limited,[19] compared to the number of *responsa* that were eventually produced.[20] This assessment has recently been challenged in the sense that the number of statutes was not that limited.[21] More importantly, in the 2nd century BCE the manner of resolving disputes with the help of the jurists' *responsa* was still in full development: their number had yet to grow.

In terms of qualitative impact it is often stated that, with regard to the development of the law, the *responsa* were more important than statute; after all, these *responsa* contain the bulk of the high-quality solutions of Roman jurists to the legal cases that they were confronted with, which has earned Roman law its reputation. However, it is questionable whether that can already be said of the *responsa* that were developed in the 2nd century: whereas the origins of the *ius civile* in the strict sense of interpretation of statute lie back a couple of centuries earlier, as we have just seen, the development of the *ius honorarium* had only just started. Moreover, in relation to disputes between citizens, Romans would continue to regard statutes as their primary source: in Pomponius' account written in the 2nd century CE, they are still presented as such.[22] As a boy, Cicero still had to learn to recite the statute of the Twelve Tables.[23] For the importance of statutes in general, see Cicero, *In Defence of Cluentius* 146:

> If I am to concede to you that this is a shame – and I shall consider the point presently – you must concede to me that it is a far greater shame, in a state which rests upon statutes, to depart from them. For statutes are the bond which secures these our privileges in the commonwealth, the

[17] For other ancient lists see Cicero, *Topics* 28 and Gaius, *Teaching Manual* 1.2.

[18] See e.g. Broggini 1959, Kaser 1986 [1978].

[19] Rotondi 1922b, 100–2 counts thirty-two statutes. Arangio-Ruiz 1970 [1938], 254 speaks of some fifty statutes.

[20] Our knowledge thereof we mainly owe to Justinian's *Digest*, a Byzantine selection of these *responsa*. See further Chapter 3.

[21] Mantovani 2018a [2012, in its original Italian], 16-31.

[22] Pomponius, *Handbook* in *Digest* 1.2.2.1. Cf. Kaser 1986 [1978], 14: 'Die *lex* ist für die Römer der Prototyp der Rechtsquelle', Ferrary 2003, Mantovani 2018a [2012], 29.

[23] See *On the Laws* 2.59: *discebamus enim pueri XII ut carmen necessarium.* See further Walter 2017, 333.

foundation of our liberty, the fountain-head of justice. Within the statutes are reposed the mind and heart, the judgement and the conviction of the state. The state without statute would be like the human body without mind – unable to employ the parts which are to it as sinews, blood, and limbs. The magistrates who administer the statutes, the judges who interpret them – all of us in short – obey the statutes to the end that we may be free.[24] (tr. Hodge, modified)

One final point needs to be considered: the relation between these sources. The assumption appears to have been that they were part of one undisputed underlying order, in which both statute and case law went organically together.[25] This undisputed background is often referred to as the *mos maiorum*, of which the statutes and decisions would be the explicit expressions. In the statutes the people themselves would make the *mos* explicit and in the cases presented to them, the judges would make clear what in the particular situation is right.[26] Law in its different forms is then the *mos maiorum* made explicit within the Roman organisation of dispute resolution.[27]

In sum: in the Republican period Rome's legal order was in full development, both with regard to the manner in which disputes were resolved, and with regard to the sources that were developed: statute, the interpretation thereof, and case law. To borrow a popular expression: Roman law developed on different 'layers'.[28] In solving a specific legal case, different levels may thus somehow have to come into play.[29] In the 2nd century BCE the different layers had yet to be more fully developed.

2.2 Hellenistic philosophy

In this section I discuss the arrival of the first representatives of the Hellenistic philosophical schools in Rome around the middle of the second

[24] *ut tibi concedam hoc indignum esse quod cuius modi sit iam videro, tu mihi concedas necesse est multo esse indignius in ea civitate quae legibus contineatur discedi ab legibus. hoc enim vinculum est huius dignitatis qua fruimur in re publica, hoc fundamentum libertatis, hic fons aequitatis; mens et animus et consilium et sententia civitatis posita est in legibus. ut corpora nostra sine mente, sic civitas sine lege suis partibus ut nervis ac sanguine et membris uti non potest. legum ministri magistratus, legum interpretes iudices, legum denique idcirco omnes servi sumus ut liberi esse possimus.* Cf. Mantovani 2018a [2012], 29.

[25] Bleicken 1995, 128.

[26] Tacitus (*c.*56–after 118 CE), *Yearbooks* 3.25–8. Cf. Mantovani 2018a [2012], 17.

[27] See e.g. Thomas 2011 [1986], 70.

[28] See e.g. Kaser 1971, 198, Wieacker 1988, 488, Waldstein and Rainer 2014, 128.

[29] For examples of the use of the different levels with regard to disputes about inheritance in the classical period, see Babusiaux 2015, 37–45, 332–4.

century BCE, with particular focus on the embassy of the philosophers of 155 BCE, and the potential of these schools with regard to interaction with the Romans, who were involved in the resolution of disputes.

As already noted in Chapter 1, section 1.4, in the Hellenistic period the study of wisdom, 'philosophy' understood in a general sense, had become school-orientated. Whereas in the 4th and 3rd centuries students interested in striving for wisdom had to travel up to Athens (most of them came from elsewhere in the Hellenised world), in the 2nd century the schools were no longer to be found in Athens alone. Their members had also moved in other directions and founded subsidiary schools there, at first in the east and south, in Alexandria and Pergamon, the capitals of the Hellenistic kingdoms, in which Alexander's empire had been divided among his successors (in the chapter on rules we will encounter a debate between philosophers from both cities), but also on the island of Rhodes and in the city of Tarsus in Cilicia, which both lay on the sea route between Pergamon and Alexandria and which had developed into important trade centres.[30]

With the rise of Rome as a world power, representatives of most of the Greek schools moved westwards and also started to present themselves in Rome.[31] The embassy of three philosophers in 155 BCE can serve as the focal point here.[32] The reason why the Athenians sent three philosophers as their ambassadors to Rome is dealt with quite extensively in our sources. The Athenians had destroyed Oropus, a town on the border between Attica and Boetia. The Oropians appealed to the Romans, who appointed the Sicyons as arbitrators in the conflict. Since the Athenians did not show up at the hearing, they were ordered by default to pay a hefty fine of 500 talents. Thereupon, the Athenians decided to appeal against the judgment and sent three envoys to Rome in order to have the fine revoked. In

[30] For Rhodes as a trade centre, see Berthold 1984, 47–58, for its intellectuals see Strabo 14.2.13, cf. Mygind 1999, 253–9. For Tarsus see Strabo 14.5.12-15, cf. Sedley 2003, 30.

[31] Cf. Ferrary 2007, a helpful overview of Greek philosophers in Rome in the period between 155 and 86 BCE.

[32] For the evidence see Garbarino 1973, frs. 77–91, cf. Schofield 2018, 570: 'One of the best documented of all interventions by Greek philosophers.' It is not documented by Diogenes Laertius, one of our main sources on Hellenistic thought, at least not in books 4 and 5, which deal with Plato's Academy and Aristotle's Lyceum respectively, but then Diogenes Laertius might have done so in book 7, on the Stoics. This book is incomplete: it breaks off in the middle of the catalogue of Chrysippus' books. According to the contents page that survived in one of the manuscripts, the lost part contained the lives and opinions of the Stoic thinkers up till Cornutus (second half of the 1st century CE), and thus included Diogenes of Babylon and the other Roman Stoics dealt with in this book. However well documented, Powell 2013 suggests that the embassy may not have been such an 'iconic moment, until Cicero made it so' (147).

accordance with a tradition that had developed in the Hellenistic period the envoys were well-respected philosophers,[33] even heads of the three most important schools of thought, who 'together carried an almost unsurpassable prestige'[34]: Carneades of Cyrene (*c.*214–*c.*129 BCE), head of Plato's Academy, Critolaus of Phaselis (2nd century BCE), head of Aristotle's Lyceum, and Diogenes of Babylon (*c.*240–*c.*150 BCE), head of the Stoic school. As ambassadors, they were partly successful: the Senate decided that the fine should be reduced to 100 talents.[35]

As philosophers, they were met with both enthusiasm and criticism. They were notably criticised by Cato the Elder, who disapproved of Greek culture and education in so far as it undermined Roman custom.[36] He therefore asked for a swift decision from the Senate, such that the philosophers could go back to their Greek students and that the young Romans could return to their earlier practice of obeying the laws and the magistrates.[37] But the philosophers were admired, too. Before they had been allowed to present the Athenian case to the Senate, they had already given lectures before the Roman public. Their lectures stunned the listeners, especially the ones delivered by Carneades.[38] In the account offered by Aulus Gellius (2nd century CE), which presumably goes back to a lost part of Polybius' *Histories* (who might even have been an eyewitness to the event[39]), each philosopher used his own style: 'Carneades spoke with a force that seized you, Critolaus to the point and smooth, and Diogenes with moderation and soberness.'[40] For Gellius, the three speeches are

33 For such public services offered by philosophers in the early Hellenistic period see Ferguson 1911, 326 and Sonnabend 1996.

34 Walbank 1979, 544.

35 See Pausanias (*fl.*150 CE) 7.11.5. 'The Athenians did not even pay this', so Pausanias immediately continues.

36 Plutarch, *Life of Cato the Elder* 23.1, where Cato used Socrates as the example of someone undermining traditional values. For a balanced assessment of Cato's hostility, apparently based on some familiarity with the Greeks, as the remark about Socrates already attests, see Astin 1967, 157–81 (the embassy is dealt with on 174–6), and more recently Humm 2018, 206–8.

37 Plutarch, *Life of Cato the Elder* 22.6-7 (Garbarino fr. 88), Pliny the Elder (23/24–79 CE), *Natural History* 7.112 (Garbarino fr. 86).

38 Plutarch, *Life of Cato the Elder* 22.2 (Garbarino fr. 88).

39 Polybius spent some sixteen years in Rome: from 167 until the end of the 150s. See, further, Erskine 2012.

40 Aulus Gellius 6.14.10 (Garbarino fr. 78, Rutilius Rufus fr. 12 *FRHist.*): *'violenta', inquiunt 'et rapida Carneades dicebat, scita et teretia Critolaus, modesta Diogenes et sobria.'* The Latin translation presumably stems from Publius Rutilius Rufus (consul 105 BCE), a student of the Stoic Panaetius and acquainted with Scipio (see below), whom Gellius also mentions (cf. Hendrickson 1933, 164). The passage is taken up in the modern reconstruction of the lost part of Polybius' *Histories*, as book 33, section 2.

examples of the three styles that can be employed in both verse and prose: grand, middle and plain respectively.[41]

Apart from their styles, what could these philosophers have brought to the Romans? Plato's Academy had become sceptical. Already in the 3rd century, Arcesilaus of Pitane (d.242 BCE), head of the Academy in the 260s, had become a 'searcher', 'suspending judgment' and 'arguing on both sides of a question'.[42] He was surely inspired by Socrates, who in Plato's *Apology* is said to have stated that in his search for wisdom he became aware of the fact that he did not know anything for sure.[43] In 155 BCE, the Romans were confronted with this scepticism when Carneades pleaded one day in favour of justice, the next day against it.[44] Like Arcesilaus, Carneades argued vehemently against the dogmatic philosophers, that is, thinkers who held 'doctrines' (*dogmata* in Greek) 'in order to be able to refute his opponents, whatever position they took'.[45] Only in 88 BCE, with the arrival of Philo of Larissa (d.*c*.79 BCE) in Rome, did the Academy begin to move away from its scepticism; with Antiochus of Ascalon (d.*c*.68 BCE) it became a dogmatic school again – its members set out Plato's thought in a systematic manner.[46] In Rome this moderate form of scepticism would appeal to Cicero and the jurist Servius Sulpicius Rufus (d.43 BCE).

With regard to Critolaus, the head of Aristotle's Lyceum, it first has to be noted that Aristotle's school at the beginning of the 2nd century appears to have been in dire straits, but that Critolaus may well have been responsible for a revival of sorts.[47] Second, familiarity with Aristotle's doctrines in the 2nd century BCE appears to have been an issue, even for the members of his own school, like Critolaus. While Critolaus clarified

[41] *et in carmine et in soluta oratione genera dicendi probabilia sunt tria, quae Graeci* χαρακτῆρας *vocant nominaque eis fecerunt* ἁδρόν, ἰσχνόν, μέσον. *nos quoque, quem primum posuimus, 'uberem' uocamus, secundum 'gracilem', tertium 'mediocrem'.*

[42] See Diogenes Laertius 4.28 (test. 1a Mette, fr. 107 Vezzoli).

[43] Socrates claimed that he did not know anything for sure (see e.g. Plato's *Apology* 23b), Arcesilaus denied that anything could be known, not even that he did not know anything for sure, see Cicero, *Varro* 45 (fr. 9 Mette, fr. 45 Vezzoli).

[44] See especially Cicero, *On the res publica*, book 3.8–28 (in favour of justice) and 3.32–41 (against justice). See Ferarry 2007, 2014, 351–81, 725–6 and Höffe 2017 for a general discussion. Carneades' virtuoso display has been assessed rather differently: Neuhausen 2008 connects it with the Oropian case, whereas Powell 2013 even considers the possibility that Cicero would have made the speeches up.

[45] See Lactantius (*c*.240–*c*.320), *Divine Teaching Manual* 5.14.4 (fr. 11b1 Mette): *quod ille facere solebat, ut alios quidlibet adferentes posset refutare.*

[46] This is one of the main themes in Engberg-Pedersen 2017. The theme of systematisation also structures Bonazzi 2015.

[47] Hahm 2007, Inwood 2014, 51–72. For the limited extant evidence on Critolaus, see Wehrli 1969b.

Aristotle's conception of the highest goal in life,[48] he also argued against rhetoric, which can be less easily reconciled with Aristotle's interest in the topic.[49] According to our sources, this has to do with the availability of Aristotle's work. If, for example, the geographer Strabo (64/3 BCE–24 CE) is to be believed,[50] few of Aristotle's writings were available, even to the Peripatetics themselves. This is Strabo's much-discussed account in *Geography* 13.1.54 (Peripatetics fr. 2A Sharples):

> The earlier Peripatetics after Theophrastus did not possess the books at all, apart from a few, chiefly those published by Aristotle himself, and were therefore not able to engage in philosophy in a serious way, but delivered theses in a hollow manner.[51] (tr. Sharples, modified)

Unfortunately, these works, which were often written in the form of dialogues and intended for a general audience, are no longer extant.[52] Aristotle's writings as we possess them now, are the notes of his lectures, or, at any rate, works intended for use within his school.[53] Just before the passage quoted above, Strabo had explained that Aristotle's pupil Theophrastus had left these to his pupil Neleus, who had taken them to his hometown Skēpsis, where they were kept until the beginning of the 1st century BCE. They were then bought by Apellicon of Teos, a wealthy (naturalised) Athenian with an antiquarian interest, who made them public in what was apparently an inferior edition.[54] In 86, when Sulla had restored the Roman order of things in a rebellious Athens, he took these lecture notes as booty to Rome, where in the 50s they were collated

48 See below Chapter 7.

49 Wöhrle and Hellmann 2011, 408. Hahm 2007, 54–6 discusses the evidence on Critolaus (without connecting it to Aristotle's *Rhetoric*). Barnes 2015 [1986], 82 may well be right that 'there really was no Peripatetic orthodoxy'.

50 See also Plutarch, *Life of Sulla* 26.2 (Peripatetics fr. 2B Sharples), Athenaeus (*fl.*200 CE) 5.214d (Peripatetics fr. 2C Sharples). For the modern discussions of the reliability of these accounts see Moraux 1973, 3–93, esp. 18ff., Sandbach 1985, Gottschalk 1987, 1083: 'Aristotle's pupils were deprived of Aristotle's writings', Canfora 1989 [1987], 173–82, Barnes 1997, Bollansée 1999, 234–5, Primavesi 2007, Sharples 2008, Nielsen 2012, Tutrone 2013, 155: 'We should avoid thinking about frequent direct use of the Peripatetic texts', Natali and Viano 2014, 6–7, Primavesi and Rapp 2016, 30–4, Horn 2018, 16. The accounts are played down by, e.g. Chroust 1962, Hahm 2007, 98–101, Sharples 2010, 28–9, Hatzimichali 2013, Griffin 2015, 219–23.

51 συνέβη δὲ τοῖς ἐκ τῶν περιπάτων τοῖς μὲν πάλαι τοῖς μετὰ Θεόφραστον οὐκ ἔχουσιν ὅλως τὰ βιβλία πλὴν ὀλίγων, καὶ μάλιστα τῶν ἐξωτερικῶν, μηδὲν ἔχειν φιλοσοφεῖν πραγματικῶς, ἀλλὰ θέσεις ληκυθίζειν.

52 For the extant bits and pieces see Gigon 1987.

53 For some incisive observations on what they may have amounted to, see Beresford 2020, xii.

54 For the storage in Skēpsis, see especially Primavesi 2007. For Apellicon's antiquarian interests – and the means which he employed, including stealing – see Posidonius in Athenaeus 5.214d–15b (fr. 253 Edelstein and Kidd, Peripatetics fr. 2C Sharples).

by the librarian Tyrannio and edited and made available to a larger audience by Andronicus of Rhodes.[55] This implies that they would have become available only towards the end of Cicero's life, perhaps even via Tyrannio, who had reorganized Cicero's library.[56] It is in this context that we can understand Cicero's remark at section 3 of his own *Topics* – which he wrote in 44 BCE, when Aristotle's lecture notes had become available – about the unfamiliarity of even most philosophers with Aristotle, 'who is not even known to the philosophers themselves, apart from a few exceptions.'[57] Even so, as John Dillon formulated it: 'There is little sign, in the works of Cicero, that he had achieved any real acquaintance with the works of Aristotle now available to us.'[58] The upshot of this is that the lecture notes may only have become available from the second half of the 1st century BCE – that is too late for them to have had a role in the developments under discussion here.

As for Diogenes of Babylon, as head of the Stoic school he was not the first Stoic to make an impression upon the Romans. In 169 BCE Crates of Mallus had visited Rome, as an envoy from Pergamon. According to the historian Suetonius (*c.*69–after 122 CE), he broke his leg on the Palatine, then the hill where the Roman nobility lived, due to a fall into a *cloaca* (sewer), and he had to stay longer in order to recover.[59] He used this time well: he 'introduced the Romans to the topic', not only in the form of tutorials, but also in numerous 'lectures'. For lectures, Suetonius uses the transliteration of the Greek *akroaseis*, if only to stress how unusual this practice must have been to the Romans, who were accustomed to private instruction.[60]

After Crates of Mallus, Diogenes of Babylon visited as part of the embassy, to be followed by other prominent Stoics and almost immediately by Antipater of Tarsus (*c.*210?–129 BCE), who would succeed Diogenes as head of the school.[61] This 'first' generation of 'Roman'

55 For Tyrannio and Andronicus see Plutarch, *Life of Sulla* 26. Cf. Barnes 1997, Hatzimichali 2013, 11–27, Roller 2018, 765–6.

56 Cicero, *Letter to Atticus* from 20 June 56 BCE, no. 78 (4.4a) Shackleton Bailey.

57 *qui* [*sc.* Aristoteles] *ab ipsis philosophis praeter admodum paucos ignoretur.*

58 Dillon 2016, 183. Even Cicero's reference to, let alone use of, Aristotle's *Topics* at the beginning of his own *Topics* (at 1, cf. *Letters to Friends* no. 334 (7.19) Shackleton Bailey), which he wrote towards the end of his life, does not yet reveal any real acquaintance with Aristotle's treatise, at least as we possess it. See further Reinhardt 2003, 177–80, 369–70.

59 See Suetonius, *On the Teachers of Grammar and Rhetoric* 2 (Garbarino fr. 72, test. 3 Broggiato), cf. Fuhrmann 1960, 159.

60 For grammar see further below, Chapter 4.

61 For Antipater see Plutarch, *Lives of the Gracchi* 8.6, *SVF* Antipater fr. 13; *pace* Garbarino 1973, 446 n. 2.

Stoics, that is, Stoics that presented themselves in Rome, was followed by a second and third generation of influential Stoics. Among the second generation was Panaetius of Rhodes (*c.*180–*c.*109 BCE), who visited Rome after 146 and became Antipater's successor in 129/128 BCE. After Panaetius the contacts between the Stoics and the Romans continued with the third generation of Roman Stoics, with Panaetius' pupils – Hecato of Rhodes (early 1st century BCE) and Posidonius of Apamea (*c.*135–*c.*50 BCE), both of whom we will encounter in subsequent chapters.

In the extant sources, Panaetius in particular is brought into contact with prominent Romans. As a student of Crates of Mallus in Pergamon, Panaetius would already have heard about Crates' stay in Rome.[62] After 146 he approached the Romans himself, notably visiting Publius Cornelius Scipio Aemilianus Africanus,[63] even becoming part of his household and accompanying him to Alexandria.[64] Next to Panaetius, the Greek historian Polybius was part of Scipio's entourage too,[65] accompanying him to Carthago.[66] According to Cicero, *On Friendship* 69, Panaetius and Polybius were part of a circle or 'herd' (*grex*) of Hellenistic and Roman intellectuals around Scipio. In his *On the res publica*, he immortalised this circle. He presents it in Scipio's villa outside Rome on the Campus Martius in the year 129. At 1.14–18, he includes among its members the Romans Publius Rutilius Rufus, Quintus Mucius Scaevola Augur, Quintus Aelius Tubero, who all studied with Panaetius (see below Chapter 6, section 6.3), as well as Manius Manilius, one of the 'founders' of the civil law (see also below, Chapter 6, section 6.3) and otherwise Scipio's predecessor as commander in the Third Punic War (149–146 BCE).[67] Both the influence of Panaetius on Scipio and the character of the circle have been much debated in modern scholarship.[68]

Two schools were not represented in the embassy: the Epicureans and the Cynics. The Athenians would surely have taken into consideration that

[62] Strabo 14.5.16 (Panaetius fr. 5 Van Straaten, fr. 5 Alesse, fr. A8 Vimercati; Crates test. 21 Broggiato).

[63] For the evidence on Scipio and Panaetius see Garbarino frs. 93–119, fr. 21–38 Alesse.

[64] Household: Cicero, *In Defence of Murena* 66 (Garbarino fr. 101, fr. 60 van Straaten, fr. 24 Alesse, fr. A25 Vimercati). Alexandria: Plutarch, *Sayings of the Romans* 200e–201a (fr. 24 van Straaten, fr. 37 Alesse, fr. A31 Vimercati). Cf. Pohlenz 1949, 423.

[65] Panaetius and Polybius: see Velleius Paterculus (*c.*20 BCE–*c.*30 CE), *Roman History* 1.13.3 (Garbarino fr. 111, fr. 15 van Straaten, fr. 27 Alesse, fr. A22 Vimercati), Plutarch, *Political Instructions* 814c–d (Garbarino fr. 112, fr. 16 Van Straaten, fr. 31 Alesse, fr. A36 Vimercati).

[66] See Polybius 38.14.3, 38.19–21.

[67] Huss 1988, 440–7. For the contacts between Polybius and Manilius see Polybius 36.11.

[68] See further Suerbaum 2002, 483–92, Ferrary 2014, 589–615, 734 and Barlow 2018. Astin 1967, who has been particularly influential, is sceptical.

the reputation of these schools among the Romans would not have helped their case. With regard to the Epicureans, the tone for their initial bad reputation among the Romans had already been set in the third century BCE.[69] In 280–279 BCE at the court of King Pyrrhus of Epirus, with whom the Romans were at war, the Roman envoy Gaius Fabricius could not believe his ears when he was confronted with the doctrine formulated by Epicurus (341–270 BCE) 'that everything we do should be measured in accordance with pleasure'.[70] In the first half of the 2nd century BCE, 'during the consulship of Lucius Postumius [this can either refer to the year 173 or 154] the Epicureans Alcaeus and Philiscus were thrown out of Rome because of the pleasures which they had introduced'.[71] A further consideration on their own part as to why they did not participate in the embassy may also have been their apolitical stance. According to Epicurus, pleasure is the overall goal in life. This notion of pleasure, which Epicurus explained in the sense of living in an undisturbed manner, free from bodily pain and mental disturbance,[72] implied abstinence from politics,[73] or – for that matter – taking part in an embassy.

Despite the Epicureans' bad reputation and their apolitical stance, in the years following 155 BCE they would gradually become more popular among the Romans.[74] First, some Romans started to make their way to Epicurus' Garden in Athens: Titus Albucius (*fl.*150? BCE) is the first-known Roman Epicurean, characterised by Cicero as an 'accomplished one'.[75] A breakthrough of Epicureanism in Rome appears to have been brought about by Gaius Amafinius, Rabirius and Catius (of uncertain dates, perhaps somewhat before 129 BCE[76]).[77] After Amafinius,

69 For an overall account of Epicureanism in Rome see Sedley 2009.

70 See Cicero, *On Old Age* 43 (Garbarino fr. 24): *omnia quae faceremus, ad voluptatem esse referenda*; cf. Plutarch, *Life of Pyrrhus* 20.6–7 (Garbarino fr. 25).

71 See the account by Athenaeus 12.547a (Garbarino fr. 73): καλῶς ἄρα ποιοῦντες Ῥωμαῖοι οἱ πάντα ἄριστοι Ἄλκιον καὶ Φιλίσκον τοὺς Ἐπικουρείους ἐξέβαλον τῆς πόλεως Λουκίου τοῦ Ποστουμίου ὑπατεύοντος, δι' ἃς εἰσηγοῦντο ἡδονάς. Athenaeus' account is followed by Aelian (*c.*175–*c.*235 CE), *Historical Miscellany* 9.12 (Garbarino fr. 74) and the Byzantine *Suidas s.v.* Epicurus (ε 2405) (Garbarino fr. 75).

72 Epicurus, *Letter to Menoeceus*, preserved by Diogenes Laertius, at 10.131-2: ὅταν οὖν λέγωμεν ἡδονὴν τέλος ὑπάρχειν [...] λέγομεν [...] τὸ μήτε ἀλγεῖν κατὰ σῶμα μήτε ταράττεσθαι κατὰ ψυχήν.

73 Epicurus, *On Lives*, book 1 according to Diogenes Laertius 10.119 (fr. 8 Usener): οὐδὲ πολιτεύσεται, ὡς ἐν τῇ πρώτῃ Περὶ βίων. For those Epicureans who exceptionally did take part in politics see Momigliano 1941, 149–57, cf. Sedley 1997, 41.

74 Castner 1988 is a useful overview of the Roman Epicureans.

75 Cicero, *Brutus* 131 (Garbarino fr. 200): *perfectus Epicureus*, cf. Grimal 1975, 300.

76 See Howe 1951, Garbarino 1973, 462–7.

77 See further Roskam 2007, 84–5.

Epicureanism would conquer 'the whole of Italy', as Cicero has it.[78] This is surely a rhetorical exaggeration on Cicero's part, but by the first half of the 1st century Epicureanism had become an established force in Rome. After 88 BCE the Epicurean Phaedrus (138–70 BCE[79]) visited Rome, if only because due to Sulla the schools in Athens were temporarily closed, when Cicero heard him as a boy.[80] Phaedrus would become head of the Epicurean school from 75 to 70 BCE. Through *On the Nature of Things* by Lucretius (see above, chapter 1 n. 28), Epicurean doctrine would become available in proper Latin too. Its late-ish arrival in Rome, but above all its apolitical character, made for limited influence on those Romans who participated in public life, including those who contributed to the resolution of disputes.[81]

With regard to the Cynics, followers of Diogenes of Sinope (*c.*412/404–*c.*323 BCE) and his pupil Crates of Thebes (*c.*365–*c.*285 BCE), if they can indeed be considered a school with a 'philosophy' (*philosophia*) rather than a group of people sharing 'a way of life' (*enstasis biou*),[82] propagated the simple life, without possessions and 'without a sense of shame' (*anaideia*).[83] If there were any in Rome, no mention is made of them in the extant sources.[84] However, Cynicism may have been present in Rome, simply because from the very beginning of the school onwards it had been an integral part of Stoicism. Zeno of Citium (334–262 BCE), the founder of the school, had originally been a pupil of Crates the Cynic;[85] his *Politeia*, the work that made him famous, was said to have been written on a dog's tail,[86] a clear allusion to the 'doggish' (Greek: *kunikos*) doctrines it contained. Cynic doctrines were also endorsed by Chrysippus of Soli (*c.*280–207 BCE), Zeno's most important successor as head of the school.[87]

[78] Cicero, *Tusculan Disputations* 4.6–7 (Garbarino fr. 206), cf. *Varro* 5–6 (Garbarino fr. 205).

[79] For his dates see Raubitscheck 1949.

[80] See Cicero, *Letters to Friends* no. 63 (13.1) Shackleton Bailey.

[81] Momigliano 1941, 156 suggested that by the end of the period we find 'Epicureans fighting against Caesar's tyranny'. He was followed by Sedley 1997, 46, who brought up an Epicurean motive behind Gaius Cassius Longinus' assassination of Caesar: 'Cassius saw in the current political situation factors which might justify even Epicurean sages in sacrificing their own tranquil detachment.' Benferhat 2005, 314 is more cautious: rather than fighting, the Roman Epicureans were after peace, and where Cassius fought against and murdered Caesar, he rather did so as a member of the Roman nobility.

[82] See Diogenes Laertius 6.103 for the ancient formulation of the question; the recent rise in interest in philosophy as a way life is especially due to Hadot, see, e.g. his inaugural lecture at the Collège de France (1984–1985), reprinted in Hadot 2002.

[83] See Chapter 7, section 7.2 for their denunciation of property.

[84] On Cynicism in second-century BCE Rome see Billerbeck 1979, 3–4, cf. Dudley 1937, 118–19 and Griffin 1993.

[85] Diogenes Laertius 7.2-3.

[86] Diogenes Laertius 7.4.

[87] Diogenes 7.187–8 (*SVF* 3.744).

In the 2nd century BCE, Apollodorus of Seleucia, nicknamed 'the one with the white spots in his eyes',[88] a student of his fellow countryman Diogenes of Babylon,[89] maintained in the ethical part of his *Introduction to the Stoic Doctrines* that the sage cynicises and that Cynicism is a shortcut to virtue.[90] Later in the 2nd century BCE, after Apollodorus had written his *Introduction*, Panaetius, head of the Stoic school from 129 BCE onwards, wanted to get rid of the Cynic aspects of Stoicism (with shamelessness surely as the most offensive characteristic for the traditional Romans), arguing against 'those Stoics that are almost Cynics': Cynicism must have been important enough.[91]

In sum: in the 2nd century, with the embassy of 155 BCE as a focal point, the Hellenistic philosophers presented themselves in Rome and the Romans became acquainted with the main Hellenistic schools of thought. While the sceptical Academy, the Peripatetics, Epicureans and Cynics had at first marginal impact on Roman thought, contact between the Stoics and Romans appears to be most promising: 'Until the middle of the first century BC[E], philosophical debate in Rome was dominated by Stoic ideas.'[92] Let us see in the next chapters what these connections brought about in law and in philosophy.

[88] ὁ ἔφηλος, see Diogenes Laertius 7.39. On the nickname see Crönert 1906, 80 n. 395, followed by von der Mühll 1976 [1963], 359–63 and in Dorandi's 2013 edition of Diogenes Laertius *ad loc.*

[89] For the relation between the two, see the catalogue of Diogenes' pupils in Philodemus (*c.*110–*c.*40 BCE), *History of the Stoics* 51.6–7 (*SVF* Diogenes fr. 11) and the contents pages in the *Parisinus graecus* 1759, one of the oldest and most reliable among the extant manuscripts of Diogenes Laertius, in which Apollodorus is mentioned immediately after Diogenes of Babylon. Unfortunately, that part of (book 7 of) Diogenes Laertius is no longer extant.

[90] Both doctrines are preserved by Diogenes Laertius 7.121, *SVF* Apollodorus fr. 13: κυνιεῖν τ' αὐτόν· εἶναι γὰρ τὸν κυνισμὸν σύντομον ἐπ' ἀρετὴν ὁδόν, ὡς Ἀπολλόδωρος ἐν τῇ Ἠθικῇ. Cf. Dawson 1992, 212 n. 1.

[91] Cicero, *On Appropriate Actions* 1.128 (and 1.148), fr. 73 Alesse, fr. C11 (and C12) Vimercati. Cf. Dawson 1992, 174.

[92] Stein 1971, 757.

CHAPTER 3

'System' in law

3.1 Introduction

The topic of this chapter is the transformation of the study of law into a science in late Republican Rome. Towards the end of the 2nd century BCE, Roman lawyers became interested in dialectical methods and were fascinated by the accounts of what the application of these methods could result in. As we will see, both with regard to method as well as the result, the Stoic understanding of science played a crucial role.

Two preliminary remarks about the term 'science' are important here. First, according to Cicero, one of our main sources about this transformation, from the 2nd century BCE onwards, law came to be considered in terms of a 'science' (*epistēmē* in Greek, *scientia* in Latin) or 'expertise' (*technē* in Greek, *ars* in Cicero's Latin). Unlike Aristotle's account – which did not play a role in the late Roman Republic (see Chapter 2, section 2.2), but would become influential in later times – the Stoics equated science and expertise. They took expertise as the model for science, following Socrates as described by, for example, Plato in his *Apology*.[1] Second, science must be understood in a general sense, rather than in its narrow meaning of 'natural science', which in the English language was after all only developed in the 17th and 18th centuries.[2] The classical definition of law as a science or expertise has been preserved at the beginning of the *Digest*, Justinian's collection of Roman case law, and ascribed to Celsus (67–130 CE), as 'the science of the good and the equitable'.[3]

How should the introduction of this notion of science in the legal domain be assessed? This question has rightly been much discussed. According to historians such as Fritz Schulz, Bruce Frier, Claudia Moatti

[1] For the Stoics on (the equation of) science and expertise see Brouwer 2014, 18–50, for the Socratic ancestry see Brouwer 2014, 146–7.

[2] See Long and Sedley 1987, vol. 1, 161–2, 263–4, Wootton 2015.

[3] *Digest* 1.1.1.1: *ars boni et aequi.*

and Aldo Schiavone, it amounted to as much as a scientific revolution.[4] Others, such as Ulrich von Lübtow, and more recently Kaius Tuori,[5] maintained that such a change did not take place in law at all. A third group of historians took up a moderate, intermediate position. Among those, the legal historian Franz Wieacker assessed the change as a more modest one.[6] Wieacker is somewhat unspecific as to what happened instead, but he seems to suggest that, with the use of Greek terminology, the jurists of the late 2nd century and the beginning of the early 1st century BCE started to develop a methodological awareness related to their existing practice.

My addition to this long-standing debate is to build on Wieacker's moderate approach, while taking Schulz's remark about differentiating between the Hellenistic philosophical schools seriously.[7] Unlike Frier's sociological analysis,[8] I will thus discuss the change against the background of a specific conception of science in the era of the late Roman Republic.[9] This means, as I have already indicated, that we have to deal with Stoic thinking about science, which put at least some of the Roman jurists on the track of applying the Stoic notions of science in terms of methods and system to their existing practice. I will argue that, even if at the time this would not amount to a radical change of the legal practice itself, it would turn out to have this effect on later generations, with a profound and still lasting impact on the jurisdictions in the European continent and in most of its former colonies.

In placing the limited evidence on the changes in law in the late second century BCE in the context of the extant, perhaps even more limited

[4] Schulz 1946/1961, 62–9/73–91, especially 67/81: 'Übertragung [...] von allergrößter Bedeutung'; Stein 1966, 26–48; Pólay 1968, 174: the change is 'epochemachend'; Frier 1985, 156: 'profound transformation'; Moatti 2015 [1997], 6 (cf. her ch. 5): 'a change of paradigm'; Schiesaro 2007, 73; Schiavone 2012/2017: 'decisive transformation' (156/153), 'intellectual revolution' (158/154), 'epistemic revolution' (202/196), with respect to Mucius filius: 'everything changed [...] qualitative leap' (183/178–9).

[5] Von Lübtow 1944, Tuori 2007.

[6] Wieacker 1969, 469: 'Schulz' wissenschaftliche Revolution hat so nicht stattgefunden.'

[7] See above, Chapter 1, n. 24.

[8] Frier 1985 is an important study, in which the 'profound transformation' (156) is analysed as a change caused by a small group of jurisconsults, like Quintus Mucius Scaevola Pontifex (*c.*140–82 BCE), who sought to counter 'disintegrative influences' on law (xiii), such as procedural reforms and rhetorical advocacy (157–8), by reconstructing their legal practice as a more autonomous and intellectual discipline, indeed as a science. Unlike Frier, in the analysis offered in this chapter I will focus on how some Hellenistic philosophers provided the Roman jurists with the intellectual instruments necessary to consider the discipline as science.

[9] Of course, we should neither anachronistically import modern conceptions of science (see Hoetink 1955) nor refrain from investigating the origins of the jurists' conception of science altogether (see e.g. Tuori 2007, followed by Thomas 2016, 17: 'Science is all things to all men').

evidence on Stoic thinking about science, I will proceed as follows: I will start with a discussion of whose conception of science the jurists picked up on (in sections 3.2 and 3.3), and then discuss the legal sources in terms of these conceptions (section 3.4).

3.2 Whose understanding of science?

What were the conceptions of science available to the Roman jurists in the late 2nd and early 1st century BCE? Two points need to be made in this respect: first, as discussed in Chapter 2, section 2.2, in Rome in this period the dominant school of thought was the Stoic one; second, unlike the other schools active in late Republican Rome, the Stoics took an active interest in thinking about and formulating a positive conception of science – as we will see in this chapter.

Among the other Greek philosophical schools, which in this period came to be represented in Rome, Epicurus and his followers can be left aside here: there is no trace in the extant evidence that they were interested in developing a conception of science as such.[10] In contrast to Epicurus, Aristotle had developed a theory of the sciences that distinguished between the theoretical, practical and productive sciences (he also referred to the latter as 'expertises').[11] However, it is at best unclear how familiar Aristotle's writings were in late Republican Rome. As discussed in Chapter 2, section 2.2, Aristotle's works as we know these today, that is his lecture notes, were presumably only made available in the second half of the 1st century. Since most modern assessments of developments in Roman law *do* take Aristotle's conception into account, they thus need to be used with caution.[12]

As for Plato's school, as already discussed in Chapter 2, section 2.2, in this period its members were sceptics; the Academy had yet to develop a dogmatic philosophical system. Only in the beginning of the 1st century

[10] This is not to say that Epicurus was not interested in scientific methodology, that is in the way nature ought to be studied. For the sources see *LS*, chapters 17 and 18, cf. e.g. Asmis 1984, Bakker 2016.

[11] *Topics* 6.6 145a15–16, *Physics* 2.1 192b8–12, *On the Heaven* 3.1 298a27–32, *On the Soul* 1.1 403a27–b2, *Metaphysics* 6.1 1025b25, 6.1 1026a18–19, 9.1 1064a16–19, 9.2 1046b1–3, *Nicomachean Ethics* 6.2 1139a26–8, 6.8 1141b29–32. Cf. Shields 2014, 34.

[12] E.g. La Pira 1934–1937, Talamanca 1977, and Giglio 2018 discuss the transformation of the study of law under the influence of Aristotle and the Stoics alike. Wieacker 1988, 622–7 starts his discussion of the beginnings of the 'Rechtswissenschaft' in Rome with an account of Aristotle's *Posterior Analytics*, mentioning Chrysippus, the third head of the Stoic school, in n. 34, in a reference to the 'Eklektiker [?] Diogenes Laertius'.

BCE, in the Academy, did Philo of Larissa, develop a moderate form of scepticism.[13] In line with Arcesilaus and Carneades, Philo and his followers still argued against the Stoic criterion of truth as the infallible impression, but they accepted that some impressions could be more convincing. In other words: whereas for the Stoics the infallible impression remained the criterion of truth, for the Philonean Academy the more probable or convincing impression already sufficed.[14] The methodology that followed from Philo's epistemological stance was therefore hearing either side on any given topic, that is: hearing the doctrines of the different, other schools of thought, and on the basis thereof choosing the most convincing doctrine. Cicero was a self-proclaimed follower of this moderate, 'cautious' sceptical methodology.[15]

In sum: with the Epicureans disinterested, Aristotle's lecture notes probably not yet known, the Academy sceptical and at any rate not having developed a positive, 'Platonist' conception of science yet, the dominant school, which indeed offered a positive conception of science in the 2nd and 1st centuries BCE, was the Stoic school. If this assessment is correct, and if one wants to discuss the change with regard to Roman law against the background of Greek thinking about science, this should thus be done against the backdrop of the Stoic school. Next to the existing concepts, a further point that should be taken into account is the interest in Stoicism among jurists in the late 2nd and early 1st century BCE, with the Stoic Panaetius being a pivotal figure in making Stoicism palatable to the Romans.[16]

3.3 The Stoic definitions of science

Let us now move on to the extant Stoic definitions of science. The admittedly pithy remains of Stoic definitions of science survived in connection with Plato's *Gorgias*. The *Gorgias* is one of the first texts in the Western tradition in which the question is put as to what a science is.[17] At the beginning of Plato's dialogue, at 448b, Socrates and his interlocutors discuss the question of whether (Gorgias') rhetoric can count as a science,

13 For Philo see Brittain 2001, for a history of the school see Bonazzi 2015 (with references to earlier literature).

14 See also Chapter 4, n. 14.

15 See, e.g. Glucker 1988, Woolf 2015, 10–33.

16 See above Chapter 2, section 2.2.

17 For the context of the debate see above, Chapter 1, section 1.5. For Gorgias and Greek rhetoric see Wardy 1996.

or whether it should rather be considered an 'experience' (*empeiria*) or, as it is referred to at 463b, a 'knack' (*tribē*).[18]

In this context, that is in his *Commentary on the Gorgias* 12.1 (*SVF* 1.73, LS 42A, *FDS* 392), the 6th-century CE Platonist Olympiodorus gives the first of the Stoic definitions of science as a system of cognitions:

> Zeno says that 'science is a system of cognitions unified by training towards some useful end in life'.[19]

The ascription of this definition to Zeno of Citium, the founder of Stoicism, is confirmed in other evidence. According to Sextus Empiricus, *Against the Professors* 7.373 (*FDS* 403), Chrysippus spoke of science as 'a system and a collection of cognitions'.[20] In a passage in a work entitled *Introduction*, at 14, 44.5–6 (*FDS* 393A), by David, presumably a student of Olympiodorus, the definition is cited anonymously, but has 'by experience' added to it.[21] Chrysippus, the third head of the school, also used this extra clause in his definition of the highest 'end' (*telos*) in life, while clarifying the definitions given by Zeno and his immediate successor Cleanthes of Assos (*c.*331–232 BCE).[22] This makes it likely that David in fact cites Chrysippus' definition, and gives further credence of Olympiodorus' attribution of the definition to Zeno.[23]

The second Stoic definition of science is also in the *Commentary*, which Olympiodorus presents immediately after the first definition, at 12.2 (*SVF* 1.490, *FDS* 392):

> Cleanthes, then, says that a science is 'a tenor [i.e. a disposition] that accomplishes everything methodically'. But this definition is considered to be incomplete, for nature is also a tenor that does methodically all it

[18] See also Plato's succinct formulation in his *Phaedrus*, at 270b: μὴ τριβῇ μόνον καὶ ἐμπειρίᾳ ἀλλὰ τέχνῃ. Cf. Scarano Ussani 1997, 31.

[19] Ζήνων δέ φησιν ὅτι 'τέχνη ἐστὶ σύστημα ἐκ καταλήψεων συγγεγυμνασμένων πρός τι τέλος εὔχρηστον τῶν ἐν τῷ βίῳ'. In reading συγγεγυμνασμένων rather than συγγεγυμνασμένον I follow von Arnim's silent emendation *ad loc.*, made explicit by Mansfeld 1983, 57, as it should be the cognitions rather than the system that are unified by training.

[20] οἱ περὶ τὸν Χρύσιππον [. . .] σύστημα καὶ ἄθροισμα καταλήψεων.

[21] τέχνη ἐστὶ σύστημα ἐκ καταλήψεων ἐμπειρίᾳ συγγεγυμνασμένη πρός τι τέλος εὔχρηστον τῶν ἐν τῷ βίῳ.

[22] See, e.g. the clarifications of Zeno's formula of the end in Stobaeus (early 5th century CE) 2.75.11–6.8 (LS 63B, *FDS* 794A): 'To Zeno's "living accordingly" Cleanthes added "with nature", and Chrysippus, wishing to clarify this further, expressed it in this way: "living according to the experience of the things happening by nature"'. More examples of this procedure of clarification are conveniently listed by Schofield 1999b, 81 n. 29.

[23] Mansfeld 1983, 64.

> does. Accordingly Chrysippus adding 'with impressions', said 'a science is a tenor to proceed in a certain way with impressions'.[24]

In the *Scholia on Dionysius Thrax* 118.13–16 (*SVF* 1.72, *FDS* 410) this definition is also ascribed to Zeno:

> Zeno says that 'science is a tenor capable of proceeding methodically', that is making something according to a certain way and method.[25]

Although in modern scholarship the attribution to Zeno has been doubted,[26] Chrysippus' variation is yet again an example of the process of clarification of an earlier formulation by the earliest heads of the Stoic school, and thus the definition must be authentic, too.

If we look more closely at these definitions, we can distinguish at least three aspects of science.[27] First, science has a useful end; second, it consists of a disposition of the mind on the basis of which the scientist can proceed methodically, bringing together or presenting dispersed notions as related;[28] and, third, it results in a system of cognitions.[29] It should be noted that the explicit mention of the notion of system – or of systematisation, for that matter – is new here.[30]

3.4 The definitions applied in law

The Stoic definitions of science can now be connected with law. As we will see, the Stoic conception of science enabled the Roman jurists of the late

[24] Κλεάνθης τοίνυν λέγει ὅτι 'τέχνη ἐστὶν ἕξις ὁδῷ πάντα ἀνύουσα'. ἀτελὴς δ' ἐστιν οὗτος ὁ ὅρος, καὶ γὰρ ἡ φύσις ἕξις τίς ἐστιν ὁδῷ πάντα ποιοῦσα· ὅθεν ὁ Χρύσιππος προσθεὶς τὸ 'μετὰ φαντασιῶν' εἶπεν ὅτι 'τέχνη ἐστὶν ἕξις ὁδῷ προιοῦσα μετὰ φαντασιῶν'.

[25] ὁ Ζήνων, λέγων 'τέχνη ἐστὶν ἕξις ὁδοποιητική' [ὁδῷ ποιητική – Festa 1932–1935, 110, Mansfeld 1983, 62], τουτέστι δι' ὁδοῦ καὶ μεθόδου ποιοῦσά τι.

[26] E.g. Pearson 1891, 27, von Arnim *ad SVF* 1.72, Festa 1932–1935, 41, Isnardi Parente 1966, 288, Ioppolo 1980, 280–1.

[27] Discussions of the Stoic definitions include Sparshott 1978 (also useful on system – see Scarano 1997, 13 n. 10), Mansfeld 1983, Ioppolo 1980, 280–1, Long and Sedley 1987, 263–4, Sellars 2009, 68–75 (who only discusses the systematic definition), Brouwer 2014, 45–6 (followed here).

[28] See e.g. Villey 1945, 10.

[29] In line with their corporealism the Stoics speak of cognitions rather than doctrines: only cognitions or 'grasps' (*katalēpseis*) exist, doctrines do not; the latter can only 'subsist'.

[30] Catana 2008. In the *Philebus* 17d Plato used system in relation to musical notes (cf. *Epinomis* 991e: in relation to numbers) and in *Laws* 686b in relation to forms of government (cf. Aristotle, *Nicomachean Ethics* 9.8 1168b32). As for the Stoics, they spoke of the world as 'a system of gods and men' (Eusebius of Caesarea (*c.*260–339 CE), *Preparation for the Gospel* 15.15.3–5, *SVF* 2.528), and of arguments as a constellation of propositions (see Diogenes Laertius 7.48, *FDS* 255). The early Stoics were the first to use system in relation to science (for further, later Stoic evidence see Epictetus (second half of the 1st century CE) 1.20.5 and Sextus Empiricus, *Outlines of Pyrrhonism* 2.173).

2nd and early 1st century to rethink their practice in terms of how to proceed and what to produce, that is to think about law in terms of method (3.4.1) and system (3.4.2). It should be emphasised that, similar to the evidence on the Stoics, the textual evidence on Roman law is limited. Again no complete treatises have survived, although with regard to law we are here somewhat better served. We can at least rely on non-hostile, albeit second-hand, accounts in Cicero's writings and in Justinian's Byzantine compilation of Roman law.

3.4.1 Method

Let us first look at the methods applied to law. The methods in the definition 'a tenor that accomplishes everything methodically' are picked up from Stoic dialectic. In Cicero's dialogue entitled *Brutus* (indeed Decimus Junius Brutus Albinus, who would later kill Julius Caesar, in order to restore the Roman Republic), at 153, Stoic dialectic is characterised as 'the greatest science among the sciences'.[31]

As already mentioned in Chapter 1, section 1.4, the Stoics regarded dialectic as a part of logic, which was itself one of the three parts of wisdom, besides physics and ethics. As for dialectic, the Stoics understood it in a broad sense. They subdivided it into the study of valid reasoning (or logic in the modern sense), of language (or grammar) and of the criterion of truth (or epistemology). Both logic and dialectic in the Stoic sense have thus a broad meaning, and differ from the modern, more limited understanding of logic as the expertise of valid reasoning.

Let us now look at the methods of Stoic dialectic. The fundamental methods of Stoic dialectic are dividing and defining,[32] which – as Long and Sedley put it in their source collection of Hellenistic thinkers – are 'especially in evidence in ethical texts'.[33] The first method of dividing is 'the dissection of a genus into the proximate species' (Diogenes Laertius 7.61, LS 32C).[34]

The second method of defining in the Stoic sense means finding the 'characteristic' (*idikon* in Greek, or *proprium* in Cicero's Latin translation).

[31] *artem omnium artium maximam* [. . .] *dialecticam.*

[32] Augustine, *On Christian Doctrine* 2.53 defines dialectic as the 'art of defining and dividing'. Cf. Moatti 1997/2015, 383 n. 3/228 n. 3.

[33] Long and Sedley 1987, vol. 1, 193.

[34] διαίρεσις δέ ἐστι γένους ἡ εἰς τὸ προσεχῆ εἴδη τομή. For the method of division in Hellenistic ethics, which is already mentioned in Plato's *Phaedrus* 265–6 and developed in his *Sophist*, *Statesman*, and *Philebus*, see e.g. Chrysippus' division of the various possible interpretations of the good life, as discussed by Algra 1997 and Annas 2007.

According to Chrysippus' *On Definitions* in Diogenes Laertius 7.60 (LS 32C), a definition is thus 'the representation of a characteristic'.[35] In the 2nd century BCE, Antipater of Tarsus clarified Chrysippus' account. According to Antipater, the characteristic must be 'necessary', i.e. must have 'reciprocal force' (*Scholia on Dionysius Thrax* 107.5-7, *SVF* 3.226, LS 32B). Antipater's definition of 'definition' thus becomes – from his first book of *On Definitions*, book 1, see Diogenes Laertius 7.60, *SVF* Antipater fr. 23, LS 32C) – 'an account of analysis exactly expressed'.[36]

These fundamental methods of Stoic dialectic were applied with regard to law. The most extensive piece of evidence is in the long celebration of the science of rhetoric, which Cicero puts in the mouth of Lucius Licinius Crassus. This celebration is part of a conversation with, among others, Quintus Mucius Scaevola Augur (consul in 117, d.82 BCE), and which Cicero situates in Tusculum in the year 91 BCE. In *On the Orator*, at 1.188–9, Crassus applies these methods of dividing and defining to Rome's *ius civile*. The method of dividing is in '[a]', and the method of defining is in '[b]':

> In the *ius civile* [...] we must [a] designate the general classes, restricting these to a small fixed number. Now a general class is that which embraces two or more species, resembling one another in some common property while differing in some peculiarity. And species are subdivisions, ranged under those general classes from which they derive; while all names, whether of general classes or species, must [b] be so defined as to show the significance of each. A definition is a concise and accurate statement, which gives the characteristic of the thing we wish to define.[37] (tr. Sutton and Rackham, modified)

The evidence for categorisation in the legal sources themselves is related to the jurists Quintus Mucius Scaevola Pontifex and Servius Sulpicius. As for Quintus Mucius Scaevola, from the extant legal evidence we can infer that – after his father Publius Mucius (and two others) had 'laid the foundations' (*fundaverunt*) of the *ius civile* (*Digest* 1.2.2.39, from

[35] ὅρος δέ ἐστιν, [...] ὡς Χρύσιππος ἐν τῷ Περὶ ὅρων, ἰδίου ἀπόδοσις. For the Stoics on definition see Crivelli 2010.

[36] ὅρος δέ ἐστιν, ὥς φησιν Ἀντίπατρος ἐν τῷ πρώτῳ Περὶ ὅρων, λόγος κατ᾽ ἀνάλυσιν ἀπαρτιζόντως ἐκφερόμενος.

[37] *in iure civili* [...] [a] *genera et ad certum numerum paucitatemque revocanda. genus autem id est, quod sui similis communione quadam, specie autem differentis, duas aut pluris complectitur partis; partes autem sunt, quae generibus eis, ex quibus manant, subiciuntur; omniaque, quae sunt vel generum vel partium nomina,* [b] *definitionibus, quam vim habeant, est exprimendum; est enim definitio rerum earum, quae sunt eius rei propriae, quam definire volumus, brevis et circumscripta quaedam explicatio. hisce ego rebus exempla adiungerem, nisi apud quos haec haberetur oratio cernerem.*

Pomponius' *Handbook*)[38] – the son would have applied the dialectical methods of, first, dividing and, second, defining.[39] About the method of dividing the material into kinds,[40] the excerpt from Pomponius' *Handbook* in *Digest* 1.2.2.41 (test. 73 FSS) tells us that 'Mucius became the first man to divide the civil law into kinds by arranging it in eighteen books.'[41] The result would eventually be – as Schiavone put it – a '"metaphysics" of social relations, reduced to a defined number of archetypal models'.[42] Here, Pomponius' account appears reliable enough (for its unreliability, see above, Chapter 1, section 1.3): elsewhere examples of Mucius' divisions survived. In Gaius' *Teaching Manual* 1.188 (fr. 24 Lenel, fr. 43 FSS) Quintus Mucius' division of kinds of 'guardianship' (*tutela*) is preserved:

> From this it can be seen how many kinds of guardianship there are. [...] Some, like Quintus Mucius have said that there are five kinds, others, like Servius, that there are three; others, like Labeo, two.[43]

In *Digest* 41.2.3.23, from Paulus, *On the Edict*, book 54 (fr. 31 Lenel, fr. 55 FSS) Mucius' division with regard to the legal notion of 'possession' (*possessio*) has been preserved, albeit in a hostile version: 'What Quintus Mucius included among the kinds of possession [...] is truly absurd.'[44] Another example of of Quintus Mucius' categorising, outside law, survived in Augustine's *On the City of God* 4.27 (fr. 102 FSS). It deals with his tripartition of traditions on the gods, divided into those developed by poets, by philosophers, and as accepted in the city respectively.[45]

38 On *fundaverunt* see further Chapter 6, section 6.3. In his discussion of the foundations of Roman law Tuori 2004 (reprinted in his 2007, 21–69) focuses on the son rather than the father as the founder of the *ius civile*. Winkel 2005 is rightly critical.

39 See e.g. Frier 1985, 160–3. Schiavone 2012/2017, 180–1/176 adds that Mucius would have dealt with layers of law, and would have used the notion of *caput*; the evidence here is Cicero, *Letters to Friends* no. 331 (7.22) Shackleton Bailey.

40 At *Topics* 28, Cicero discusses the distinction between *partitio* and *divisio* respectively (for the Stoic origin of the distinction see Diogenes Laertius 7.61–2), illustrated with the legal examples of the partition of sources of law and the division of the kinds of transfer of property. According to Nörr 1972a, the distinction would have been taken over by the Roman jurists, whereas Talamanca 1977, 105 maintains that the distinction may well have been too sophisticated for the jurists' taste.

41 *Quintus Mucius Publii filius pontifex maximus ius civile primus constituit generatim in libros decem et octo.*

42 Schiavone 2012/2017, 202/196.

43 *ex his apparet, quot sint species tutelarum.* [...] *hoc totum <omittimus. hoc solum> tantisper sufficit admonuisse, quod quidam quinque genera esse dixerunt, ut Quintus Mucius, alii tria, ut Servius Sulpicius; alii duo, ut Labeo.*

44 *quod autem Quintus Mucius inter genera possessionum posuit,* [...] *ineptissimum est.*

45 Cf. Schiavone 1976, 6–66 and Schiavone 2012/2017, 226/224–5, who discusses its likely Stoic origin and Mucius' criticism of the first two traditions.

About the second method of defining, Quintus Mucius, dealt with definitions in his book entitled *Definitions*, of which the title – in Greek – survived in the *Index Florentinus* of the *Digest*, at 3.1.[46] He must have done so in the footsteps of his father, from whom the definition of the 'free space' (*ambitus*) around a house survived in Cicero's *Topics*, at 24.[47] The Greek in the title has sometimes been taken as proof of its inauthenticity; it seems more appropriate to take it as evidence for the novelty of the terminology, which had yet to be translated into Latin.[48]

With Servius Sulpicius the dialectical methods of dividing and defining were applied even more consistently. In Cicero's *Brutus* the interlocutors Cicero and Brutus discuss Servius' place in the development of law. At 152, Cicero claims that it was Servius who made law into a science by using the dialectical methods of categorising, defining, and interpreting the obscure and ambiguous, in order to produce general rules that can be applied to specific cases.[49] Brutus is somewhat hesitant here, such that Peter Stein's assessment of the difference between Mucius' and Servius' methods as a change of emphasis rather than of nature is probably correct. As one might expect in a subsequent generation, Servius applied these dialectical methods more strictly and consistently than Mucius.[50]

Of course, to us, the application of these methods of dividing and defining may seem all too simple. But here Brian Frier's words can be brought to mind: 'A modern lawyer will find nothing unusual in all this activity. But there is simply no evidence that any human being, let alone any Roman, had ever previously worked with such sustained effort on the materials of a secular legal system.'[51]

[46] *Q. Mucius Scaevola*, ὅρων βίβλιον ἕν.

[47] *ambitus aedium* [...], *quod parietis communis tegendi causa tectum proiceretur, ex quo tecto in eius aedis qui protexisset aqua deflueret.* See, e.g. Reinhardt 2003, 252–4 and Schiavone 2012/2017, 170/166.

[48] Scherillo 1952, cf. Schmidlin 1976, 107, who characterises the book as 'the doubtlessy most spectular attempt to make dialectic work for the legal discipline' (my translation).

[49] Cicero's Latin reads: *quae doceret rem universam tribuere in partes, latentem explicare definiendo, obscuram explanare interpretando, ambigua primum videre, deinde distinguere, postremo habere regulam, qua vera et falsa iudicarentur et quae quibus propositis essent quaeque non essent consequentia.* See Miglietta 2010 for extensive references to discussions of this passage in modern scholarship.

[50] Stein 1978, who characterises Mucius as 'insufficiently rigorous' (184).

[51] Frier 1985, 163. The expression 'legal system' is question-begging: its systematic character had yet to be made explicit.

3.4.2 System

Let us move on to the application of the second Stoic definition of science as a system of cognitions unified by training towards some useful end in life. Again a preliminary, terminological remark must be made: a standard Latin translation of the Greek word *sustēma* did not come into being. In the Latin translations of the Stoic definition of science as a system, either *constructio* or *ratio* is used. In Cicero's extant writings a uniform translation cannot be found.[52] It can therefore be no surprise that in the Latin tradition a uniform equivalent for the Greek *sustēma* is missing.[53] In the 4th century CE Diomedes, incidentally ascribing the Stoic definition to Cicero, would use *constructio*, whereas also in the 4th century, Marius Victorinus would use *ratio* instead.[54]

Even though a standard Latin translation of the Greek term is lacking, in the late 2nd or early 1st century BCE the production of systematical accounts had become fashionable. In his *On the Orator*, at 1.187–9, with the year 91 BCE as its dramatic date, Cicero's character Crassus gives the examples of (1) music, (2) geometry, (3) astronomy, (4) grammar (including the study of poetry and history), and (5) rhetoric:

> Nearly all elements, now forming the content of the sciences, were once without order or correlation: [1] in music, for example, rhythms, sounds and tones; [2] in geometry, lines, figures, distances and sizes; [3] in astronomy, the revolution of the sky, the risings, settings and movements of heavenly bodies; [4] in grammar, the study of poets, the investigation of the stories, the explanation of words and proper intonation in speaking them; [5] and lastly in this very theory of rhetoric, invention, style, arrangement, memory and delivery, once seemed to all men things unknown and widely separate one from another. And so a certain science [i.e. Stoic dialectic] was called in from outside, derived from another definite sphere, which philosophers arrogate wholly to themselves, in order that it might give coherence to things so far disconnected and sundered, and bind them in some sort of system.[55]

[52] See *SVF* 1.73: *Lucullus* 22: *constat*; *On Ends* 3.18: *ratio*; *On the Nature of the Gods* 2.148: *collatis et conparatis*. Cf. *Varro* 43: *veteris Academiae ratio et Stoicorum.*

[53] Hager 1998, 824–5.

[54] Diomedes, *Science of Grammar* 2, p. 421 Keil (*SVF* 1.73): *ars est perceptionum exercitarum constructio ad unum exitum utilem vitae pertinentium;* Marius Victorinus, *Science of Grammar* 1, p. 1 Keil: *ars est summa rerum ratio comprehensarum atque exercitarum ad aliquem vitae finem tendentium.* Cf. Mariotti 1967, 106–7.

[55] *omnia fere, quae sunt conclusa nunc artibus, dispersa et dissipata quondam fuerunt; ut* [1] *in musicis numeri et voces et modi;* [2] *in geometria lineamenta, formae, intervalla, magnitudines;* [3] *in astrologia caeli conversio, ortus, obitus motusque siderum;* [4] *in grammaticis poetarum pertractatio, historiarum cognitio, verborum interpretatio, pronuntiandi quidam sonus;* [5] *in hac denique ipsa ratione dicendi excogitare, ornare, disponere, meminisse, agere, ignota quondam omnibus et diffusa late videbantur.*

Cicero's suggestion is obvious: the Roman practitioners of law could not stay behind.[56] Indeed, law *was* no exception, and attempts were made to present it in a systematic manner, too.[57] Somewhat later in the 1st century BCE, Roman religious law was presumably presented in a systematic manner by the polymath Varro (116–27 CE) in his *Antiquities*.[58] Also somewhat later than 91 BCE the Roman statesmen Pompey (106–48 CE) and after him Julius Caesar (100–44 CE) formulated proposals to systematise statutes.[59] The first instance of systematisation in law, however, would become the *ius honorarium*, the law developed on the basis of the praetor's *imperium* (see above Chapter 2, section 2.1). What is more, different from Pompey's and Caesar's, the proposals with regard to the *ius honorarium* were in the end put into practice by the Roman jurists. In the dialogue *On the Orator*, Cicero lets Crassus make the following plan at 1.190:

> Now I will briefly summarise my plan. For if I am permitted to do what I have long been projecting, or if someone else anticipates me, preoccupied as I am, or does the work when I am dead, first dividing the entire *ius civile* into general kinds, which are very few, and next distributing what I may call the subdivisions of those classes, and after that making plain the proper significance of each by definition, then you will have a complete system of the *ius civile*, magnificent and copious but neither inaccessible nor obscure.[60]

adhibita est igitur ars quaedam extrinsecus ex alio genere quodam, quod sibi totum philosophi adsumunt, quae rem dissolutam divulsamque conglutinaret et ratione quadam constringeret. The translation is based on Sutton and Rackham 1942 as well as May and Wisse 2001.

56 See further Rawson 1978, Mette 1954, 51 n. 1, Fuhrmann 1960 (offering an ahistorical, systematic approach here), Moatti 1997, Reinhardt 2003, 59–66. Griffin 2013a also discusses the relation between Roman law and philosophy in the late Roman Republic, but with emphasis on the influence of philosophy on law.

57 In the literature on Roman law some attention is paid to the Stoic definition of science as a system: La Pira 1936–1937, 150–1, followed by Wenger 1953. The definition is mentioned by Behrends 1976, 40, Scarano Ussani 1997, 12–15, 113–14.

58 On Varro as a systematiser of religious law, see Cicero's characterisation in his *Varro* 9: tu [sc. Varro] *sacrorum iura et sacerdotum* [. . .] *aperuisti*; see further Macrae 2017, Smith 2018 (on Varro's 'antiquarianism' in general), and Leonardis 2019, chapters 3 and 4.

59 See Isidorus of Sevilla (*c.*600–636 CE), *Etymology* 5.1.5: *leges autem redigere in libris primus consul Pompeius instituere voluit, sed non perseveravit obtrectatorum metu. deinde Caesar coepit id facere, sed ante interfectus est.* Cf. – with the mention of the *ius civile*, too – Suetonius, *Caesar* 44: *ius civile ad certum modum redigere atque ex immensa diffusaque legum copia optima quaeque et necessaria in paucissimos conferre libros.* See further Sanio 1845, 79–126, Pólay 1965a, 1965b, Talamanca 2009, 98–100.

60 *nunc complectar, quod proposui, brevi: si enim aut mihi facere licuerit, quod iam diu cogito, aut alius quispiam aut me impedito occuparit aut mortuo effecerit, ut primum omne ius civile in genera digerat, quae perpauca sunt, deinde eorum generum quasi quaedam membra dispertiat, tum propriam cuiusque*

In this proposal method and result are connected: the application of the Stoic dialectical methods makes a systematisation of law possible.

Of course, in theory the Stoic definition can be applied to law in various manners. First, as both Peter Stein and Elisabeth Rawson have reminded us, the scope of a system can be complete or partial.[61] Second, the types of systematisation can differ. Here, a distinction can be made between on the one hand systematic accounts of all cases judged in the civil law and on the other hand such accounts based on the praetor's annual edict; that is, on the basis of the list of the types of cases that could be heard by a judge.[62]

As for the first manner, Quintus Mucius aimed at the wide scope of the *ius civile* as a whole. As we have seen, according to Pomponius, *Digest* 1.2.2.41, Mucius arranged the *ius civile* in a compendium of eighteen books. Second, as for the types of systematisation, Mucius devised his compendium of the *ius civile*, whereas according to Pomponius, *Digest* 1.2.2.44, Servius produced a first, although 'very brief' commentary on the praetor's edict, dedicated to Brutus, in two books.[63]

Just as with regard to method, the achievements of Mucius and Servius as systematisers were assessed differently. In the *Brutus*, at 152, Cicero is willing to concede Mucius a 'great familiarity with the law' (*iuris civilis magnum usum*), but less systematisation, whereas he attributes the greater systematisation of law to Servius.[64] Cicero would not have been his ambitious self if he had not attempted to outdo these jurists by producing his own systematic account of Roman civil law, entitled *On Arranging the Civil Law into a Science* (*De iure civile in arte redigendo*).[65] That is to say: if the book had delivered on its title. We cannot be sure, however: the text is

vim definitione declaret, perfectam artem iuris civilis habebitis, magis magnam atque uberem quam difficilem et obscuram.

61 Stein 1978, Rawson 1978.

62 Cerami 1998, 83–4. Next to the basic types, Cerami also distinguishes between derivative types of systematisations that are based either on other jurist's *Digests*, such as the ones by Celsus or Salvius Julianus, or on *Teaching Manuals*, such as the one by Gaius. With regard to the latter type: one of the reasons why Gaius' *Teaching Manual* would become so important is because the praetor's edict had become 'eternal' – see Mette 1954, 64.

63 *Servius duos libros ad Brutum perquam brevissimos ad edictum subscriptos reliquit.* According to Schiavone 2012/2017, chapter 14, Servius would have stopped Mucius' efforts to systematise the law.

64 Cf. Schulz 1946/1961, 96/113, Schiavone 2012/2017, chapter 14, Kaster 2020, 100 n. 243, who are all downplaying Servius' role in systematisation altogether: Servius' focus would have been on the cases. Even so, as Schiavone formulates it, referring to von Savigny, Servius' 'case examination' would be about 'regulating cases' (248/243) and 'ontological forms' (247/243).

65 The two extant fragments are in Garbarino's collection of Cicero's fragments, at 93–4; on the treatise see further Mette 1954. Bretone 1982 [1970], 275–86 suggested that Cicero's treatise would have been used by Pomponius. See further Mantovani 2009.

lost. But after Mucius', further systematic accounts were produced, among which Gaius' and Justinian's teaching manuals (from the 2nd century and 6th century CE, respectively) are the most famous.[66]

3.5 Conclusion and outlook

It can be concluded that in the late 2nd and early 1st century BCE the Stoics presented their conception of science to the Roman jurists. The jurists could thus apply the Stoic methods of dialectic to their unique, or at any rate typically Roman, practice of solving disputes on a specialist basis. They were therefore able to produce systematic accounts of the cases they had judged in the *ius civile*.

The question can now be addressed whether this application implied a fundamental change. The answer, I suggest, is twofold. The answer is affirmative with regard to the study of law: with the tools of Stoic dialectic the study of law changed and systematic accounts of the *ius civile* became possible. The study of law was thus transformed and became scientific. The answer is negative, I believe, with regard to the operations of the law itself: in the words of Antonio Guarino, Publius Mucius and his successors the practice remained – unsurprisingly in the Roman context – 'fundamentally traditional'.[67]

A parallel can be drawn here with Blackstone's *Commentaries on the Laws of England* in the common law tradition, which Blackstone published in the middle of the eighteenth century. These *Commentaries*, one of the most influential systematic accounts of the common law, facilitated the study of law, but did not change the nature of English law itself.[68] Only when the *Commentaries* themselves became an important legal source, as in the newly established United States,[69] did the nature of the US variant of the common law change. In fact, a similar development took place with regard to Roman law: with the tools of Stoic dialectic, it was the study of law that was facilitated. The nature of law itself was changed only at a later date, at the latest at the beginning of the 6th century CE, when the

66 A helpful overview can be found in Scherillo 1953.

67 Guarino 1981, 149: 'fondalmente tradizionalist[i]'. On the limited popularity of abstract thought in Rome (as expressed in Ennius' words *philosophari paucis*, used by Cicero, *On the res publica* 1.30; cf. Aulus Gellius 5.19.9) see also Vesperini 2012, especially 207–47.

68 For a vivid account of the challenges the student of common law faced before Blackstone, see Hale's preface to Rolle's 1688 *Abridgment* as quoted and translated in Jones 1973, xxiv.

69 Of course, in English law the *Commentaries* became a source of law, too, as a 'book of authority'. However, in comparison with case law (or even statute) its relevance was – and in a way still is – limited.

Byzantine Emperor Justinian declared his systematic account of law – which thus goes back to at least Gaius' systematic account[70] – to be a legal source itself. This systematic account would become the model for legal codes on the European continent, including the French, Dutch, Belgian and – again, somewhat later – German civil codes.

In sum: towards the end of the 2nd century BCE, Roman jurists started to think about their legal practice in terms of method and system – under the influence of Stoic thought about science. For methods, they looked at the Stoic definition of science in terms of method, and taking over the methods of dividing and defining developed in dialectic as presented to them by the Stoics in late Republican Rome. For system, they looked at the Stoics' other definition of science, which helped them to produce systematic overviews of law, and which enabled them to study and teach their tradition more comfortably. Only over time would these teaching manuals transform law itself, culminating into – much than 500 years later – Justinian's *Teaching Manual*, the system of which is still surviving in one form or other in the contemporary continental legal codes.

It might even be the case that the study of law as a science influenced the new approaches to the study of 'nature' in the 16th and 17th centuries, or, if that is more to the reader's taste, contributed to the Scientific Revolution, as so much of the terminology of this development or revolution has a background in law – David Wootton in his study *The Invention of Science* rightly drew attention to the notion of 'fact' and 'evidence'.[71] But, of course, that is an altogether different topic.

[70] Kelly 1979 hence presents Gaius' 'institutional scheme' as one of the substructures of Western social thought.

[71] For the notion of 'fact', from the Latin *factum*, 'something that has been done' (to be distinguished from (questions of) law), see Wootton 2015, chapter 7; for 'evidence', presented in courts of law, see Wootton 2015, chapter 11.

CHAPTER 4

'Rule' in law

4.1 Introduction

The systematisation of law into categories with accompanying definitions asks for an account of the relations between and within the categories. In this chapter I will discuss how the term 'rule', *kanōn* in Greek or *regula* in Latin, gradually came to be used, at first with regard to the study of law, and, much later, also in law itself. Contemporary jurists in the Western traditions, both in continental European or civil law but also in the English or common law tradition, often take the notion of rule for granted. In this chapter, then, I want to make a contribution towards a better understanding of the origins of this notion as it was developed in Hellenistic thought and, from there, transferred into Roman law and beyond.

The introduction of the notion of rule in law has been a matter of some debate. Some fifty years ago, Peter Stein suggested that the Roman jurists took over the notion of rule from the grammarians; that is from the students of language.[1] As Stein set out, the grammarians used rules – in the plural – in a debate on how to study the inflexion of words, on whether the focus ought to be on the inflexion of each word (anomalists) or on the regularities between the words (anomalists). Stein may well be right that here the jurists were influenced by the grammarians, and that the jurists under the influence of the analogists started to focus on the regularities between the cases they had decided. Some (later) jurists, such as Labeo (died between 5–22 CE), most likely were. As Aulus Gellius, *Attic Nights* 13.10.1 tells us, Labeo 'had delved deep into grammar and dialectic',[2]

[1] Stein 1966, 49–73, especially 53.

[2] *Labeo Antistius iuris quidem civilis disciplinam principali studio exercuit et consulentibus de iure publice responsitavit; set ceterarum quoque bonarum artium non expers fuit et in grammaticam sese atque dialecticam litterasque antiquiores altioresque penetraverat Latinarumque vocum origines rationesque percalluerat, eaque praecipue scientia ad enodandos plerosque iuris laqueos utebatur.*

which might be taken as (indirect) evidence for the fact that jurists introduced 'rules' in law, out of their interest in grammar and philosophy.[3]

Here I would like to discuss other evidence with regard to the use of rule in Hellenistic thought, both in epistemology as well as in ethics. In epistemology, in the vigorous debate among the philosophical schools about the criterion of truth, the notion of rule was first used in its metaphorical sense, also in the plural: how to decide whether a sensory impression or a statement about that impression is true or false. Among the Stoics, the notion of rule was also used in the domain of ethics, as the criterion of right: how to decide whether an action is right or wrong, or just or unjust. In ethics, especially among the 'Roman' Stoics from the second half of the 2nd century BCE onwards, a focus towards the use in the plural can be discerned: they focused less on the single standard by which to distinguish between right and wrong in a specific situation, but rather on types of actions and the precepts that go with these types. In addition to grammar, Hellenistic epistemology and ethics can thus have served as two other contexts, against which the introduction of rules in law can be explained. What is more, Stoic ethics can here be understood as an intermediate between what otherwise appear to be the rather distant topics of grammar on the one hand and law on the other.

Taking over the late Hellenistic understanding of rule, the Roman jurists were thus able to use it with regard to the cases that they had decided, extracting the rule out of the cases – in the phrase used by the medieval lawyers – proceeding from *casus* to *regula*, and then applying the rule again to similar cases.[4] Different from these medieval (or indeed modern) lawyers, however, for the Roman jurists the use of the notion of rules remained restricted to the study of law. In solving actual cases they rarely referred to rules. Only when one of the teaching manuals that they had produced came to be considered as a legal source, under Justinian, did the notion of rules start to dominate law itself.[5]

The plan of this chapter is as follows. I will start with the notion of rule in Hellenistic epistemology (section 4.2) and ethics (section 4.3). In section 4.4, I will discuss the development in Stoic ethics, from the single standard to types of actions. In section 4.5, I will deal with the parallel in grammar. In section 5.6, finally, I will discuss the introduction of the notion of rule in Roman law, against the background of these debates in epistemology, ethics and grammar.

[3] Cf. Stein 1966, 63, Stein 1971, 764–6.
[4] See e.g. Cairns and Du Plessis 2010.
[5] See e.g. Ioro 2010.

4.2 'Rule' in Hellenistic epistemology

Before I start to discuss the ocurrences of rule in Hellenistic thought, the original meaning of *regula* should be considered.[6] *Regula*, a derivation of the verb *regere*, 'to keep straight',[7] has the basic sense of a straight line (cf. *rectum*, straight). Already in a transferred, metaphorical sense, it came to mean the carpenter's rule along which physical object could be measured. In an even wider sense it acquired the meaning of 'standard'. It is in this sense that we encounter *regula* in Hellenistic thought, or *kanōn* as its Greek equivalent. (Just as the Latin *regula*, the Greek word *kanōn* underwent a similar shift in meaning: from the litteral meaning 'straight line' to the metaphorical meaning of 'standard'.)

In Hellenistic thought, rule in the sense of standard is above all used in epistemology, but it also occurs in ethics. I will first deal with epistemology, in which *regula* refers to the means of distinguishing truth from falsehood, also referred to as the 'criterion of truth'. This usage may well have started with Epicurus.[8] According to Diogenes Laertius, at 10.31 (fr. 35 Usener, LS 17A) – in his book entitled *Rule* (or *On the Criterion* as in 10.29, *De regula et iudicio* in Cicero's translation at *On the Nature of the Gods* 1.43, LS 23E) Epicurus offered three criteria of truth: 'sensations, preconceptions and feelings'.[9] Whether they here followed Epicurus or not, the Stoics used these terms, rules and criteria, too, declaring the topic one of the three (or four) (sub-)parts of logic: 'Next to dialectic, rhetoric (and according to some a part about definitions) the third (or fourth) part is about rules or criteria.'[10] According to the Stoics, the part on rules or criteria dealt with the means of the discovery of truth, since there guidance is offered for the differences between impressions.[11] Different from Epicurus, who declared all impressions to be true, the Stoics presented the 'cognitive impression' as their criterion of truth.[12]

[6] Compare Moatti 1997/2015, 166/171: '*Regula*: the word is clear.'

[7] See e.g. Lewis and Short 1879, Glare 2012 *s.v.*

[8] See e.g. Long and Sedley 1987, vol. 1, 88.

[9] ἐν τοίνυν τῷ Κανόνι λέγων ἐστὶν ὁ Ἐπίκουρος κριτήρια τῆς ἀληθείας εἶναι τὰς αἰσθήσεις καὶ προλήψεις καὶ τὰ πάθη.

[10] Diogenes Laertius 7.41 (*SVF* 2.48, LS 31A, *FDS* 1, 33): τὸ δὲ λογικὸν μέρος φασὶν ἔνιοι εἰς δύο διαιρεῖσθαι ἐπιστήμας, εἰς ῥητορικὴν καὶ εἰς διαλεκτικήν. τινὲς δὲ καὶ εἰς τὸ ὁρικὸν εἶδος, τὸ περὶ κανόνων καὶ κριτηρίων· ἔνιοι δὲ τὸ ὁρικὸν περιαιροῦσιν.

[11] Diogenes Laertius 7.42 (LS 31A, *FDS* 33): τὸ μὲν οὖν περὶ κανόνων καὶ κριτηρίων παραλαμβάνουσι πρὸς τὸ τὴν ἀλήθειαν εὑρεῖν· ἐν αὐτῷ γὰρ τὰς τῶν φαντασιῶν διαφορὰς ἀπευθύνουσι.

[12] Diogenes Laertius 7.54 (*SVF* 2.105, LS 40A, *FDS* 255): κριτήριον δὲ τῆς ἀληθείας φασὶ τυγχάνειν τὴν καταληπτικὴν φαντασίαν.

The different interpretations of what counts as the correct criterion of truth and the subsequent debates on these positions constitute one of the highlights of ancient thought.[13] Here, the debate between Stoics and Academics must be singled out. The Academics Arcesilaus and Carneades were critical about the Stoics' account of the criterion of truth as the cognitive impression: as a consequence the Stoics modified their account. In the 80s of the 1st century BCE, in his 'Roman books' the Academic Philo of Larissa introduced the probable or persuasive impression as criterion of 'truth', thus proposing a less demanding standard.[14]

The specifics of this debate need not concern us here. What is important, however, is that the term rule or criterion became a central term in the debate among the Greek thinkers. Its importance is well captured in Cicero, *Lucullus* 29 (*FDS* 353), in a quote ascribed to Antiochus of Ascalon, a contemporary of Philo of Larissa and his main rival in becoming the head of the Academy:

> The determination of what is true and false and of what is known and unknown is, after all, the criterion for the complete study of wisdom.[15]

Apart from its importance, we should thus already note the trite point that in Hellenistic epistemology *regula* was not only used in the singular: not only did different schools propose their own *regulae*, also within the same school different *regulae* were proposed.

Less obvious perhaps is that also in logic proper or dialectic, as the ancients would call it, the term *regula* appears to have been applied in more than one way. An example can be found in Cicero's *Brutus* 152, where Cicero presents Servius Sulpicius Rufus, who, as we have seen in the previous chapter, would have made the study of Roman law into a 'science' by making use of the expertise of logic:

> He [Servius] could never have attained through knowledge of the law alone had he not previously acquired the expertise that teaches [...] to have a standard by which true and false impressions can be distinguished and which conclusions follow from certain premises and which ones do not.[16]

13 See especially Striker 1996 [1974], Brunschwig 1995 [1988]. For Epicurus, see Lefebvre 2004.

14 See Cicero, *Lucullus* 18, Sextus Empiricus, *Outlines of Pyrrhonism* 1.235, cf. Brittain 2001, 129–68, Brittain 2006, 13.

15 *hanc enim esse regulam totius philosophiae, constitutionem veri falsi cogniti incogniti.*

16 *quod numquam effecisset ipsius iuris scientia, nisi eam praeterea didicisset artem, quae doceret* [...] *habere regulam, qua vera et falsa iudicarentur et quae quibus propositis essent quaeque non essent consequentia.*

This passage thus implies the use of standard in different contexts, and hence of two standards: *regula* is the standard that allows us, first, to distinguish between truth and falsehood, and, second, also between validity and invalidity of arguments.[17]

4.3 'Rule' in early Hellenistic ethics

Until now, I have focused on the metaphorical use of rule as standard in Hellenistic epistemology and dialectic. Here, I will move on to its use in Hellenistic ethics. Among the Stoics, the notion of rule is used with regard to law. According to them, law is the criterion which serves as the standard to distinguish between justice and injustice. A passage in Cicero's treatises *On Laws* is an example thereof, at 1.19 (*SVF* 3.315):

> Law is the power of nature, it is the mind and reason of the wise person, it is the standard of justice and injustice.[18]

Cicero's usage of *regula* in the sense of standard goes back at least as far as Chrysippus, the third head of the Stoic school. The beginning of Chrysippus' *On Law* survived in the *Digest*, at 1.3.2 (*SVF* 3.314, LS 67R), in a passage taken from Marcian's *Teaching Manual*:

> Law is king of all human and divine matters. Law must preside over what is virtuous and bad as ruler and as guide, and thus be the standard of what is just and unjust, ordering animals that are political by nature what they should do, and prohibiting them from what they should not do.[19]

In order to make sense of this use of *regula*, a few words must be devoted to the Stoic doctrine of law.[20] The Stoics, from Zeno of Citium, the founder of their school, onwards, identified law with the one active force of nature that shapes the world. Cicero, *On the Nature of the Gods* 1.36 (*SVF* 1.162) is an important witness here: 'Zeno thinks that the law of nature is divine and that it has the power to order the right things and to forbid the

[17] Schulz 1936, 50; Stein 1966, 52 is sceptical about the distinction between the standards here.

[18] *ea [sc. lex] est enim naturae vis, ea mens ratioque prudentis, ea iuris atque iniuriae regula.* The singular *lex* is Cicero's translation of Chrysippus' *nomos*: for Chrysippus *nomos* should be contrasted with the plural *leges* (*nomoi* in Greek) as statutes created or formulated by human beings (see below, n. 31). For the different meanings of *lex* and *nomos* see further Chapter 2, n. 1.

[19] ὁ νόμος πάντων ἐστὶ βασιλεὺς θείων τε καὶ ἀνθρωπίνων πραγμάτων· δεῖ δὲ αὐτὸν προστάτην τε εἶναι τῶν καλῶν καὶ τῶν αἰσχρῶν καὶ ἄρχοντα καὶ ἡγεμόνα, καὶ κατὰ τοῦτο κανόνα τε εἶναι δικαίων καὶ ἀδίκων καὶ τῶν φύσει πολιτικῶν ζῴων προστακτικὸν μὲν ὧν ποιητέον, ἀπαγορευτικὸν δὲ ὧν οὐ ποιητέον.

[20] See further, e.g. Vogt 2008, Brouwer 2008, Brouwer 2011a, Boeri 2013, Wildberger 2018.

opposite things.'[21] The Stoics thus equated law with the power or force that brings order in the world. According to standard Stoic doctrine, human beings stand in a special relationship vis-à-vis this rational force in nature. At some point in their lives (the sources differ here, one makes it the age of 7, the other the age of 14) reason has developed naturally. However, thereafter human beings themselves need to develop this reason further. According to the Stoics, then, the highest goal in life is the perfection of rationality such that human beings acquire virtuous dispositions, and thus become active parts of this rational force.[22]

The Stoics called the actions done out of this disposition in accordance with the law as 'right actions' (*katorthōmata*), for which Stobaeus 2.85.20-6.1 (*SVF* 3.494, LS 59B) can be consulted:

> Right actions are activities in accordance with virtue, such as thinking and acting justly.[23]

The Stoics qualified such an act in accordance with virtue as 'perfect', 'complete'[24] or – as is attested in several sources – 'containing all the numbers'.[25] This intriguing expression is best understood as a musical metaphor, referring to the fact that such an act is wholly in tune, or in harmony or symphony with the nature of the whole, without the presence of a false note.[26] By inference, an imperfect act is thus an act which misses out on a 'single number' and that thus destroys the harmony.

It has to be said, then, that such a perfect disposition is difficult to achieve: the Stoics notoriously maintained that the perfect human being living in accordance with the law and performing the right actions had not yet come into existence – with the exception perhaps of Socrates.[27]

21 *Zeno* [. . .] *naturalem legem divinam esse censet, eamque vim obtinere recta imperantem prohibentemque contraria.* Cf. the evidence preserved by Aristocles of Messene (1st century CE?) in Eusebius of Caesarea, *Preparation for the Gospel* 15.14.1–2 (*SVF* 1.98, LS 45G, 46G).

22 See Brouwer 2014, 18-41.

23 κατορθώματα δ' εἶναι τὰ κατ' ἀρετὴν ἐνεργήματα, οἷον τὸ φρονεῖν, τὸ δικαιοπραγεῖν.

24 Stobaeus 2.85.19 (*SVF* 3.494, LS 59B): τῶν δὲ καθηκόντων τὰ μὲν εἶναί φασι τέλεια, ἃ δὴ καὶ κατορθώματα λέγεσθαι.

25 Stobaeus 2.93.14–15 (*SVF* 3.500, LS 59K): κατόρθωμα δ' εἶναι λέγουσι καθῆκον πάντας ἐπέχον τοὺς ἀριθμούς. Cf. Cicero's translation in Latin, in *On Ends* 3.24 (*SVF* 3.11, LS 64H): *quae autem nos aut recta aut recte facta dicamus, si placet, illi autem appellant* κατορθώματα, *omnes numeros virtutis continent.*

26 Long 1991/1996, 113/219.

27 For the rarity of the sage see Brouwer 2014, 92–135, for Socrates as a sage in the final days of his life see 163–6.

Rational human beings, who have not yet achieved that virtuous and perfectly rational disposition in accordance with the law, can have a true insight into their place in the order of things, but lacking this solid disposition, they will most of the time have to live according to the order of the whole, like – as in the famous Stoic image – the dog tied behind the cart,[28] suffering if they attempt to go against it.[29]

An implication of this interpretation of law as the rational force in which the sage on the basis of his perfectly rational, virtuous disposition participates is that *in the end* law cannot be captured in generally formulated statutes. According to the Stoics, the description of law in such general terms cannot be but an imperfect reflection of the actual course of this force in the world order. The Stoics thus criticised *all* existing statutes and constitutions in no uncertain terms.[30] Zeno did so in his *Politeia*; Chrysippus did so, too, as can be inferred from the reproach that an otherwise unknown Diogenianus in Eusebius of Caesarea, *Preparation for the Gospel* 6.8.14 (*SVF* 3.324) directs at him: 'How can you say that all current statutes and constitutions are wrong?'[31]

4.4 The Roman Stoics

Of course, these radical Stoic doctrines – that the force of right reason in the world is the one and only standard of justice and injustice, that a right action needs to be complete and that performing such a right action is almost impossible for ordinary human beings[32] – would not have got an enthusiastic reception everywhere, certainly not among conservative Romans. Stoics, such as Panaetius, who tried to make Stoic thought acceptable to them, hence attempted to present a more down-to-earth version of Stoicism. Such a change of perspective with more attention to ordinary human beings can be found in Cicero's writings, as in his *On Friendship* 18:

[28] [Hippolytus of Rome?], *Refutation of All Heresies* 1.21 (*SVF* 2.975, LS 62A). For the text and a discussion of its authorship, see Litwa 2016.

[29] The Stoic theory of emotions as incorrect judgments about one's place in the order of things finds its origins here. See further Graver 2002 and 2007.

[30] *Politeia* is notoriously difficult to translate: its meanings range from the general 'state of the polis' to the more specific 'constitution'.

[31] πῶς δὲ τοὺς κειμένους νόμους ἡμαρτῆσθαι φῄς ἅπαντας καὶ τὰς πολιτείας;

[32] Schofield 1999b, 67–74, Sellars 2007, Atkins 2015. On the Cynic background of these early Stoic doctrines see Brouwer 2020a, 32–3.

> We should pay attention to those things, which are available in our own experience and in ordinary life, not things that are merely imagined or wished for.[33] (tr. Atkins)

or in his *On Appropriate Actions* 3.15:

> Such appropriate actions, which I am treating in these books, are said to be virtuous in a second-rate way, not confined to sages only, but shared with the whole human race.[34] (tr. Atkins)

The approach Cicero describes here goes back to at least Panaetius.[35] In his *On Appropriate Actions*, at 3.13 (fr. 101 van Straaten, fr. 75 Alesse, fr. A69 Vimercati), Cicero describes Panaetius as a Stoic, holding on to the doctrine that virtue is the only good, but he then continues:

> The virtuous that is properly and truly so called, is found in sages only and can never be severed from virtue. With those who do not possess perfect wisdom, this virtuous, perfect as it is, can in no way exist; however, semblances of the virtuous exist.[36] (tr. Atkins)

These Stoics, like Panaetius, thus put more emphasis to the 'intermediate' phase in human development, stressing the role of what the founder of Stoicism, Zeno of Citium, had already introduced as 'intermediate appropriate actions'.[37] These appropriate actions are called intermediate rather than perfect, since only 'a reasonable justification can be given as to why they have been done'.[38] In the final analysis, that is from the point of view of the disposition of the perfect human being, in line with early Stoic rigour, these intermediate actions are morally bad too, since they are not completely and hence perfectly in consistency with the law.[39]

[33] *nos autem ea, quae sunt in usu vitaque communi, non ea, quae finguntur aut optantur, spectare debemus.*

[34] *haec igitur officia, de quibus his libris disserimus, quasi secunda quaedam honesta esse dicunt, non sapientium modo propria, sed cum omni hominum genere communia. Officium* is Cicero's translation of Zeno's *kathēkon*, with which he struggled (see his *Letter to Atticus* from 12 November 44, 16.14.3, no. 425 Shackleton Bailey: *aut da melius?* 'Or give me something better.'). In order to stress this origin – at the cost of losing the Roman association of 'public task' that comes with Cicero's translation – *officium* and *kathēkon* will both be rendered as 'appropriate action' here. For Zeno's neologism as 'appropriate action' see immediately below and Chapter 6, n. 27.

[35] See Tieleman 2007, Brouwer 2008, Brouwer 2011a, Fiori 2011, Fiori 2014.

[36] *atque illud quidem honestum, quod proprie vereque dicitur id in sapientibus est solis neque a virtute divelli umquam potest. in iis autem, in quibus sapientia perfecta non est, ipsum illud quidem perfectum honestum nullo modo, similitudines honesti esse possunt.*

[37] See further Chapter 6, section 6.2.

[38] Stobaeus 2.85.13–14 (*SVF* 3.494, LS 59B), Diogenes Laertius 7.107 (*SVF* 3.493, LS 59C): καθῆκόν φασιν εἶναι ὃ πραχθὲν εὔλογόν [τε] ἴσχει ἀπολογισμόν.

[39] Diogenes Laertius 7.108 (*SVF* 3.495, LS 59E), Cicero, *On Appropriate Actions* 1.8; cf. Luschnat 1958, 178–214.

Nevertheless, the Stoics attached some value to intermediate appropriate actions, for which already Zeno was criticised by his pupil Aristo of Chios (3rd century BCE). According to Aristo, understanding and implementing Stoic doctrine, such as 'living in accordance with nature etc.' into one's own life is the only thing that matters. For the deviant Stoic Aristo, the part of ethics that deals with precepts on appropriate actions (see Chapter 6, section 6.2) has no value whatsoever, since such general precepts are incapable of sinking into the right mind: they are but 'advice from old women'[40] – presumably meant to be a reference to Zeno and his followers.[41]

In comparison with Zeno, Panaetius moves a step further: on Panaetius' second order level of the semblance of the virtues, such as they are 'available in our own experience and in ordinary life' (*On Friendship* 18, quoted above, n. 33) – reference is sometimes made to the *vir bonus* of Roman law, the good and just citizen, who acts according to the law,[42] these intermediate actions are good enough.

In our sources on the early Stoics, lists of examples survived in Diogenes Laertius 7.108 (*SVF* 3.495, LS 59E) with 'honouring parents, brothers and country, spending time with friends';[43] Seneca, *Letter* 94.1 (*SVF* 1.538), with reference to Cleanthes: 'For each social role, such as advising a husband on how he should behave to his wife, a father on how to raise his children, or a master on how to regulate his slaves'[44] (tr. Graver and Long), and Stobaeus 2.86.3–4 (*SVF* 3.494, LS 59B): 'Marrying, growing old, conversing and such things.'[45]

In contrast to these arid accounts about the early Stoics, Cicero's *On Appropriate Actions*, in which he above all follows Panaetius, is a rich handbook of practical ethics, addressed explicitly to his son, but implicitly also to the other members of the next generation of the Roman ruling class. In the first book Cicero discusses the intermediate actions to be

[40] Seneca (*c*.4 BCE–65 CE), *Letter* 94.2 (*SVF* 1.358, LS 66I, in part): *Ariston Stoicus e contrario hanc partem levem existimat et quae non descendat in pectus usque, anilia habentem praecepta.*

[41] For the satirical characterisation of Zeno as a babbling old woman see Timon of Phlius (*c*.320–230 CE) in Diogenes Laertius 7.15 (*SVF* 1.22, fr. 812 Lloyd-Jones and Parsons, LS 3F, *FDS* 108, fr. 38 Di Marco): 'And I saw a greedy old Phoenician woman.' On this passage see further Brouwer 2014, 154–6.

[42] See above, Chapter 1, section 1.5.

[43] γονεῖς τιμᾶν, ἀδελφούς, πατρίδα, συμπεριφέρεσθαι φίλοις· παρὰ τὸ καθῆκον δέ, ὅσα μὴ αἱρεῖ λόγος, ὡς ἔχει τὰ τοιαῦτα, γονέων ἀμελεῖν, ἀδελφῶν ἀφροντιστεῖν, φίλοις μὴ συνδιατίθεσθαι, πατρίδα ὑπερορᾶν καὶ τὰ παραπλήσια.

[44] *cuique personae praecepta nec in universum componit hominem sed marito suadet quomodo se gerat adversus uxorem, patri quomodo educet liberos, domino quomodo servos regat.*

[45] τὸ γαμεῖν, τὸ πρεσβεύειν, τὸ διαλέγεσθαι, τὰ τούτοις ὅμοια.

derived from (the semblances of) the virtues, and offers plenty of Greek as well as Roman examples. One of the main intermediate actions that go with justice is that one should treat common things as common, and private ones as one's own.[46] Here Cicero, or rather Panaetius, makes private property into a central feature of justice, analysing the origins of private property in a historical perspective and making social harmony dependent on respecting the legal arrangements that protect private property.[47]

To sum up: whereas for early Stoics like Chrysippus the focus is on 'right actions' in accordance with right reason, for Roman Stoics like Panaetius the focus shifts to the intermediate appropriate actions 'with a reasonable justification', which are good enough, in a second-rate way. Their focus now shifts from those actions which have all the numbers and are thus in complete harmony with the universal law to types of actions for which a reasonable justification can be given. It should perhaps be noted that Panaetius does not appear to have given up on law or right reason as the standard of justice; he rather emphasises the value of intermediate appropriate actions. It can also be noted that this shift in focus would give rise to the conception of law 'of nature' as a set of general precepts that can reasonably be applied in most cases. I will briefly return to this topic in Chapter 8, section 8.1.

4.5 The parallel with Hellenistic grammar

Let us now turn to grammar, a topic which, as we have seen in Chapter 3, also started to attract the attention of the Hellenistic thinkers.[48] In the study of language one of the issues became: should the study of language be focused on the specifics or rather focus on its regularities? According to Varro, *On the Latin Language*, some thinkers focused on the study of all aspects of the inflexion of words, giving attention to each specific case, whereas others rather focused on the regularities or the 'rules' (*kanōnes* in Greek, *regulae* in Latin) of language.

Varro mentions Chrysippus among the thinkers who are said to have focused on the anomalies. Chrysippus' interest in grammar should not surprise us. For the Stoics, or Chrysippus for that matter, grammar was classified as a part of logic, in their broad conception of this part of the study of wisdom. According to the Stoics, as stated in Diogenes Laertius 7.41–3 (*FDS* 33, LS 31A), logic consists of dialectic and rhetoric; dialectic

[46] *On Appropriate Actions* 1.20. [47] See Chapter 7, below. [48] See Chapter 3, section 3.4.

is subdivided into the part that deals with the signified and with utterance. This is how Varro, *On the Latin Language* 9.1 (*SVF* 2.151, *FDS* 640, Crates of Mallus fr. 104 Broggiato) brings up Chrysippus:

> The distinguished grammarian Crates relied on Chrysippus, a man of great acumen, who left four books *On Anomaly*. On the basis thereof Crates opposed analogy and Aristarchus.[49]

Varro immediately continues with a comment that Crates would have misunderstood Chrysippus and Aristarchus. In an ingenuous interpretation Michael Frede argued that Varro may well have been incorrect here, that 'Crates may have had good reason, after all, to see a conflict between Alexandrian and Stoic positions on this matter'.[50] This is not the place to deal with this question in much detail; what suffices here is that the passage shows that Chrysippus was clearly interested in the specifics or irregularities of language, that he was presumably an anomalist and that Crates followed suit. In the catalogue of Chrysippus' books, partly preserved by Diogenes Laertius, at 7.192 (*SVF* 2.14, *FDS* 194), we find the title *On Anomaly in Sayables, Addressed to Dion, in Four Books*.[51] Since the title is longer here, it is unclear whether Varro in fact referred to this book. Of course, if Chrysippus had even written two books on grammatical anomaly, this would confirm his interest in the matter further.[52]

As Varro informs us, Crates of Mallus as an anomalist would continue the debate with the analogists.[53] Among them Aristarchus of Samothrace (also 2nd century BCE), the founder of the Alexandrinian school,[54] and in the 1st century BCE, Gaius Julius Caesar can be singled out.[55]

As for later Stoics, there is evidence that Panaetius also focused on the regularities of the language. According to the 12th-century CE Byzantine scholar Eustathius of Thessalonica in his *Commentary on the Odyssey*, at ψ 220, vol. 2, 305.30 Stallbaum (fr. 92 van Straaten, fr. 155 Alesse, fr. A119 Vimercati), a certain Heraclides contrasted the regularities of the inflection of verbs ending with the letter alpha in Homer's Greek with the

[49] *Crates, nobilis grammaticus, qui fretus Chrysippo, homine acutissimo qui reliquit* περὶ ἀνωμαλίας *IV libros contra analogian atque Aristarchum est nixus.* For the text (especially the conjecture of IV for the corrupt *lei* in the manuscript) see De Melo's edition *ad loc.*, cf. Fink 1952, 378, Blank 2005, 236. For Varro's position in the debate see further Ax 1996, Cardauns 2001, 35–7, cf. Taylor 2015, 19–32.

[50] Frede 1978, 73.

[51] Περὶ τῆς κατὰ τὰς λέξεις ἀνωμαλίας πρὸς Δίωνα δ'.

[52] Brunschwig 1995 [1977], 66–7.

[53] On this *querelle*, which some scholars hold to be an oversimplification (references in Dickey 2007, 6 n. 15 and Montana 2015, 150), see further Cavazza 1981, 106–53, Broggiato 2001, xxxiii–xli, Bod 2013 [2009], 14. For Crates see Broggiato 2001.

[54] See Matthaios 1999.

[55] See Garcea 2012, Pezzini 2017, cf. Papke 1988.

regularities in Attic Greek, where the same verbs end with the letter ēta.[56] Eustathius then continues: 'Panaetius states that he found such regularities in Plato's writings [in Attic Greek].'[57] This is obviously only a tiny passage, and unfortunately Eustathius does not elaborate on Panaetius. Even though he may have still followed Chrysippus and considered himself an anomalist, as most modern commentators have assumed,[58] the passage makes at least clear that Panaetius became interested in analogies.

The parallel between the debate in ethics among Stoics on the one hand and the debate in grammar between anomalists and analogists on the other hand now becomes clear. In grammar the issue was: should we study the specifics in language or rather focus on its regularities? In ethics the issue was: should the focus be upon the virtuous actions of the sage, which contains all the numbers, as the earlier Stoics had proposed, or should it rather be on types of actions which have a reasonable – although not perfect – justification, based on an analysis of ordinary human experience? The parallel is thus: should the focus be on the specifics or should it rather be on the regularities? The connection between grammar and ethics now almost speaks for itself. Both in grammar as well as ethics, Chrysippus focuses on the specifics. By contrast, in the Roman settings Panaetius develops an interest in regularities, both in grammar and perhaps most prominently in his ethics, focusing in his *On Appropriate Action* on types of action that have a reasonable rather than a perfectly rational justification.

4.6 'Rule' in the study of Roman law (and beyond)

We have seen that the notion of rule is prominent in Hellenistic thought – not just in grammar, but also in epistemology and in ethics. In their contacts with the Hellenistic, especially Stoic, thinkers the Romans would thus have been able to introduce the plural *regulae iuris* in legal discourse. In line with the Hellenistic use in first epistemology, grammar and ethics,

56 Perhaps Heraclides of Pontus, the 4th-century BCE follower of Plato and Aristotle: in his catalogue of writings, preserved by Diogenes Laertius, at 5.87, under the heading 'Works on grammar', two writings on Homer can be found. Cf. Alesse 1997, 297. The passage is neither in Wehrli 1969a nor in Schütrumpf 2008, the modern collections of the evidence on Heraclidus of Pontus.

57 The passage runs in full: περὶ δὲ τοῦ ᾔδη, ὅ πέρ ἐστιν ἠπίστατο, εἴρηται μὲν καὶ ἐν τῇ ἄλφα τῆς Ἰλιάδος. διαρθρωτέον δὲ μᾶλλον ἐνταῦθα, ὅτι οὐχ' ἁπλῶς τὸ ᾔδειν καὶ ἐνενοήκειν καὶ ἐπεποιήκειν διαλύει τὸ ᾔδεα καὶ ἐνενοήκεα καὶ ἐπεποιήκεα, ἀλλὰ τὰ ἐξ αὐτῶν Ἀττικὰ τὰ διὰ τοῦ ἦτα. παραδίδωσι γὰρ Ἡρακλείδης, ὅτι Ἀττικοὶ τοὺς τοιούτους ὑπερσυντελίκους ἐν τῷ ἦτα μόνῳ περατοῦσιν, ᾔδη λέγοντες καὶ ἐνενοήκη καὶ ἐπεποιήκη. καὶ οὕτω φησὶ Παναίτιος ἔχειν τὰς γραφὰς παρὰ Πλάτωνι.

58 Alesse 1997, 297, Vimercati 2002, 278 n. 124, Vimercati 2004, 85–6.

for the jurists, then, rules – in the plural – can serve as a yardstick to be applied in similar types of cases.

Three questions, as to where, when and how the jurists used the concept, can now be dealt with. With regard to the first question, 'where did the jurists use the concept?': as discussed in Chapter 2, section 2.1, one of the layers of Roman law is the *ius honorarium*, developed on the basis of the decisions of the judges when they were allowed to do so by the praetor. In dealing with the dispute at hand, a judgment is foremost the solution of a particular dispute between two parties, expressing the state of right as established by the judge – usually prepared by an *iurisconsultus*, the legal expert consulted by the judge. It must gradually have become clear that these judgments did not only affect the *res iudicata* itself, the case as judged between the parties, but should have implications with regard to similar or analogous cases. A case can thus become a precedent for similar types of cases. If similar facts are presented to a judge, the earlier judgment, or more precisely the reason underlying the decision, should be found and applied too. If the facts are distinct, the reason should be left aside. So here, the notion of rule makes its entry into the legal domain: out of the earlier case a 'rule' (*kanōn*, *regula*) can be extracted. Lawyers start understanding cases not only as particular decisions, but also as types, which can be reformulated in terms of rules.

In the 3rd century CE in his *Commentary on Plautius*, book 16, and preserved at *Digest* 50.17.1 pr.1, Paulus, perhaps the most famous among the classical lawyers, offers the following account of a rule:

> A rule is something which briefly describes how a thing is. The law may not be derived from a rule, but a rule must arise from the law as it is. By means of a rule, therefore, a brief description of things is handed down and, as Sabinus says, is, as it were, the summary of a case, which loses its function as soon as it becomes in any way defective.[59] (tr. Crawford in Watson 1998, adapted)

A rule is discovered in the case, 'from the law as it is'. A rule is a brief description or summary of the reason(s) underlying the decision.[60] A decision can thus be understood under the aspect of rule against which similar disputes in the future can be measured. In law, rule has thus developed into the concise formulation of the state of right with regard

[59] *regula est, quae rem quae est breviter enarrat. non ex regula ius sumatur, sed ex iure quod est regula fiat. per regulam igitur brevis rerum narratio traditur, et, ut ait Sabinus, quasi causae coniectio est, quae simul cum in aliquo vitiata est, perdit officium suum.*

[60] Stein 1962, 1966, 1967.

to a certain topic.[61] Schmidlin speaks of a 'case rule' (*Fallregel*),[62] as a 'bundle of legal experience'.[63]

Among the extant examples of rules, the Catonian Rule deserves pride of place.[64] It survived in Justinian's *Digest*, at 34.7.1 preface, from Celsus, *Digest*, book 35: 'The Catonian Rule is as follows: "Any legacy which would have been invalid if the testator had died at the time of the making of the will is invalid whenever he dies."' In short: if a will is invalid and the testator dies, the will remains invalid. It cannot be validated any more.

Let us move on to the second question: when was the use of the concept in law first attested? As we have just seen, Paulus' account was preserved in the *Digest*, where Justinian's 6th-century CE compilers presented the term under the heading 'On the different rules from ancient law'.[65] As can be inferred from the *Index Florentinus*, the list of titles of the around 1,600 books that can be found at the beginning of the Florentine copy of the *Digest*, and which offers an indication of the books consulted by the compilers,[66] includes more than sixty that had a title with 'rule' in it.[67] In his account Paulus refers back to Sabinus' usage of rule in the 1st century CE, so the word was already used in the legal context by then. Some have pushed back its origins even further. Jörs suggested that the introduction of the notion of rule went back to Cato the Elder himself, and should thus be dated before 152 BCE, the year of his death; Cato would thus have marked the beginning of what Jörs called 'Regularjurisprudenz'.[68] For the date of the introduction of the notion of *regula* Cato is perhaps too early and Sabinus likely too late. As for Cato, the rule would surely not in his own days have been called after him: in Republican times adjectives are usually derived from the family name rather than the nickname (however much the nicknames have become standard in modern times: Cicero rather than Tullius, Caesar rather than Julius, or Cato rather than Porcius).[69] As for a candidate earlier than

[61] Stein 1966, 61–73. [62] Schmidlin 1970, 17.

[63] Schmidlin 1970, 17: 'Sammelpunkt juristischer Erfahrung'.

[64] Further examples are assembled in Schmidlin 1970, 29–35, and discussed in the remainder of his book.

[65] *Digest* 50.17: *De diversis regulis iuris antiqui.*

[66] On the Index see Rotondi 1922a, Pugsley 1993.

[67] Neratius (8.1, in 15 books), Pomponius (9.8, in one book), Cervidius Scaevola (18.4, in four books), Gaius (20.11, in one book), Ulpian (24.8 and 24.15, in seven books and in one book respectively), Paul (25.8, in seven books, 25.9, 25.23, 25.32, each in one book, the latter on the Catonian Rule only), Marcian (29.2, in five books), Modestinus (31.3, in ten books), Rufinus (35.1, in twelve books). Cf. Humfress 2015, 96.

[68] Jörs 1888, 290, cf. Schiller 1978, 292.

[69] Stein 1966, 66, Schmidlin 1970, 19, Nörr 1972b, 19.

Sabinus, Stein suggested that at the beginning of the 1st century CE, the jurist Labeo, given his interest in grammar, might have been the first to introduce the notion of rule.[70] But if my reconstruction in this chapter is correct, the introduction may well already have taken place in the late 2nd or in the beginning of the 1st century BCE, due to the extensive contact between jurists and especially Stoic philosophers,[71] and given the developments in Hellenistic thought. Both in logic and ethics, philosophy was 'brought down from heaven and placed in the cities' even further – to borrow Cicero's phrase from the *Tusculan Disputations* 5.10 – to the realm of everyday life in Rome. The exact date must remain speculative, of course. What is important here, though, is that the notion of rule was introduced in or shortly after the period when in Hellenistic thought the metaphorical usage of rule had been developed.

Finally, the third and last question: how did the jurists use the concept? What was the function of rule in the legal domain? Were rules applied in law itself? Would these rules have been legally binding? Some have argued that only the older ones, formulated by the Republican jurists, would have been,[72] others that only some jurists (the Sabinians as opposed to the Proculians) would have accepted their binding force.[73] However, in their answers to the questions presented to them, the jurists rarely refer to rules. As Honoré nicely formulated it, rules are 'presupposed'.[74] Hence, rather than in law itself, the use of rule played a role in the domain of the *study* of law, in the first place as a mnemotechnic device, as a reminder of what is important about a case from a legal point of view.[75] In the second place, the notion of rule came to be used with regard to the teaching manuals as descriptions of the relations between and within the categories. The systematic overviews organised on the basis of the main categories of 'person', 'things' and 'actions', that were devised in the late Republic and early Empire, as discussed in Chapter 3, can then be regarded as a *summa summarum*, as a systematic collection of the summaries that were found in the cases decided.

[70] See Stein 1966, 64–6, Stein 1967, 374, cf. Schiavone 2012/2017, 336/325. Bremer 1898, 17–18 offers eleven examples of Labeo's analogies from the *Digest*: 21.1.64 pr., 43.23.2, 43.20.1.13, 8.3.10, 43.24.13.5, 28.5.65 pr., 14.3.5.7, 9.2.5.2, 50.16.43, 1.9.7.1, 47.10.15.7.

[71] See further Chapter 6, section 6.5. [72] Schmidlin 1970, 46, 70. [73] Stein 1966, 65, 73.

[74] Honoré 1973, 60. Cf. definitions, which are presupposed, too. In this sense rules and definitions are related; they should neither be regarded as synonyms as Schulz 1946/1961, 173/209-10 suggests, nor sharply distinguished as Carcaterra 1966, 23 does, cf. Schmidlin 1970, 6. According to Nörr 1972b, 82 n. 300 (cf. Nörr 1972b 28) the connection between rules and definitions could go back to the Stoics.

[75] Finkenauer 2015.

Via Emperor Justinian, who brought Gaius' *Teaching Manual* as revised by his civil servant Tribonian (*c.*485–542 CE) within the domain of law itself by giving it statutory status, Justinian's set of rules served as the model to be emulated for most of the modern civil codes on the European continent, especially those based on the French Civil Code. Rule is no longer a mnemotechnic device, which ought to remind the jurists of the underlying case; in the codes the rules as such have come to be considered as the law itself. Whereas on the continent this background to the notion of rule is often forgotten, in English law the relation between case and rule is anything but severed: if a new case is similar to one already decided, the judge will have to find and apply the *ratio decidendi* from the earlier case. Even so, in contemporary analytical Anglo-American jurisprudence, the notion of rule is also often used without reference to its historical background, which would surely allow us to understand its role in law better.[76]

[76] See e.g. Hart 2012 [1961], who makes a 'fresh start' (80) in terms of rules, without further ado (as an alternative to Austin 1995 [1832] and his notion of command), Dworkin 1977, who devised his own conception of rule (see e.g. Twining and Miers 2010, 82–5), or Schauer 1991.

CHAPTER 5

'Person' in law

5.1 Introduction

In discussing the influence of Greek philosophy on Roman law I have, thus far, concentrated upon method and discussed the introduction of 'system' and 'rules', initially in the domain of the study of law, and later also in law itself. This influence can also be discerned with regard to substantive legal terms, especially with respect to the notion of 'person'. In this chapter I want to deal with the origins of the notion of person, and how it came to be applied in law. I will show that the history of the term is a history of transfers, which starts out from Etruscan burial rituals (see section 5.2), as well as from the beginnings of Greek theatre (section 5.3). From both origins the notion of person was picked up in philosophy, notably by the Stoic Panaetius of Rhodes (section 5.4), and in other sciences, as they were systematised towards the end of the Roman Republic (section 5.5), among which the transfer to the study of law was perhaps the most important (section 5.6).[1]

As we will see, the notion of person started out as a venerable Etruscan–Roman institution, at first referring to a mask that is used to represent the deceased, with a grand moral purpose. Under the influence of the Greeks, its abstract potential emerged: masks can transcend the individual (role, character), and they were hence presented in taxonomies, presented according to more and less general categories. The application of masks outside the context of funeral rites or theatre is owed to the Roman Stoic Panaetius of Rhodes, who started thinking about the self ('personal identity') as well as about what human beings universally may have in common ('personhood'). The Roman jurists could thus make use of their own

[1] Among recent work on the origins of the notion of person and how it ended up in law see Faro 2010, Sacchi 2008, Sacchi 2010, Ribas Alba 2012, and Ribas Alba 2014. Among earlier work on the origins of the notion can be mentioned Trendelenburg 1908, von Blumenthal and Düll 1937, Nédoncelle 1948.

venerable notion of person and apply it with regard to all human beings. In their attempts at systematising law, the notion of person thus served as an ideal starting point for a taxonomy in law.

5.2 Etruscan funeral rituals

The origin of the Latin word *persona* has been much discussed. Most scholars these days accept that the Latin word goes back to the Etruscan word *phersu*. The word is inscribed on the right- and left-hand walls in the Tarquinian Tomb of the Augurs (no. 42 Steingräber 1985), which is dated around 520 BCE.[2] On its right wall *phersu* is winning a bloody fight, with a leashed dog biting an already wounded figure; on the left wall *phersu* is fleeing. A similar figure, without inscription, is depicted in the Tomb of the Pulcinella (no. 104 Steingräber), dated some ten years after the Tomb of the Augurs. Here, clearly in a less martial setting, he dances.[3] Unfortunately, not much else is known about this figure – although speculative remarks abound, especially in the older literature.[4] *Phersu* is perhaps most safely described as a figure participating in games of more or less violent sorts that honour the deceased, with a bearded mask as his most conspicuous attribute.[5]

From *phersu* (or perhaps *Phersu* as the proper name of the figure) *phersuna* can be derived.[6] Even though we are still waiting for a major bilingual text, the Etruscan variant of the Rosetta Stone, through the discovery of a growing number of smaller texts our understanding of the Etruscan language is slowly improving. According to Steinbauer's *Handbuch des Etruskischen*, the suffix *-na* is the most productive in the Etruscan language.[7] It is the typical way by which the possessive adjective is formed out of a noun.[8] *Phersuna* in Etruscan would thus mean 'belonging to *phersu*'. In the Roman world the Etruscan word *phersuna* would thus become the Latin *persona*, denoting *phersu*'s most conspicuous possession: his mask.[9] The change from 'ph' to 'p' is perfectly common too: The Etruscans prefer 'ph', where the Romans favour 'p', see, for example, the Latin *nepos*, which is *nephts* in Etruscan.

2 Cf. Pallotino 1968, 80 (*s.v. phersu*), Benelli 2009, 418 (*s.v. phersu*).
3 For other representations of *phersu* see Haynes 1963.
4 See e.g. Friedländer 1909, Altheim 1929, Nédoncelle 1948.
5 See Krauskopf 1985, Breyer 1993, Jannot 1993.
6 Bonfante and Bonfante 2003, 203.
7 Steinbauer 1999, 121.
8 See also Bonfante and Bonfante 2003, 99.
9 See Krauskopf 1985, 218, Rix 1995. Wallace 2008, 129–30, expresses reservations about the derivation: 'The long vowel [o] is not easy to explain.'

It is not just the word that the Romans took over from the Etruscans: they also appear to have taken over the related customs.[10] At any rate the role of masks in Roman burial rituals is prominent. A major source here is the Greek historian Polybius, who in his *Histories* analysed the causes of Rome's astonishing rise to becoming a world power.[11] According to Polybius, *Histories* 6.53.5 and 6.54.1–3 (fr. 61 Flower 1996), in his vivid description of Roman funeral rites the masks were supposed to be an exact representation of the ancestor:

> The image [of the deceased] consists of a mask that has been moulded and made up, to a remarkably exact likeness. [. . .] Whenever a notable family member dies, they take them [the masks] out for the funeral procession and put them on those who seem to bear the closest resemblance to the dead men, in height and appearance. [. . .] When they reach the rostra, they all sit in a row on ivory chairs. [. . .] It is hard to imagine a finer sight for an ambitious young man who aspires to excellence. [. . .] And then, once the person who delivers the encomium of the man being buried has finished speaking about him, he does the same for each of the ancestors who are represented there, starting with the most ancient, and describes their successes and achievements.[12] (tr. Waterfield)

In the continuation of the passage, Polybius' interest in the phenomenon becomes clear. He uses it in his overall scheme of explaining Rome's greatness: 'The most important thing is that young men are inspired to heroic feats of endurance, in order to gain the fame that accrues the brave.'[13] (tr. Waterfield) According to Polybius, then, the Roman, presumably Etruscan, burial ritual of the mask representing the deceased with great exactness contributed to Rome's rise to becoming a world power, in the sense that it inspired new generations to great deeds.[14]

[10] Camporeale 2003 [2000], 53, who further suggests that *Phersu*'s bloody games would have been taken over as gladiator games. For the introduction of the gladiator games see Livy 1.35.710 and 7.2.

[11] See Brouwer 2011a, with further references.

[12] ἡ δ' εἰκών ἐστι πρόσωπον εἰς ὁμοιότητα διαφερόντως ἐξειργασμένον καὶ κατὰ τὴν πλάσιν καὶ κατὰ τὴν ὑπογραφήν. [. . .] ἐπάν τε τῶν οἰκείων μεταλλάξῃ τις ἐπιφανής, ἄγουσιν εἰς τὴν ἐκφοράν, περιτιθέντες ὡς ὁμοιοτάτοις εἶναι δοκοῦσι κατά τε τὸ μέγεθος καὶ τὴν ἄλλην περικοπήν. [. . .] ὅταν δ' ἐπὶ τοὺς ἐμβόλους ἔλθωσι, καθέζονται πάντες ἑξῆς ἐπὶ δίφρων ἐλεφαντίνων. [. . .] οὗ κάλλιον οὐκ εὐμαρὲς ἰδεῖν θέαμα νέῳ φιλοδόξῳ καὶ φιλαγάθῳ. [. . .] πλὴν ὅ γε λέγων ὑπὲρ τοῦ θάπτεσθαι μέλλοντος, ἐπὰν διέλθῃ τὸν περὶ τούτου λόγον, ἄρχεται τῶν ἄλλων ἀπὸ τοῦ προγενεστάτου τῶν παρόντων, καὶ λέγει τὰς ἐπιτυχίας ἑκάστου καὶ τὰς πράξεις.

[13] τὸ δὲ μέγιστον, οἱ νέοι παρορμῶνται πρὸς τὸ πᾶν ὑπομένειν ὑπὲρ τῶν κοινῶν πραγμάτων χάριν τοῦ τυχεῖν τῆς συνακολουθούσης τοῖς ἀγαθοῖς τῶν ἀνδρῶν εὐκλείας.

[14] See further Flower 2014, 391.

5.3 Greek theatre

For the second source of the use of 'person' in Rome we have to go back to Greek theatre and the origins thereof. In the context of the Athenian festival in which a choir sang and danced in honour of Dionysius, we come across the shadowy figure of Thespis (late 6th century BCE). In a 3rd-century BCE inscription known as the Marmor Parium, Thespis is described as the first actor.[15] According to Diogenes Laertius 3.56, in a side remark in his biography on Plato, Thespis invented the theatre by allowing one actor to step out of the choir. Aeschylus would have added a second actor, Sophocles a third and so tragedy would have been brought to completion.[16] According to another later source, the Byzantine *Suidas s.v.* Thespis (θ 282, test. 1 Snell), this stepping out was accompanied by the invention of the mask, *prosōpon* in Greek. Thespis did so initially with a white face, then with a mask made out of linen:

> Thespis, of Ikarion, a city in Attica, the sixteenth after Epigenes of Sicyon, the first writer of tragedies, but some say that he was the second after Epigenes, others that he was the first tragedian. At first he performed having rubbed his face with white lead, then he covered his face with purslane in his performance, and after that he also introduced the use of masks made purely out of linen. He produced his plays in the first Olympiad [535–532]. He is remembered for his plays *The Games of Pelias or Phorbas*, *The Priests*, *The Youths*, *Pentheus*.[17] (tr. Pickard-Cambridge and Webster, modified)

According to Tièche's ingenious interpretation,[18] whereas the choir were presumably wearing animal masks, this may well mean that Thespis is credited here with the invention of the human mask. At any rate, the human mask became a standard attribute in Greek theatre. Against this

[15] *Inscriptiones Graecae* 12.5, number 444, at 43.58b: Θέσπις ὁ ποιητὴς [ὑπεκρίνα]το πρῶτος, ὃς ἐδίδαξε [δρ]ᾶ[μα ἐν ἄστ[ει. See further Fuhrer and Hose 2017, 6.

[16] Diogenes Laertius 3.56 (fr. 11 Pickard-Cambridge and Webster, fr. 7 Snell), in a parallel with Plato, who would have brought philosophy to perfection, adding dialectic to the ancients' physics and Socrates' ethics: τὸ παλαιὸν ἐν τῇ τραγῳδίᾳ πρότερον μὲν μόνος ὁ χορὸς διεδραμάτιζεν, ὕστερον δὲ Θέσπις ἕνα ὑποκριτὴν ἐξεῦρεν ὑπὲρ τοῦ διαναπαύεσθαι τὸν χορὸν καὶ δεύτερον Αἰσχύλος, τὸν δὲ τρίτον Σοφοκλῆς καὶ συνεπλήρωσεν τὴν τραγῳδίαν.

[17] Θέσπις, Ἰκαρίου, πόλεως Ἀττικῆς, τραγικὸς ἑκκαιδέκατος ἀπὸ τοῦ πρώτου γενομένου τραγῳδιοποιοῦ Ἐπιγένους τοῦ Σικυωνίου τιθέμενος, ὡς δέ τινες δεύτερος μετὰ Ἐπιγένην: ἄλλοι δὲ αὐτὸν πρῶτον τραγικὸν γενέσθαι φασί. καὶ πρῶτον μὲν χρίσας τὸ πρόσωπον ψιμυθίῳ ἐτραγῴδησεν, εἶτα ἀνδράχνῃ ἐσκέπασεν ἐν τῷ ἐπιδείκνυσθαι, καὶ μετὰ ταῦτα εἰσήνεγκε καὶ τὴν τῶν προσωπείων χρῆσιν ἐν μόνῃ ὀθόνῃ κατασκευάσας. ἐδίδαξε δὲ ἐπὶ τῆς πρώτης καὶ ἑξηκοστῆς Ὀλυμπιάδος μνημονεύεται δὲ τῶν δραμάτων αὐτοῦ Ἆθλα Πελίου ἢ Φόρβας, Ἱερεῖς, Ἠΐθεοι, Πενθεύς.

[18] Tièche 1933; see also Lesky 1956, 44, Lesky 1971, 267.

background, the meaning of the Greek word *prosōpon* changed: it accrued the transferred senses of role and character.

With the introduction of the theatre in Rome,[19] clearly under the influence of the Greeks, presumably those from the city of Tarentum,[20] both the human mask and the transferred senses of role and character became standard conventions in Roman theatre as well. This can be seen in the prologue from Terence (first half 2nd century BCE), *The Eunuch* 31–4, where he informs his readers that he will offer an adaptation of a Greek comedy:

> The playwright [i.e. Terence] does not deny that he has imported these characters into his *Eunuch* from Menander's [*c.* 342–*c.*290 BCE] Greek play. But he does most definitely deny any knowledge of the prior existence of the Latin versions.[21] (tr. Barsby)

An explicit piece of textual evidence for the use of masks, that is for the use of *persona* in the literal sense, on the Roman stage survived from the 1st century BCE.[22] Aulus Gellius, *Attic Nights* 5.7 offers it in passing, in a further explanation for the Roman word *persona*, which he ascribes to Gavius Bassus (1st century BCE):

> Cleverly, by Hercules! and wittily, in my opinion, does Gavius Bassus explain the derivation of the word *persona*, in the work that he composed *On the Origin of Words*; for he suggests that that word is formed from *personare*. 'For,' he says, 'the head and the face are shut in on all sides by the covering of the *persona*, or mask, and only one passage is left for the issue of the voice; and since this opening is neither free nor broad, but sends forth the voice after it has been concentrated and forced into one single exit, it makes the sound clearer and more resonant. Since then that covering of the face gives clearness and resonance to the voice, it is for that reason called *persona*, the o being lengthened because of the formation of the word.'[23] (tr. Rolfe, modified)

[19] See Cicero, *Brutus* 72–3. The year 240 BCE is usually given, when a play by Livius Andronicus was staged in order to celebrate Rome's victory over Carthago.

[20] See Cicero, *Brutus* 72, cf. Manuwald, 2011, 188–9, Brown 2014, 401.

[21] *eas se non negat personas transtulisse in Eunuchum suam ex Graeca. sed eas fabulas factas prius Latinas scisse sese, id vero pernegat.*

[22] See also Cicero, *On the Orator* 2.193, 3.221, cf. Saunders 1911, Boyle 2006, 19, Manuwald 2011, 79–80.

[23] *lepide mi Hercules et scite Gavius Bassus, in libris quos de origine vocabulorum composuit, unde appellata persona sit, interpretatur; a personando enim id vocabulum factum esse coniectat. nam caput, inquit, et os coperimento personae tectum undique unaque tantum vocis emittendae via pervium, quoniam non vagam neque diffusam set in unum tantummodo exitum collectam coactamque vocem ciet, magis claros canorosque sonitus facit. quoniam igitur indumentum illud oris clarescere et resonare vocem facit, ob eam causam persona dicta est, O littera propter vocabuli formam productiore.*

As an aside, nowadays Gavius Bassus' etymology of the word *persona* is generally rejected.[24] Aulus Gellius may well have expressed his scepticism about the etymology, too, by prefacing this account with 'cleverly and wittily'.

An interesting feature accompanies the notion of masks, and that is categorisation. As the French anthropologist Claude Lévi-Strauss (1962) described it the first chapter of his *La pensée sauvage*, the categorisation of masks is a common phenomenon in many societies and already occurs among 'primitive' or *chthonic* people. In this respect, Lévi-Strauss speaks of the 'science du concret'.[25]

Also among the Greeks in the Hellenistic period masks were categorised. The first written taxonomies of masks were presumably produced in Ptolemaic Alexandria.[26] One example has survived – in an *onomastikon*, a *thesaurus*, compiled by the second century CE sophist Julius Pollux of Naucratis (close to Alexandria).[27] The passage is of considerable length: twenty-one pages in Bethe's (1900–1937) modern edition (4.133–54). It offers a classification of masks for each type of play, that is tragedy, satyrplay and comedy. Within each category subdivisions are made, described in some detail.[28] For comedy alone, forty-four types of masks are distinguished. The main distinction is between old men, young men, slaves and women, with a remarkable eye for detail. In Wiles' words, this is 'an exercise in taxonomy',[29] 'rooted in sociological assumptions about the Hellenistic world'.[30]

5.4 'Person' in philosophy

So far I have discussed, two geographically distinct origins for the use of masks in Rome: Etruria, where masks representing ancestors were used in funeral rituals, and Athens, where human masks were worn in the theatre and where 'mask' obtained its transferred sense of role or character. Both were transferred to Rome: the Etruscan usage was picked up in Roman funeral rituals, in order to represent the deceased with fidelity, and with a

[24] See e.g. Nédoncelle 1948, 285–6.
[25] Lévi-Strauss 1962, chapter 1. I owe this reference to Smith 2016, 73.
[26] Callimachus' pupil Aristophanes of Byzantium (*c.*257–180 BCE) may have started the tradition: according to Athenaeus 14.659a–b (= p. 276 Nauck 1848, fr. 363 Slater), he wrote the treatise *On Masks*, in which he dealt with different types of masks. Athenaeus refers to it in the context of the etymology of *maisōnikon*: against Chrysippus (no reference in *SVF* or *FDS*), Aristophanes would have been correct in deriving it from the comic actor Maison, who invented the roles (and hence the masks) of cook and servant. Cf. Cohn 1896, 1004, Gudeman 1934, 146, Matthaios 1999, 392.
[27] On Pollux's sources see Rohde 1870 (with a useful stemma at 82), Bieber 1930, 2076.
[28] See Bieber 1930, 2076–105, still the fullest discussion to date.
[29] Wiles 1991, 75.
[30] Wiles 1991, 77.

protreptic, moral purpose. The Greek usage was picked up when Greek theatre was introduced in Rome, where masks represented characters or roles on stage. With the theatre mask, the potential for a more abstract use of the notion must have become clear, too.

A decisive turn in the already rich history of the notion of person begins in the 3rd century BCE, when the Stoics start to reflect on it. As we will see in a moment, these philosophers – among whom in the 2nd century BCE Panaetius of Rhodes deserves pride of place – distinguish between the use of *persona* in a specific sense ('personal identity') as well as a more general, indeed universal sense ('personhood', 'being treated as a person'). From there, from Stoic thought, the notion of person appears to have spread out to the other disciplines as well.

In the 3rd century BCE, for the first generation of Stoics the theatrical person was already a major topic. The Stoics were surely inspired by the radical and anti-conventional thought of the Cynics. As already noted in Chapter 2, section 2.2, Zeno of Citium, the first head of the Stoic school, started studying philosophy with these notorious anti-conventionalists. The Cynics had a clear interest in theatre. Diogenes of Sinope, the 'founder' of Cynicism (or, rather, the first among those who called themselves Cynics) wrote tragedies: in the catalogue of his books (extant in Diogenes Laertius, at 6.80) seven titles have been preserved. Aristo of Chios, a contemporary of Zeno of Citium, used the notion of person in relation to the sage, that is the human being who has brought his or her rational faculties to perfection, for which see Diogenes Laertius 7.160 (*SVF* 1.351, LS 58G): 'For the wise man is like the good actor who, whether he puts on the mask of Thersites or Agamemnon, plays either part in the proper way.'[31] (tr. LS) According to standard Stoic doctrine, the sage lives the good life, that is he or she lives his or her life in accordance with cosmic reason or the order of things, whether this implies playing the role of Thersites, ugly and low born (see Homer, *Iliad* 2.212), or of Agamemnon, the king.[32]

Panaetius of Rhodes, who became head of the Stoic school around 129 BCE, gave a decisive twist to the notion of person.[33] As discussed above (in Chapter 2, section 2.2; cf. Chapter 4, section 4.4) Panaetius successfully

[31] εἶναι γὰρ ὅμοιον τὸν σοφὸν τῷ ἀγαθῷ ὑποκριτῇ, ὃς ἄν τε Θερσίτου ἄν τε Ἀγαμέμνονος πρόσωπον ἀναλάβῃ, ἑκάτερον ὑποκρίνεται προσηκόντως.

[32] See e.g. Ioppolo 1980, 196–7, Nagy 2017, 112.

[33] On Panaetius and person see further Kerferd 1972–1973, Puhle 1987, Gill 1988, Engberg-Pedersen 1990 (partially reprinted in Stephens 2006, 364–78), Long 1997, Forschner 2001, Sorabji 2006, 157–71, Gill 2009, Schofield 2012, Machek 2016, Rist 2020, 26–9.

tried to make Stoic philosophy acceptable among the Roman elite, hiding the anti-conventional, 'Cynicised' doctrines held by the founders of their school. Unlike early Stoics (such as Aristo of Chios), Panaetius, in a clearly anti-Cynic move, applies the notion of *persona* to non-perfect human beings. Rather than aiming to move beyond human imperfection, like the early Stoics, for Panaetius the imperfect *condition humaine* became the vantage point from which to consider whether one's life can be considered good enough.

In this focus on ordinary human beings, in a discussion of the virtue of 'seemliness' (*prepon* in Greek, *decorum* in Latin), of being able to act fittingly in the eye of the traditional public, Panaetius developed the notion of person: just as in the theatre actors play more than one role by wearing different masks, so in ordinary life human beings play various roles, too, to be distinguished as it were by the various masks they wear. In his unfortunately lost *On Appropriate Action* Panaetius distinguished at least two roles, the content of which has been transmitted via Cicero, *On Appropriate Actions* 1.107 (LS 66E, fr. 61 Alesse, fr. B14 Vimercati):

> Furthermore, one must understand that we have been dressed, as it were, by nature for two roles: *one* is common, arising from the fact that we all have a share in reason and in the superiority by which we surpass the brute creatures. Everything honourable and seemly is derived from this, and from it we discover a method of finding out what is appropriate. The *other*, however, is that assigned specifically to individuals. For just as there are enormous bodily differences [. . .], similarly, there are still greater differences in men's spirits.[34] (tr. Atkins, modified)

The first role is common to all human beings, arising from the fact that they all have a share in reason and thus stand above brute animals. The second role is based on mental qualities, the natural talents and abilities which account for the differences between human beings.

A little bit further, at *On Appropriate Actions* 1.115 (fr. 64 Alesse, fr. B15 Vimercati), two further specific roles are distinguished, the role imposed on us by chance or circumstance, and the role based on life choices human beings make in relation to their careers or the kind of virtue they want to excel in:

[34] *intellegendum etiam est duabus quasi nos a natura indutos esse personis; quarum una communis est ex eo, quod omnes participes sumus rationis praestantiaeque eius, qua antecellimus bestiis, a qua omne honestum decorumque trahitur et ex qua ratio inveniendi officii exquiritur, altera autem quae proprie singulis est tributa. ut enim in corporibus magnae dissimilitudines sunt* [. . .], *sic in animis existunt maiores etiam varietates.*

> To the two roles [. . .] a *third* is added: this is imposed by some chance or circumstance. There is also a *fourth*, which we assume for ourselves by our own decision. Kingdoms, military powers, nobility, political honours, wealth and influence, as well as the opposite of these are in the gift of chance and governed by circumstances. In addition, assuming a role that we want ourselves is something that proceeds from our own decision; as a consequence, some people apply themselves to philosophy, others to civil law, and others again to rhetoric, while even in the case of the virtues, different men prefer to excel in different of them.[35] (tr. Atkins, modified)

For the specific roles defined here Cicero may well yet again have been following Panaetius;[36] it has also been assumed that the latter two roles would go back to Cicero himself.[37] At any rate, in either case the Roman background seems to play a role here. In terms of the double origin of the notion of person, it is not only the Greek background of the theatre mask that is put to use, also the Etruscan–Roman background of the specific mask must have been taken into consideration.

The implications of the distinction between these common and more specific roles in the history of Western thought are momentous. The first, common role marks the starting point of the Western universalist tradition in ethics, according to which each human being as a person ought to perform some types of appropriate actions: these can be regarded as the precursors of Kant's 'duties' (*Pflichten*), that is – as he set out most famously in his *Groundwork* of 1785 – acts of which rational beings want that they be performed universally, and subsequently of the universal (human) rights that correlate with these duties.[38] The use of the notion of person in the universal sense is accompanied by a reinterpretation of the traditional Roman value of *dignitas* and the introduction of the notion of *humanitas*. *Dignitas*, in the Roman context traditionally understood as referring to the higher standing of the politically powerful, is here put on a par with 'outstandingness' (*excellentia*), and now understood as the status

[35] *ac duabus iis personis* [. . .] *tertia adiungitur, quam casus aliqui aut tempus imponit, quarta etiam, quam nobismet ipsis iudicio nostro accommodamus. nam regna, imperia, nobilitatem, honores, divitias, opes eaque, quae sunt his contraria, in casu sita temporibus gubernantur; ipsi autem gerere quam personam velimus, a nostra voluntate proficiscitur. itaque se alii ad philosophiam, alii ad ius civile, alii ad eloquentiam applicant, ipsarumque virtutum in alia alius mavult excellere.*

[36] See Schofield 2012. [37] Schmekel 1892, 39–41.

[38] Kant, *Grundlegung*, Ak. 4:421–4. The difference is that for the Stoics an appropriate action is an action that in most situations is in accordance with reason that pervades common nature and as such has a reasonable justification, whereas for Kant a duty exists if a human being using his rational faculty comes to the conclusion that the prospective course of action is wanted universally. See further e.g. Gill 1988, Nussbaum 2000, Forschner 2001, and Faro 2010, 363.

of a human being as a human being,[39] who because of his 'mind nourished by learning and reasoning' surpasses other living beings, that – in what surely is an anti-Epicurean move – 'perceive nothing except pleasure'.[40] Also, next to *dignitas*,[41] Panaetius and Cicero used *philanthrōpia* and *humanitas* as 'the fellowship and community of human beings',[42] and which included a more humane approach to the imperfections of the human kind.[43] Here, too, Kant was inspired: next to person and appropriate actions, in the *Groundwork* he also took dignity and humanity on board.[44] The specific role marks the beginning of thinking about personal identity, in an ethical context, in which each human being, as a rational being, has to deal with character and circumstance in order to give shape to his or her own life.[45]

In sum: with Panaetius (perhaps inspired by Polybius' depiction of the Roman usage of masks and by the categorisation of the theatre mask), who was followed by Cicero, the Greek–Etruscan notion of person became an important notion in ethics, and would remain popular with later thinkers in antiquity, notably Seneca, Epictetus and Boethius.[46] But the proliferation of the term in the late Roman Republic did not stop with ethics. Its popularity was such that it also started to play a role in the systematisation of the emerging scientific disciplines, such as rhetoric, grammar and the study of law.

5.5 'Person' in other disciplines

As discussed in Chapter 3, in section 4.2 especially, in the Hellenistic period most disciplines transformed from a 'knack' into a science. Whereas the term 'person' is missing in the earliest Hellenistic systematisations, it becomes a popular term from the 2nd century BCE onwards, especially in rhetoric, grammar and the study of law. So let us have a brief look at the emergence of the notion of person in each of these disciplines.

39 To clarify: *dignitas* did not loose its political connotations altogether. Cicero continued to use *dignitas* as a political notion, while attempting to protect the values of the Rome's constitutional arrangements against monarchical ambitions. See e.g. Atkins 2000, 513.

40 Cicero, *On Appropriate Actions* 1.105–6 (fr. 81 Alesse, fr. B12 Vimercati), cf. Wegehaupt 1932, 34–6, Pöschl 1989, 38–41, Atkins 2000, 482, 503, 513, Sensen 2009, 312–3, Sensen 2011, 71–91, Ribas Alba 2012, xix, Griffin 2017.

41 According to Griffin 2017, 57, fellowship and dignity are connected: the fellowship of human beings is the result of their superiority over non-rational animals.

42 *On Appropriate Actions* 1.50 (fr. 91 Alesse, B27 Vimercati).

43 Schadewaldt 1973, 52–61, especially 57 n. 43.

44 For humanity see *Groundwork*, Ak. 4:429, for dignity see *Groundwork*, Ak. 4:434.

45 Long and Sedley 1987, vol. 1, 427–8: 'Panaetius' theory intriguingly anticipates modern conceptions of personality.'

46 See Brouwer 2019, 40–4.

Rhetoric is the oldest among these disciplines that is transformed into a science. The question of whether rhetoric can be considered a science was brought up in Plato's *Gorgias*, as we saw earlier (see Chapter 1, section 1.5, and Chapter 3, section 3.3). For Plato's contemporary Isocrates, the answer was clear: it can already be derived from the title of his treatise *The Science of Rhetoric*. Among the other systematisers of rhetoric should of course be mentioned Aristotle, but also the author of the 4th-century *Rhetoric to Alexander* (see above, Chapter 1, section 1.5). It is remarkable that in these early manuals of the 4th and 3rd century BCE the notion of *persona* (or rather its Greek equivalent *prosōpon*) does not yet occur. Only in later manuals, from the 2nd century onwards, such as the one written by Hermagoras of Temnos, can the notion of person be found: in the evidence that we still possess that presumably stems from this manual, person occurs in one passage.[47] In the Latin language the first systematic accounts were written in the first part of the 1st century BCE, of which are still extant the *Rhetoric to Herennius,* erroneously transmitted as if written by Cicero, and Cicero's early *On Invention.*[48] In these treatises the notion of person is used. Also in his *On the Orator* Cicero uses person. At 2.102 Cicero describes the preparation for a trial, using person in the sense of role: 'Then, when he [the client] has departed, on my own and with fairness I play three roles [*tres personas*]: myself, the other party, and the judge.'[49] (tr. Sutton and Rackham, modified) At 3.53, Cicero distinguishes between things and persons:

> It is those whose speeches are clear, explicit and full, perspicuous in matter and in language, and who in the actual delivery achieve a sort of rhythm and cadence—that is, those whose style is what I call ornate. Those who manage this same ornate style as the relative importance of the things and persons concerned directs, deserve to be applauded on the score of the sort of distinction that I designate appropriateness and suitability of style.[50] (tr. Rackham, modified)

Let us move on to the study of language. Grammar could only develop into a science after the debate on how to study language had been settled.

[47] See especially [Augustine], *On Rhetoric* 8 (= fr. 7 Matthes, not in Woerther).
[48] See e.g. Clarke 1971, 30–1.
[49] *itaque cum ille discessit, tres personas unus sustineo summa animi aequitate, meam, adversarii, iudicis.*
[50] *qui distincte, qui explicate, qui abundanter, qui inluminate et rebus et verbis dicunt et in ipsa oratione quasi quendam numerum versumque conficiunt, id est, quod dico, ornate. qui idem ita moderantur, ut rerum, ut personarum dignitates ferunt, ei sunt in eo genere laudandi laudis, quod ego aptum et congruens nomino.*

As we have seen in Chapter 4, according to the anomalists the focus should be on the specifics of language, whereas according to the analogists language should be studied with a focus on its regularities or rules. With the analogists eventually winning the debate, grammar finally developed into the study of language from a systematic perspective.[51]

The earliest example of a systematisation in grammar in which the notion of person occurs is the *Science of Grammar*, ascribed to Dionysius Thrax (*c.*170–*c.*90 BCE), a pupil of the Alexandrian scholar Aristarchus of Samothrake (see above, Chapter 4, section 4.5), himself a pupil of Aristophanes of Byzantium (see above n. 26).[52] Person is discussed in chapter 13, at p. 51.20–1 Uhlig: 'There are three persons: first, second, and third. The first is from whom the utterance orginates, the second is to whom it is addressed, the third is topic of the utterance.'[53] (tr. Kemp, modified) A couple of generations after Dionysius Thrax, Varro wrote a treatise *On Persons*, in three books,[54] and dealt with persons in his *On the Latin Language*. Unfortunately *On Persons* is lost, but *On the Latin Language* survived partly. Person is discussed at 8.20:

> In the class of words which indicate times, because these were three, past, present, and future, a threefold inflection had to be made [...] Since likewise the nature of persons was threefold, the one who was speaking, the to whom, and about whom, these were inflected from the same word, there are these derivative forms of each and every verb.[55] (tr. De Melo)

This is sometimes referred to as the Aristotelian 'Dreipersonenlehre' of speaker, audience and subject, which would have its origins in Aristotle's *Rhetoric*.[56] However, as we have seen, this is an anachronism: Aristotle did not yet use the word person in this context.[57]

[51] For the systematisation of the discipline see above Chapter 3, section 3.4. See further Frede 1978, Desbordes 1990, 45–6, Wolff 2015, 144: 'L'ars grammatica a fini par s'identifier au système.'

[52] For a challenge of authorship and date see Law 2003, 56–7, with further references.

[53] πρόσωπα τρία, πρῶτον, δεύτερον, τρίτον· πρῶτον μὲν ἀφ' οὗ ὁ λόγος, δεύτερον δὲ πρὸς ὃν ὁ λόγος, τρίτον δὲ περὶ οὗ ὁ λόγος. Cf. Diomedes, *Science of Grammar* 1, 334.20–3 Keil: *persona est substantia rationalis. personae in verbo sunt tres, per quas universus administrabitur sermo. prima est quae loquitur, ut dico, secunda quacum sermo habetur, ut dicis, tertia de qua quis loquitur et relatio indicitur, ut dicit,* and Charisius, *Science of Grammar* 214.17–19 Barwick and Kühnert: *persona est substantia nominis ad propriam significationem dicendi relata, personarum notitia est triplex, primae secundae tertiae.*

[54] See the catalogue of Varro's writings in Hieronymus, as printed by Cardauns 2001, 86.

[55] *in verborum genere quae tempora adsignificant, quod ea erant tria, praeteritum, praesens, futurum, declinatio facienda fuit triplex* [...]. *cum item personarum natura triplex esset, qui loqueretur, ad quem, de quo, haec ab eodem verbo declinata, quae in copia verborum explicabuntur.*

[56] Matthaios 1999, 507.

[57] Matthaios 1999, 392–5.

Let us finally move on to law. Just like grammar or rhetoric, towards the end of the 2nd century BCE the study of law also changed from a 'knack' into a 'science', to use the terms of Plato's *Gorgias* again – with *persona* playing an important role. As we have seen in Chapter 3, in the change of the study of law into a science, Quintus Mucius Scaevola Pontifex was a pivotal figure, who – in Pomponius' words at *Digest* 1.2.2.41 – 'divided the civil law into kinds by arranging it into eighteen books'. In his systematisation of the legal material a major role is attributed to the notion of *persona*.[58] First, in the extant evidence, at *Digest* 41.3.24, from Pomponius, *Quintus Mucius*, book 24, the contrast between persons and things is made:

> Where statute prohibits *usucapio* [acquisition of ownership through possession], possession in good faith avails no one. Sometimes, though, even though it was not the deceased who initiated possession, the possession runs for his heir; suppose, for instance, that a defect, emanating from the person of a possessor, but relating to the thing itself, should be remedied, as when the thing ceases to belong to the treasury to be stolen or possessed by force.[59] (tr. Thomas in Watson 1998)

Second, we have evidence of Mucius' taxonomical use of person in a passage that survived in Cicero, *On Laws* 2.48–9:

> There is a question about those who are bound by the sacred rites. The cause of the heirs is most just, for there is no person who comes nearer the place of him who has departed from life. Next, [. . .] In the third place, [. . .] Fourth, [. . .] Last is the person who owed money to the death person and has paid it to no one; he should be held to have acquired this as money. We have learned these things from Scaevola. They were not thus arranged by the ancients.[60] (tr. Fott)

In the still extant teaching manuals that were produced in the subsequent centuries, the notion of person takes on its position in the now firmly established tripartite classification of law. See Gaius, *Teaching Manual* 1.8: 'All law, which we use, is about persons, things or actions.'[61] Tripartition

58 Cf. Ribas Alba 2012, xxiv, 210, Paricio 2012, 455.

59 *ubi lex inhibet usucapionem, bona fides possidenti nihil prodest. interdum etiamsi non fuerit inchoata usucapio a defuncto, procedit heredi eius: veluti si vitium, quod obstabat non ex persona, sed ex re, purgatum fuerit, ut puta si fisci res esse desierit aut furtiva aut vi possessa.*

60 *quaeruntur enim qui adstringantur sacris. heredum causa iustissima est; nulla est enim persona quae ad vicem eius qui e vita emigrarit propius accedat. deinde* [. . .] *tertio* [. . .] *quarto* [. . .] *extrema illa persona est ut, si is qui ei, qui mortuus sit, pecuniam debuerit neminique eam solverit, proinde habeatur quasi eam pecuniam ceperit. haec nos a Scaevola didicimus, non ita descripta ab antiquis.*

61 *omne autem ius, quo utimur, vel ad personas pertinet uel ad res vel ad actiones.*

into person, things, and actions has thus been rightly characterised as a crucial theme in Gaius' thought, with a lasting influence.[62] Gaius' subdivisions with regard to persons start immediately thereafter, at 1.9, and will remain the topic of the remainder of the first book until the very end at 1.199: 'The highest division in the law of persons is this: all human beings are either free or slaves.'[63] At the instigation of Justinian, at the beginning of the 6th century Tribonian and his fellow-lawyers adapted Gaius' textbook and turned it into Justinian's *Teaching Manual*, where the law of persons is introduced in chapter 3 of the first book and developed in the subsequent twenty-three chapters. It is this *Teaching Manual* that would become the model for most of the modern continental legal codes (see above Chapter 3, section 3.5).

Among the first drafts for such a modern code, usually adaptations of Justinian's *Teaching Manual* to their own time and place,[64] Grotius' *Introduction to the Study of the Law of Holland* (*Inleiding tot de Hollandse Rechts-Geleerdheid*), which he wrote between 1619 and 1621, is most notable.[65] Book 1 is devoted to the law of persons. In his adaptation Grotius goes as far as to render all Latin terminology into his vernacular Dutch, translating *persona* into 'gestaltenis'. In Grotius' appendix to the *Introduction*, which is printed in the modern Dutch, but not the English editions,[66] we get a taxonomy of the use of person in law, nicely set out in tree form, remarkably similar to Pollux's taxonomy of masks used in the theatre. Similar taxonomies could be produced for the modern codes.

5.6 Conclusion and outlook

While the usual *caveats* apply, given the state of the limited, if not outright meagre evidence available, the following questions can now be answered. Where and when was person introduced in law? As we have seen, towards the end of the second and at the beginning of the 1st century BCE the interest in *persona* in Roman circles is attested for Polybius, Panaetius and

[62] Kaser 1971, 188: 'Die Institutionen von Gaius zeigen, angeregt von Vorbildern aus der griechischen Philosophie und Grammatik, Gegenüberstellung der *personae* und der *res* ein Grundschema, das sich für alle Zukunft als fruchtbar erwiesen hat.' Cf. Stroux 1934, Villey 1945, Wieacker 1953, Quadrato 1986.

[63] *et quidem summa divisio de iure personarum haec est, quod omnes homines aut liberi sunt aut servi.*

[64] See Glenn 2014, 142–4. [65] See e.g. Wieacker 1967, 288.

[66] For the original edition in Dutch see Dovring and others 1965; for an English translation see Lee 1953.

the Mucius family, and may thus have been picked up by jurists like Mucius in their efforts to systematise the law.

Why whould they have chosen the notion of person? As we have seen, *persona* referred to a venerable Roman institution – a mask that represented the deceased – with a grand moral purpose. With the introduction of the mask in Greek theatre, its abstract potential emerged too: masks can transcend the individual (role, character), and can be used in taxonomies. Its application outside the context of funeral rites or theatre is owed to the 'Roman' Stoic Panaetius of Rhodes, who started thinking about the self ('personality identity') as well as about what human beings universally may have in common ('personhood'). In other disciplines, such as rhetoric and grammar, person also became a popular notion, both as an overall term and as a term that allows for subdivisions.

Already in Roman law, then, the notion of person came to be applied to all human beings, expressing the trait of universality,[67] while allowing for subdivisions, and was thus an ideal starting point for a taxonomy in law. In Gaius' *Teaching Manual*, the first extant systematisation of Roman law, person was given pride of place. With the elevation of Justinian's adaptation of Gaius' manual to a legal source in the Byzantine period and its subsequent reception in Western Europe from the 12th century onwards, person also has become a pivotal term in contemporary substantive law, at least in those jurisdictions that belong to the two main Western legal traditions, the civil law as well as the common law tradition, which originated on the European continent and in England respectively. In the jurisdictions belonging to the civil law tradition the notion of person gives its name to one of three main categories of private law, next to the law of property rights and the law of obligations. In the French Civil Code the first book out of three is devoted to the law of persons. In the Dutch Civil Code of 1992 the law of persons is dealt with in the first two books out of the current ten. In the German Civil Code the rules with regard to natural and legal persons can be found at the very beginning, too, in the first section of the first book (articles 1–89). Beyond the civil law tradition, via Church (or Canon) law, person even became a pivotal term in the common law tradition.

[67] Ribas Alba 2012, xix, presents it as the triumph of the idea of universality, which – incorrectly – would already have been a 'basic' characteristic of Roman law.

CHAPTER 6

Casuistry in philosophy

6.1 Introduction

In Chapter 4, we saw how the Roman jurists started to use the notion of *regula* in law under the influence of notably Hellenistic epistemology and ethics, as instruments to generalise (or memorise[1]) the reasoning underlying their decisions in specific cases, with its wider implications for similar cases in the future. Jurists thus moved from the specific case to general rules. This chapter can be considered as its counterpart. In this chapter, I will discuss how philosophers moved away from the general to the specific. They became fascinated by the focus of the Roman jurists on solving cases as such. In the late Republican period, then, we find Stoic thinkers discussing real-life disputes, trying to determine the underlying reasons for deciding them correctly.

Whereas it has sometimes been maintained that the Roman Stoics, notably Diogenes of Babylon, Antipater of Tarsus, Panaetius of Rhodes, Posidonius of Apamea and Hecato of Rhodes, invented casuistry,[2] in this chapter I intend to show that they adopted the topic of casuistry from the Roman jurists. From the second half of the second century onwards we find these philosophers discussing cases as 'quasi legal controversies', as Cicero in his *On Appropriate Actions* 3.91 (not in *SVF*) formulates it.[3] I will argue that Cicero uses *quasi* here in order to make clear that the controversies the philosophers discussed had their origins in law, but that these thinkers brought them within the overall domain of the study of wisdom.

A word on casuistry is surely useful. In modern parlance, casuistry has been characterised in different ways: as reasoning where a rule cannot easily be applied ('low casuistry'), or where two rules are in conflict ('high casuistry'),[4] as reasoning without rules,[5] or – again in a modern, influential

[1] Finkenauer 2015. [2] Thamin 1884, 274, Jonsen and Toulmin 1988, 76.
[3] *hae sunt quasi controversiae iura Stoicorum.* [4] Veillard 2015, 210.
[5] Hart 2012 [1961], Sunstein 1996, 10.

formulation – of dealing with 'hard cases'.[6] Among contemporary moral philosophers, casuistry is often distinguished from generalist ethics, e.g. by G.E. Moore in his *Principia ethica*,[7] or more recently by Jonathan Dancy, who prefers the term particularism to casuistry.[8] For particularists, like Dancy, the focus on cases is usually justified with the argument that ideal justice is flexible, and that cases are not settled by rules.[9] In Chapter 4, we have seen that the understanding in law of the implications that a particular decision may have upon later similar disputes is only gradually emerging. In this development, the notion of rule was taken over from Hellenistic epistemology. In this chapter I will focus on casuistry as dealing with difficult real-life cases.[10]

In order to substantiate the hypothesis that the Roman Stoics took over their interest in cases from the Roman jurists, I will proceed as follows. I will deal with the question, whether in philosophy before the second century this focus on cases can be found (section 6.2), and argue that they became a core topic in Roman law, especially in relation to the *ius honorarium*; that is, the law which developed under the power of a Roman magistrate (section 6.3). The arrival of Greek, especially Stoic, thinkers in Rome in the 2nd century BCE, which coincided with a growing reflection on the side of the jurists on their own activities, allowed for a fertile exchange of ideas between these two groups. With regard to the jurists, it has to be borne in mind that in this period they started to write these solutions down rather than giving them orally as used to be the case. This new practice of writing would surely have incited them to reflect on their activities anew. In section 6.4, I will discuss the new developments among the Roman Stoics: their shift in focus – in comparison with the early Stoics – that is, first, to 'second-rate' virtues and 'intermediate' appropriate actions, and, second, to conflicts between possible actions. In section 6.5, I will pull the threads together to see the occurrence of casuistry in philosophy under the influence of law, a lasting development.

[6] Griffin 2013b, 120–2. The formulation 'hard cases', influential among modern lawyers, goes back to Dworkin 1977, who built his influential theory of underlying legal principles on an attack at Hart's loosely made remark that in difficult cases judges exercise discretion (see Hart 2012 [1961], 131). For Hart's response see the Postscript as printed in the second (1994) and third (2012) editions.

[7] Moore 1993 [1903], section 1.4.

[8] Dancy 2004, Dancy 2017. Cf. Woolf 2007 (on Cicero), Brouwer 2012 (on the particularism of the Austrian twentieth-century novelist Musil).

[9] See Dancy 2004 and Dancy 2017, cf. Sunstein 1996, 121.

[10] The distinction between casuistry as bottom-up and generalist ethics as top-down is not useful here, since bottom-up fits a generalist ethics with a focus on actions, too: the generalist would thus look at whether a particular action fits his overall theory. As we will see below, the early Stoics can be regarded as generalists with a bottom-up interest in actions.

6.2 Casuistry in philosophy before the Roman Stoics?

Let me first deal with the question of whether casuistry can already be found in Greek thought before the Roman Stoics. I will do so by looking – briefly – at other possible candidates: Socrates, as depicted by Plato in his early dialogues, Plato himself, Arcesilaus and Carneades, as Plato's successors in the Academy, Aristotle and finally the early Stoics.

If we look at the accounts of Socrates that Plato offers us in his early dialogues, we find him depicted as searching for an understanding of the perfect mental states with which human beings ought to live: *aretai* in Greek, literally 'excellences' or in the traditional, standard translation 'virtues', with which I will stick for the sake of convenience. The examples are familiar: in the *Euthyphro* Socrates searches for an answer to the question: 'What is the virtue of piety?', in the *Laches* he asks the same question with regard to courage, in the *Charmides* with regard to moderation, and in the first book of the *Republic* with regard to justice (as a mental state, that is). In discussing the answers given to him, Socrates makes clear that he is not satisfied with simple instances of piety, courage, moderation or justice. In so far as the answers are of a more general nature, Socrates is not satisfied with them either: they allow for counter-examples. Cases are thus discussed by Socrates, but are either rejected or serve as 'refutations' of the answer given to him – *elenchoi*, as they are now commonly referred to, due to Gregory Vlastos' influential work.[11] An example is Polemarchus' answer to Socrates' question about justice in *Republic* 1: the definition of justice as 'to pay everyone what is owed to him' (331e) is refuted by Socrates with the case of the return of someone's weapons if that someone is no longer of sound mind: 'When someone goes out of his mind, and then asks it back, isn't returning it completely out of the question?' (332a, tr. Griffith).[12] In Plato's early dialogues a focus on cases as such can thus not be found. If they are brought up, they are rather the means by which Socrates makes clear that he is someone who does not have the answers to questions about the nature of virtue.[13]

In Plato's later writings casuistry does not appear either. In his ethics, Plato is above all interested in giving general answers to the Socratic questions about the virtues or the good life, which are given in the most elevated manner possible in the continuation of the *Republic*,

[11] Vlastos 1983, Vlastos 1991.

[12] ἀποδοτέον δέ γε οὐδ' ὁπωστιοῦν ἰότε ὁπότε τις μὴ σωφρόνως ἀπαιτοῖ;

[13] Cf. Jonsen and Toulmin 1988, 62–3.

books 2–10, and with more emphasis on the human condition in the *Statesman* and the *Laws*.

Plato's successors Arcesilaus and Carneades, heads of the 'sceptical' Academy, as the institution is nowadays usually referred to, used cases in good Socratic fashion as counter-examples in order to refute the doctrines of the 'dogmatic' philosophers, both in ethics and in epistemology. Perhaps most famously, in epistemology Carneades brought up the counter-example of the identical twins, which he used against the Stoics in order to refute their doctrine of the cognitive impression as the criterion of truth.[14] In the case of the identical twins – say Castor and Pollux – the alleged cognitive impression may well be false, if it is an impression of Castor as though it were of Pollux: 'For the virtuous man will get a false impression [. . .] if the impression he gets from Castor is one of Pollux' (tr. Bett).[15] In the debates with the Stoics the sceptical Academics thus operate like Socrates, using cases in order to refute: they do not show an interest in a methodology to arrive at positive answers.[16]

Does casuistry appear in Aristotle's writings? In his *Nicomachean Ethics*, Aristotle famously states that the study of human conduct deals with what is particular and contingent, as opposed to the study of nature, which deals with what is universal and necessary.[17] However, this does not seem to imply a focus on hard cases. If there are any, they rather seem to serve as illustrations of Aristotle's general accounts. A first example from the *Rhetoric* is Antigone's dilemma whether to bury Polynices as just by nature or to refrain from doing so on the basis of Creon's decree.[18] A second example that has been suggested is Aristotle's discussion of the 'puzzles' (*aporiai*) with regard to friendship in the *Nicomachean Ethics* 9.2, at 1164b22–6, such as whether one should always agree with one's father, whether one should trust one's doctor, or whether one should elect as a general someone capable in warfare or not.[19] A third example are the cases Aristotle brings up in his *Topics*. The *Topics* deals with the expertise of dialectical argument, and is presumably an early work, which has its origins in the conversational approach while he was still in the Academy:

[14] See Sextus Empiricus, *Against the Professors* 7.410 (Carneades fr. 2 Mette, LS 40H). For a list of further cases see Mette 1985, 124–5.

[15] λήψεται γὰρ ψευδῆ φαντασίαν ὁ σπουδαῖος [. . .] ἐὰν ἀπὸ Κάστορος ὡς ἀπὸ Πολυδεύκους φαντασιωθῇ.

[16] For an introduction to the history of the Academy, also in the Hellenistic period, see Bonazzi 2015; for the debate between Academics and Stoics as a debate about Socrates' legacy see Brouwer 2020b.

[17] See Aristotle, *Nicomachean Ethics* 6.5 1140b, 6.7 1141b, 6.9 1142b, cf. Nussbaum 1986, Jonsen and Toulmin 1988, 65–6.

[18] Aristotle, *Rhetoric* 1.13 1373b8–13.

[19] See e.g. Griffin 2013b, 121.

it thus deals with the question how to converse correctly. A *topos* can hence be defined as 'a location where a number of arguments can be stored for ready recall'.[20] The cases discussed in the *Topics*, then, once again serve as a means, illustrating the types of arguments.[21] Overall: if we find Aristotle discussing cases in his now extant work, these cases are either exceptional or used in order to illustrate his more general account.

Even so: if one were to accept these cases as examples of casuistry, it is questionable whether they exerted any influence on the philosophers or even jurists of the late 2nd and the beginning of the 1st century BCE. After all, as discussed in Chapter 2, section 2.2, Aristotle's writings as we know them were presumably not even available to the thinkers in his own school, let alone – in the Hellenistic system of higher education, in which students were educated within one particular school of thought – outside his school.

Finally, were the early Stoics interested in casuistry? With Plato and Aristotle, the early Stoics shared their focus on virtue. But different from these ancient thinkers, they already developed an interest in actions as such. This interest is expressed in the Stoic subdivision of ethics as one of the three parts of wisdom, next to physics and logic.[22] Unfortunately, this subdivision only survives in one source and, at the relevant point, the text is difficult. The source is Diogenes Laertius 7.84 (*SVF* 1.178, 3.1, LS 56A), where the division is ascribed to Chrysippus and later Stoics:

> They divide the ethical part of philosophy into the topics of [i] impulse, [ii] good and bad things, [iii] emotions, [iv] virtue, [v] the end, [vi] primary value and actions, [vii] appropriate encouragements and discouragements. This is how Chrysippus subdivides ethics, along with Archedemus, Zeno of Tarsus, Apollodorus, Diogenes, Antipater and Posidonius.[23]

The difficulty relates to (vii), which is usually understood as a reference to two topics. Long and Sedley offer 'appropriate functions and encouragements and discouragements',[24] Inwood and Gerson 'on appropriate actions, and on encouragements and discouragements to actions',[25] and Boeri and Salles 'on obligations, on exhortations and discouragement'.[26] However, this usual reading presupposes that in the Greek text the

[20] Smith 1997, xxviii. [21] Düring 1968. [22] See above, Chapter 1, section 1.4.

[23] τὸ δ' ἠθικὸν μέρος τῆς φιλοσοφίας διαιροῦσιν εἴς τε τὸν [i] περὶ ὁρμῆς καὶ εἰς τὸν [ii] περὶ ἀγαθῶν καὶ κακῶν τόπον καὶ εἰς τὸν [iii] περὶ παθῶν καὶ [iv] περὶ ἀρετῆς καὶ [v] περὶ τέλους [vi] περί τε τῆς πρώτης ἀξίας καὶ τῶν πράξεων καὶ [vii] περὶ τῶν καθηκόντων προτροπῶν τε καὶ ἀποτροπῶν. οὕτω δ' ὑποδιαιροῦσιν οἱ περὶ Χρύσιππον καὶ Ἀρχέδημον καὶ Ζήνωνα τὸν Ταρσέα καὶ Ἀπολλόδωρον καὶ Διογένην καὶ Ἀντίπατρον καὶ Ποσειδώνιον.

[24] LS 56A. [25] Inwood and Gerson 2008, 110.

[26] Boeri and Salles 2014, no. 21.1: 'a los actos debidos, a los exhortaciones y las disuasiones.'

preposition 'about' would have been omitted. In a literal reading, however, the final *peri* governs phrase (vii), which suggests that the words should be read together as 'appropriate [as an adjective] encouragements and discouragements'. Diogenes Laertius (or his underlying source) thus offers us a contrast between (vi) primary value and actions on the one hand and (vii) appropriate encouragements and discouragements on the other hand. If 'primary' is understood in a hierarchical (rather than temporal) sense, the division suggests a contrast between (vi) perfect actions of primary value on the one hand and (vii) imperfect (dis-)couragements in general, which have relative value only, on the other hand. In terms of the neologisms that the Stoics were happy to introduce in the Greek language, the contrast can hence be reformulated as between perfect 'right actions' (*katorthōmata*) that are in accordance with the sage's virtuous disposition, and 'appropriate actions' (*kathēkonta*) that apply to ordinary, not yet perfect human beings and that have a reasonable justification.

'Appropriate action' was already introduced by Zeno, the founder of the school. See Diogenes Laertius 7.108 (*SVF* 1.230, LS 57C):

> Zeno was the first to use this term *kathēkon* [appropriate action], the name being derived from *kata tinas hēkein*, 'coming to some people'. Appropriate action is an activity appropriate to constitutions that accord with nature.[27]

'To some people' can refer to most human beings or to the sage. With regard to most human beings 'appropriate action' is used as the general term for the type of activities that are in accord with the nature of most human beings; with regard to the sage, the appropriate action refers to his right action, that is in accordance with perfect(ed) reason. A perfect action is thus – in standard Stoic doctrine[28] – a special kind of appropriate action.

If this interpretation of the passage of the division of ethical topics is correct, the Stoics were thus interested in actions in accordance with nature, both in the sense of acting in accordance with the nature of most human beings or of acting in accordance with perfect reason as the specific circumstances demand. Examples of appropriate actions in general are showing respect for one's parents or meeting up with friends (see Diogenes Laertius 7.108, *SVF* 3.495, LS 59E); with regard to the right

[27] κατωνομάσθαι δ᾽ οὕτως ὑπὸ πρώτου Ζήνωνος τὸ καθῆκον, ἀπὸ τοῦ κατά τινας ἥκειν τῆς προσονομασίας εἰλημμένης. ἐνέργημα δ᾽ αὐτὸ εἶναι ταῖς κατὰ φύσιν κατασκευαῖς οἰκεῖον.

[28] See e.g. Stobaeus 2.85.18–6.1 (*SVF* 3.494, LS 59B): τῶν δὲ καθηκόντων τὰ μὲν εἶναί φασι τέλεια, ἃ δὴ καὶ κατορθώματα λέγεσθαι. κατορθώματα δ᾽ εἶναι τὰ κατ᾽ ἀρετὴν ἐνεργήματα, οἷον τὸ φρονεῖν, τὸ δικαιοπραγεῖν.

actions in specific circumstances the Stoics included sexual intercourse with family members and eating human corpses (see Diogenes Laertius 7.188, *SVF* 3.744, 3.747), actions which the Stoics' adversaries, such as the Epicurean Philodemus in his *On the Stoics* were all too eager to exploit.[29]

However, the early Stoics' interest in actions, both of the perfect and the not (yet) perfect human being, apparently did not bring about an interest in casuistry – to judge by the extant sources, that is. Perhaps this was due to the early Stoics' focus on the sage and his right actions: here a conflict between courses of actions is obviously not possible, since the sage, by his or her perfect nature, will live in harmony with the nature of the whole.[30] If the early Stoics focused on 'conflicts', they did so between common opinion on the one hand and their Stoic doctrines with regard to the sage on the other hand, between the common *doxai* and the Stoics' *paradoxai*. These *paradoxai* drew the attention of the ancients and have been well preserved: even if captured by the notorious tyrant Phalaris, who used to roast his enemies, the sage is free; even as a beggar, the sage is rich, etc.[31] What the Stoics maintain about the sage appears to be contradicting common opinion, but can in the end be appropriately explained in the context of Stoic thought: the sage's virtuous disposition makes him both free and rich in the real – i.e. Stoic – sense of the words.

So, even though this interest in the topic of actions did not imply an interest in casuistry yet, it could have prepared the grounds for the appeal the lawyers' discussion of hard cases could have had to the Roman Stoics, especially where these Roman Stoics became more interested in the appropriate actions of not yet perfect human beings, as we will see shortly.

6.3 Casuistry in Roman law

Before doing so, let us first take a closer look at Roman law. In the Roman system of dispute resolution, especially in the 2nd century BCE, casuistry becomes the heart of the matter. As we have seen in Chapter 2, section 2.1, in the 2nd century BCE disputes had come to be resolved by respectable members of the community. When these lay-judges had to decide difficult cases, they started to consult self-proclaimed specialists. These legal experts offered an advice or 'answer' (*responsum*). If the problem related to how to apply a phrase in a particular statute, such as that in the Twelve Tables, the lay-judges asked the legal expert to interpret this phrase. The products of

[29] See Dorandi's 1982 edition, cf. Brouwer 2021.
[30] See further, e.g. Brouwer 2014, 29–41.
[31] See e.g. Cicero, *On the Paradoxes of the Stoics*, chapters 5 and 6, cf. *SVF* 3.589–603.

juristic interpretation as applied by the judge came to be known as the *ius civile* in a strict sense.

With regard to disputes that were not covered by statute, the praetor, the magistrate-politician responsible for adjudication, had the power to decide whether they could be heard by a judge. Upon his election he would make clear in an edict which types of cases could be heard. Parties would present the praetor their dispute, whereupon he would decide whether it would fit one of the types. If so, he would offer them a *formula*, in which their dispute was rephrased in the wordings of his edict. Thus moulded, the dispute could then be presented to the judge. Here the lay-judge (and indeed the praetor himself) could take the services of a legal expert on board. This legal expert would formulate an answer by making Roman custom explicit. The products of the expert finding what is right according to Roman tradition came to be known as the *ius honorarium* or as the *ius civile* in the broad sense.

Like the decisions, the *responsa* were initially oral: after all, what was of interest to the parties to the dispute as well as to those involved in deciding it was its resolution. Only the statutes and the praetor's edict were written down: the statutes inscribed on bronze, the annually changing edicts on wooden tablets.[32] In the 3rd century BCE an exception appears to have been made with regard to the *responsa* about public matters, which Coruncanius (consul in 280 BCE) wrote down in the priesterly books, as Pomponius in his *Handbook*, at *Digest* 1.2.2.35 and 38 (Coruncanius test. 23 and 24 Viarengo), presents it.[33] With regard to most cases, however, writing remained inessential.[34]

If Pomponius' developmental account is to be believed (as with Coruncanius he is our only source here), this started to change in the first half of the 2nd century BCE, when the first collection of juristic *responsa* by a legal expert was put together. According to Pomponius' *Handbook* in *Digest* 1.2.2.38 (Sextus test. 25 Bottiglieri), Sextus Aelius (consul in 198 BCE) wrote a work with the title *Partitioned in Three* (*Tripertita*), which contained the text of the Twelve Tables, his interpretation thereof, and the accompanying *actio(-nes)*. 'Three' in its title presumably refers here not so much to a treatise in three parts, but rather to the fact that in connection with each specific passage of the statute its interpretation and the accompanying *actio(-nes)* will be given.[35]

32 Fögen 2002, 184.
33 Ibbetson 2015, 38, Waldstein and Rainer 2014, 147, 149, Domingo 2018, 54.
34 Liebs 2002, 561.
35 Cf. Liebs 2002, 563: 'Dreigeteiltes'.

In the middle of the 2nd century BCE a further development takes places, at least so it is reported in Pomponius' *Handbook*, in *Digest* 1.2.2.39, already brought up in chapter 3, section 3.4.1: 'Publius Mucius, Brutus and Manilius laid the foundations for the civil law.' Let me first try to assess the reliability of Pomponius' account by taking a closer look at other extant evidence relating to these jurists and their *responsa*, before moving on to the much-discussed question as to what might have made these men the 'founders' of the civil law.

As for Publius Mucius Scaevola (*c.*175–115 BCE, consul 133, pontifex maximus 131),[36] according to Pomponius' *Handbook* at *Digest* 1.2.2.39, he wrote ten short books, which may well have been collections of his own *responsa*. At any rate, Cicero, *On the Orator* 1.212, mentions him among those who gave *responsa*, of which several survived.[37] These *responsa* dealt among others with the retro-active effect of the Lex Atinia on theft,[38] the definition of the confines of a building,[39] and – perhaps most famously – the ownership of the baby of a slave: does the baby belong to the slave owner as fruit of his ownership or to the mother?[40]

As for Marcus Junius Brutus (praetor in 142 BCE), he wrote a work *On the Civil Law* in three books (mentioned by Pomponius in *Digest* 1.2.2.39). Unique among the Roman lawyers, he did so in the form of a dialogue, surely modelled after the writings of the Greek philosophers: each book contained a conversation, which was held in a different place, i.e. Brutus' villas in Priverno, Albano, and Tivoli respectively.[41] The work may also have contained his *responsa*, about which Cicero, *On the Orator* 2.142, complains that Brutus still used the names of the parties, thus distracting from the 'matter' (*res*) or legal problem as such.[42]

As for Manius Manilius (born shortly after 200, consul in 142 BCE), 'our interpreter of the law' as Cicero calls him,[43] he provided answers on questions relating to legacies and inheritances of women. He did so while walking across the forum (Cicero, *On the Orator* 3.133, not referred to by

[36] Kunkel 2001, no. 17, Bona 1973 (reprinted 2003), Guarino 1981, Talamanca 1981, 21, Schiavone 1992, 5, Wieacker 1988, 547.

[37] Cf. Lenel 1889, 755–6.

[38] Aulus Gellius, *Attic Nights* 17.7.3 (fr. 4 Lenel).

[39] Cicero, *Topics* 24 (fr. 3 Lenel).

[40] Cicero, *On Ends* 1.12.

[41] See Cicero, *In Defence of Cluentius* 141, *On the Orator* 2.223–4 (Brutus frs. 1–3 Lenel). Cf. Bretone 1971, 108, Liebs 2002, 566, Schiavone 2012, 168/2017, 164.

[42] *video enim* [. . .] *in Bruti libris nominatim fere referri, quid alicui de iure viro aut mulieri responderit; credo, ut putaremus in hominibus, non in re consultationis aut dubitationis causam aliquam fuisse.*

[43] Cicero, *On the res publica* 3.17 (Manilius fr. 9 Lenel): *iuris interpres noster.*

Lenel), and presumably wrote them down in his work in seven books that in Pomponius' 2nd century CE was still available on papyrus rolls.[44]

So it is clear that these three jurists provided *responsa*. What is it that, according to Pomponius makes them founders of the civil law; what does Pomponius in the passage preserved at *Digest* 1.2.2.39 mean by *fundaverunt*? It should first be noted that the focus on founders or origins is standard in Roman (or Greek) historical accounts. Pomponius is particularly fond of it: he already used the word at 4, and uses it again at 44. It has thus been argued that at 39, Pomponius does not use *fundaverunt* in the strong sense of being the first, but rather of stabilising: the three jurists would thus have firmly established an oral practice.[45] If one were to retain the sense of being the first, *fundaverunt* could rather be taken to refer to their activity of giving *responsa* as reasoned independently from statute, simply because many of the disputes were no longer covered by statutes like that of the Twelve Tables: rather than offering an 'interpretation of statute' (*interpretatio legis*), as an activity that had already been started by priests, the three jurists discovered the law in the cases at hand: they were thus the first to present an *interpretatio iuris*.[46]

Whether Pomponius' attribution of this new type of interpretation to these three jurists in particular is historically correct or not, it is clear that this new type did come into being, fitting in well with political and economic developments in the 2nd century BCE. With the remarkable and fast rise of Rome as a world power (in the Eastern Mediterrenean in 168 BCE the Romans defeated the Macedonians at Pydna, in the Western part in 146 BCE they razed Carthago to the ground), its economy became more global. In a rural society, the existing statutes may well have offered appropriate arrangements. In the more global economy, different disputes arose, especially with regard to foreigners and commerce. In the 3rd century a special magistrate, the *praetor peregrinus*, started to allow disputes to be judged in which foreigners were involved, in the 2nd century the praetor also started to deal with such disputes among Roman citizens. It is

[44] See Pomponius, *Handbook* in *Digest* 1.2.2.39: *et extant volumina scripta Manilii monumenta*. For *monumenta* as a reference to papyrus rolls see Baviera 1909, 37–73, cf. Liebs 2002, 563, Schiavone 2012, 169.

[45] Nörr 1976, 537, Guarino 1969, 104–7, Tondo 1979, 33–51, Talamanca 1981, 15, Cannata 1997, 223, Schiavone 2017, 160.

[46] Archi 1970, 19, cf. Bretone 1971, 108, Bretone 1982, 266. A different interpretation of *fundaverunt* in the stronger sense is offered by Behrends 1980a, 73, Behrends 1980b, 53, Behrends 1982, who here discerns the influence of what he refers to as Antipater of Tarsus' 'humanist' version of the Stoic theory of natural law (unfortunately without referring clearly to evidence for this 'humanist' version).

here then that we find the origins of casuistry in Roman law, of adjudication beyond the existing statutes, where the praetor allows such cases to be judged on the basis of his edict and by reformulating the disputes in *formulae*.

The written form of such a *responsum*, on which the *ius civile* came to be built, is concise: the dispute is brought back to its core, in line with or based on the *formula* that goes with the case.[47] Different from later *responsa*, at least in the ones written by among others Brutus, as we have just seen (n. 42), parties are still referred to by their names. However, it would become standard for these *responsa* to be more abstract: the names of the parties and specific, but otherwise legally irrelevant circumstances, such as place and date, would be left out.[48]

Together with the rise of the written *responsum*, we find the jurists giving different *responsa* on the same question: the 'legal controversy' (*controversia*) comes into existence.[49] Two examples should suffice here. For the *ius civile* in the strict sense, an example can be found in Aulus Gellius, *Attic Nights* 17.7.3, which deals with the question of the possible retro-active effect of the *lex Atinia* about 'theft' (*furtum*): 'Mucius, Brutus and Manilius were in doubt as to whether the statute applies to future cases of theft only or also to theft already committed.'[50] For the *ius honorarium*, Cicero, *On Ends* 1.12 offers an example:

> We have our leading citizens debate the question of whether the offspring of a female slave is to be regarded as *in fructu*, with Publius Scaevola and Manius Manilius on one side, and Marcus Brutus dissenting.[51] (tr. Woolf)

According to Publius Mucius Scaevola and Manius Manilius, a baby is a by-product (the 'fruit') that as such belongs to the owner of the slave; according to Marcus Brutus, it does not.[52]

Next to statute, then, the written *responsum* came to play an important role in the resolution of disputes, eventually developing into a core source of Roman law. In the next generations *responsa* were formulated by

[47] Wieacker 1970, 204. [48] Wieacker 1970, 204, Rawson 1985, 204; cf. Thomas 2011 [1986].

[49] Heumann 1909 *s.v. controversia*. Cf. Bretone 2008.

[50] *Q. Scaevola patrem suum et Brutum et Manilium, viros adprime doctos, quaesisse ait dubitasseque utrumne in post facta modo furta lex valeret an etiam in ante facta.*

[51] *an, partus ancillae sitne in fructu habendus, disseretur inter principes civitatis, P. Scaevolam M'. que Manilium, ab iisque M. Brutus dissentiet.* Via Ulpian, it would survive in the *Digest* too, at 7.1.68, from Ulpian, *To Sabinus*, book 7, with reference to Brutus only (Brutus fr. 4 Lenel): *vetus fuit quaestio, an partus ad fructuarium pertineret: sed Bruti sententia optinuit fructuarium in eo locum non habere: neque enim in fructu hominis homo esse potest.*

[52] For discussion, especially as to why Brutus dissented, see Wieacker 1988, 588, with further references.

Quintus Mucius Scaevola, the son of founder Publius, by Servius Sulpicius Rufus,[53] and by their pupils, such as Quintus Aquilius Gallus, Alfenus and Ofilius,[54] and in Imperial times by the classical jurists. The relevance of this development of consulting an expert in the process of dispute resolution cannot easily be underestimated.[55] In giving their *responsa* the legal experts made the system of Roman law explicit. See the later (2nd century CE) definition of *responsum* in Gaius, *Teaching Manual* 1.7, who speaks of jurists who in giving these responses build up the law: 'Juristic answers are the judgments and opinions of those entrusted with the task of building up the law' (tr. Gordon and Robinson in Watson 1998).[56] Many of these *responsa* survived the ages and exerted their influence, especially on the continental legal systems through Emperor Justinian's *Digest*, the ultimate collection of written *responsa*.

6.4 The Roman Stoics

Let us move on to the Roman Stoics, the first three generations of Stoics that came in contact with Rome, including Diogenes and Antipater as the first, Panaetius as the second, and Posidonius and Hecato as the third generation (see above, Chapter 2, section 2.2). As we have already seen in Chapter 4, section 4.4, in comparison with the early Stoics, for these Roman Stoics the focus shifts from perfection to imperfection, in two ways. First, the shift occurs with regard to virtue, from the sage to the 'good man' (*vir bonus*), or, to put it in in other words: from the human being that is virtuous to the human being that resembles the virtuous person. Second, with regard to actions, the Roman Stoics move away from the right actions of the sage and focus instead on the appropriate actions of the not yet perfect human being that have a reasonable justification.

Perhaps these shifts had already occurred with Diogenes and Antipater: they can be found in Cicero's discussion of their controversies in his *On Appropriate Actions*, to which I will turn in a moment, and presumably also in Stobaeus 2.83.10–4.17 (*SVF* Diogenes fr. 47, Antipater fr. 52), where Diogenes and Antipater, next to 'primary value', distinguish and hence emphasise the lesser senses of 'exchange value' and 'selective value'.

[53] Pomponius, *Handbook* in *Digest* 1.2.2.43: *Servius Sulpicius in causis orandis primum locum.*

[54] For Mucius' pupils see Pomponius, *Handbook* in *Digest* 1.2.2.41, cf. Wieacker 1988, 600–2; for Servius' pupils see Pomponius, *Handbook* in *Digest* 1.2.2.44, cf. Bauman 1985, 70–113, Wieacker 1988, 607–11.

[55] Glenn 2014, 136, following Watson 1995a, 472.

[56] *responsa prudentium sunt sententiae et opiniones eorum, quibus permissum est iura condere.*

Primary value is the value according to nature, whereas exchange value is the value that people are prepared to attribute to something. According to Antipater, things with selective value are chosen when circumstances allow, such as health over illness, life over death, and wealth over poverty.

Against the background of these developments within the Stoic school itself, first, of the interest in actions among the early Stoics, and, second, of the more moderate, down-to-earth approach of the Roman Stoics, with their shift in focus from the right actions of the sage to the still imperfect, but reasonable actions of the good man, we find the Roman Stoics discussing hard cases. As I will argue, they did so under the influence of the Roman jurists, appropriating their casuistry, both in form and in content.

For the first three generations of these Stoics we have yet again to rely on the later source of Cicero's *On Appropriate Actions*, book 3. Here Cicero presents two sets of cases, at 50–67 and at 89–92. The first set includes two cases discussed by Diogenes and Antipater, the 'first' generation of Roman Stoics. The second set of ten cases stems from the 'third' generation Roman Stoic Hecato, a pupil of Panaetius, from his *On Appropriate Actions*, book 6 (fr. 11 Gomoll). Perhaps surprisingly, from the 'second' generation, from Panaetius, cases are not extant. This is not due to lack of interest: Panaetius was interested in casuistry. In his *On Appropriate Action* he apparently even promised to deal with this topic. However, he did not fulfill this promise for a somewhat remarkable reason.[57] According to Posidonius, one of Panaetius' pupils, who has it from his fellow-student Publius Rutilius Rufus (consul 105 BCE), what Panaetius had already written on appropriate action was so excellent that he himself (or anyone else for that matter) did not dare finishing the unfinished.[58] Here a comparison is made with Apelles' painting 'Venus of Cos', which was already so good that neither Apelles himself nor anyone else dared finishing it.

Let us start with the first set of cases. The first case therein, at *On Appropriate Actions* 3.50 (*SVF* Diogenes fr. 49, Antipater fr. 61), deals with the case of a seller of grain, who has commercially relevant information, where the question is whether he ought to share this with the buyer:

[57] Cicero, *On Appropriate Actions* 3.7 (fr. 35 van Straaten, fr. 94 Alesse, fr. A69 Vimercati): *de tertio autem genere deinceps se scripsit dicturum nec exsolvit id, quod promiserat.*

[58] Cicero, *On Appropriate Actions* 3.9–10 (Panaetius fr. 35 van Straaten, fr. 94 Alesse, fr. A69 Vimercati, Posidonius fr. 41C Edelstein and Kidd): *quae Panaetius praetermisisset et non perfecisset, propter eorum, quae perfecisset, praestantiam neminem persecutum.*

> For example, suppose that a good man had brought a large quantity of corn from Alexandria to Rhodes at a time when corn was extremely expensive among the Rhodians because of shortage and famine. If he also knew that several more merchants had set sail from Alexandria, and had seen their boats en route laden with corn and heading for Rhodes, would he tell the Rhodians? Or would he keep silent and sell his own produce at as high a price as possible?[59] (tr. Atkins)

The second case, at 3.54, concerns the sale of a house with defects, where the question is whether the seller should inform the buyer:

> Suppose that a good man is selling his house because of certain faults that he knows and that others do not know, say, that it is unsanitary but thought to be salubrious, or that it is not generally known that vermin can be found in all the bedrooms, or that it is structurally unsound and crumbling, but no one except the owner knows this.[60] (tr. Atkins)

For both cases Cicero presents the different answers formulated to these questions by Diogenes and Antipater respectively. It has been argued that this debate or these different answers for that matter are in fact a Ciceronian construction.[61] This is quite unlikely, though. In the second set of cases, at 3.91, which stems from Hecato's *On Appropriate Action* 6, we find two cases, in which Diogenes and Antipater are yet again shown to be in dispute. One is similar to the first two cases, at 3.91 (not in *SVF*, fr. 11 Gomoll):

> If a man is knowingly selling a wine that will not keep, ought he to say? Diogenes thinks it unnecessary, Antipater considers that a good man would do so. Such matters are for the Stoics like legal controversies (tr. Atkins),[62]

the other deals with the use of counterfeited money, again at 3.91 (not in *SVF*, fr. 11 Gomoll):

[59] *si exempli gratia vir bonus Alexandrea Rhodum magnum frumenti numerum advexerit in Rhodiorum inopia et fame summaque annonae caritate, si idem sciat complures mercatores Alexandrea solvisse navesque in cursu frumento onustas petentes Rhodum viderit, dicturusne sit id Rhodiis an silentio suum quam plurimo venditurus?*

[60] *vendat aedes vir bonus, propter aliqua vitia, quae ipse norit, ceteri ignorent, pestilentes sint et habeantur salubres, ignoretur in omnibus cubiculis apparere serpentes, male materiatae <sint et> ruinosae, sed hoc praeter dominum nemo sciat; quaero, si haec emptoribus venditor non dixerit aedesque vendiderit pluris multo. quam se venditurum putarit, num id iniuste aut improbe fecerit?*

[61] Annas 1989. Cf. Powell 2013, who argues that it cannot be excluded that Carneades' lectures in favour and against justice in book 3 of *On the res publica* are in fact a Ciceronian invention (see above, Chapter 2, section 2.2).

[62] *qui vinum fugiens vendat sciens, debeatne dicere. non necesse putat Diogenes, Antipater viri boni existimat. haec sunt quasi controversia iura Stoicorum.*

> If a wise man has foolishly accepted counterfeit coins for good ones, when he discovers it, would he pay with them any debt he may have, instead of with good coins? Diogenes says yes; Antipater says no, and I agree rather with him.[63] (tr. Atkins)

So Diogenes and Antipater themselves offer different answers as to what the appropriate course of action would be. Here we need not be concerned with the actual differences between their answers: what is important is that both Diogenes and Antipater bring legal cases into the general domain of the study of wisdom. Diogenes follows the responses of the jurists that the appropriate action is that the seller need not inform the buyer, whereas Antipater argues that the appropriate action is rather that the seller ought to tell the buyer everything, since the seller ought to take the common benefit into account. Diogenes does not simply reproduce the legal answer, as has been maintained.[64] He may, rather, have argued that pursuing one's self-interest is not unjust,[65] or – surely more elegant and philosophically interesting – that pursuing one's self-interest is the appropriate action from an overall moral point of view. Here Adam Smith's invisible hand springs to mind: egoism brings the greatest benefit to all.[66]

The next, third, generation of Roman Stoics also engaged themselves with cases and treated them as philosophically rewarding. Among these Stoics, Posidonius and especially Hecato can be mentioned. Whereas Posidonius stated that no topic is so important, he nevertheless only briefly dealt with cases in some commentaries.[67] Unfortunately, nothing of his brief dealings with them has survived. This is different for his contemporary Hecato of Rhodes, who like Posidonius was a pupil of Panetius.[68] Just like Panaetius, Hecato wrote a book *On Appropriate Action*, of which book 6 dealt with casuistry: in Cicero's words, *On Appropriate Actions* 3.89 (fr. 11 Gomoll), it was 'full of questions of this kind'.[69] We get ten examples in Cicero's *On Appropriate Actions* 3.89–92 (fr. 11 Gomoll), an

63 *quaerit etiam, si sapiens adulterinos nummos acceperit imprudens pro bonis, cum id nescierit, soluturusne sit eos, si cui debeat, pro bonis. Diogenes ait, Antipater negat, cui potius assentior.*

64 Backhaus 2006, 7. 65 Pohlenz 1934b, 26, cf. 17.

66 Schofield 1999a. Another interpretation is offered by Fiori 2011, whose (not unproblematic) starting point is that positive law should be considered as an imperfect instantiation of the law of nature: according to Diogenes, the inferior person is bound by positive law, whereas according to Antipater, the inferior person is also bound by the law of nature.

67 *On Appropriate Actions* 3.8 (fr. 41C Edelstein and Kidd): *quem locum miror a Posidonio breviter esse tactum in quibusdam commentariis, praesertim cum scribat nullum esse locum in tota philosophia tam necessarium.*

68 On Hecato, see Abel 1987, Veillard 2015, 239–40. For collections of evidence on Hecato see Gomoll 1933. Veillard prepares a new edition.

69 *plenus est sextus liber de officiis Hecatonis talium quaestionum.*

account that has been characterised as 'lifeless and hasty'.[70] But perhaps Cicero simply wanted to give an impression of the sheer amount of the cases and hence of the relevance of this Roman topic of casuistry for the Greek Hecato.[71] I will briefly run through them: (1) if corn has become extremely expensive, should the good man still feed his slaves?;[72] (2) if cargo must be thrown overboard at sea, should it be an expensive horse or a cheap slave?;[73] (3) if in a shipwreck a not yet perfectly rational being seizes a plank, is the sage allowed to wrest it from him if he can?[74] (4) what if he is not a sage, but the captain?; (5) what if both are sages?; (6) is it relevant whether one sage serves his country and the other does not?; (7) if a father despoils a temple, or digs a tunnel to the treasury, will his son denounce him to the magistrates?[75]; (8) what if the son finds out that his father wants to betray his country? The next two cases, about the counterfeited coins and the cheap wine, we already encountered in the context of Diogenes and Antipater giving different answers. The final two cases, if indeed still from Hecato rather than from Cicero himself, concern the question of whether a seller ought to give information about a slave's character defects, or whether a good man should interfere in a commercial action when a seller thinks that he is selling brass but in fact is selling gold. As with Diogenes and Antipater, Hecato's answers as such need not concern us here: what matters is that a Roman Stoic like Hecato is fully immersed in dealing with hard cases.

6.5 Casuistry from law to philosophy

The threads can now be pulled together. As we have seen, in philosophical discourse in the 2nd century BCE, before the arrival of the first Stoics in Rome, discussion of cases as such is absent. This is different in the legal domain: in the 2nd century BCE casuistry became one of the jurists' key activities, whether developed either on the basis of the interpretation of statute (*ius civile* in the strict sense) or with regard to the disputes that could be heard if the praetor allowed so (*ius honorarium*). The contents of

70 Lefèvre 2001, 176: 'ebenso lieblos wie hastig ausgeführt'. 71 Dyck 1996, 612–3.

72 *plenus est sextus liber de officiis Hecatonis talium quaestionum, sitne boni viri in maxima caritate annonae familiam non alere. in utramque partem disputat, sed tamen ad extremum utilitate, ut putat, officium dirigit magis quam humanitate.*

73 *quaerit, si in mari iactura facienda sit, equine pretiosi potius iacturam faciat an servuli vilis. hic alio res familiaris, alio ducit humanitas.*

74 *si tabulam de naufragio stultus arripuerit, extorquebitne eam sapiens, si potuerit?*

75 *si pater fana expilet, cuniculos agat ad aerarium, indicetne id magistratibus filius?*

the cases are drawn from real life, with the emphasis on commercial transactions. The form of the cases is simple: the problem is formulated in a condensed manner, but not yet in the abstract manner, without reference to the actual names of the parties. Where we suddenly find the Roman Stoics discussing these practical, real-life cases, with content often remarkably similar to the legal cases, and in a condensed form that yet again resembles the legal *responsa*, they thus seem to take over these legal cases and bring them in the general realm of the study of wisdom: how can these practical real life questions be resolved, on the level of the good man? Legal controversies thus transform into philosophical controversies.[76]

Next to the similarities in content and form, further evidence for the thesis that the philosophers were influenced by the Roman jurists, relates to the contact between these two groups, which – especially against the background of the overall paucity of the evidence in this period – are relatively well recorded. As for Diogenes, it seems likely that on his visit as ambassador to Rome in 155 (see Chapter 2, section 2.2) he could have been introduced to legal casuistry. It has been objected that a Greek-speaking philosopher could not have joined the jurists' debates in Latin – for most Greeks surely a barbaric language – with reference to the fact that senator Gaius Acilius undertook the task of acting as their interpreter in their deliberations in the Senate.[77] But given the Roman interest in things Greek, with part of their education in Greek, most educated Romans would have been able to speak the language and hence to discuss matters with the Athenians, and thus to present their real-life cases to Diogenes.[78]

As for Antipater, after Diogenes' return to Athens, Diogenes himself would have been able to introduce Antipater to the legal cases. But it is likely that Antipater himself was in direct contact with the jurists: he even appears to have been in Rome, in the company of Blossius of Cumae.[79] As a 'house friend' (*hospes*) of the Mucii (see Cicero, *On Friendship* 37), Blossius (d.128 BCE), who according to Plutarch, *Lives of the Gracchi* 8.6

[76] Schwartz 1951, 206. His understanding of the difference between legal and philosophical controversies is misleading: the difference is not that, unlike philosophical controversies, legal controversies cannot exist. The difference is rather that the judge will have to solve the dispute, declaring the law on the basis of his authority, whether the answer is 'right' or not.

[77] See Aulus Gellius, *Attic Nights* 6.14.9, cf. Plutarch, *Life of Cato the Elder* 22; for the asymmetrical attitudes towards each other's language see Momigliano 1971, 19 ('The Greeks had no choice. They could only speak Greek to the Romans, and it was for the Romans to decide whether they wanted an interpreter'), Fiori 2011, 286, 295.

[78] Cf. Suerbaum 2002, 27.

[79] Plutarch, *Lives of the Gracchi* 8.6 (*SVF* Antipater fr. 13); *pace* Garbarino 1973, 446 n. 2.

(*SVF* Antipater fr. 13), was the inspiration behind Tiberius Gracchus' proposals for land reform, was surely familiar with legal casuistry.[80] Antipater even dedicated some of his writings to Blossius.[81]

For subsequent generations even more evidence for the contact between Greek philosophers and Roman lawyers has been preserved. As for Panaetius, contacts are attested with Quintus Aelius Tubero, Quintus Mucius Scaevola Augur and Publius Rutilius Rufus. As already mentioned in Chapter 2, section 2.2, they are all presented together by Cicero in the dramatic setting of the first book of *On the res publica*. Whereas the dramatic setting of *On the res publica* might be regarded as purely fictional, further evidence of the contact between Panaetius and the Roman lawyers exists. Publius Rutilius Rufus attended Panaetius' lectures.[82] Quintus Mucius Scaevola Augur did so too.[83] As for Tubero, grandson of Sextius Aelius and Scipio's nephew, he was a jurist as well as a Stoic. As a jurist he is mentioned by Pomponius (*Handbook* in *Digest* 1.2.2.40) among the pupils of the founders of the *ius civile*.[84] According to Cicero, in a fragment from his otherwise lost *On Arranging the Civil Law into a Science*, preserved by Aulus Gellius, *Attic Nights* 1.22.7 (Cicero, fr. 1 Garbarino), 'Tubero did not fall short of his predecessors in knowledge of the law, in teaching even outdid them.'[85] As a Stoic, with his Stoicism presumably learned from Panaetius, he had mediocre rhetorical skills but was good at dialectic.[86] At any rate, Panaetius wrote him a letter about how to endure pain,[87] advising him to learn by heart *On Grief*, a treatise written by Crantor of Soli (late 4th century BCE), the Academic philosopher and a close friend of Arcesilaus.[88] In another letter to Tubero, Panaetius praised Appius Claudius Caecus' collection of maxims, written in around 300.[89] Tubero is furthermore known for his contacts with

80 On Blossius and the modern debate on his underlying reasons for pursuing the land reform (whether he was influenced by Stoicism or by the inequality he witnessed in Italy or both), see further Dudley 1941, Smuts 1957, Erskine 1990, 161–7, Vesperini 2012, 175–205, La Greca 2016, Alesse 2017.

81 Plutarch, *Lives of the Gracchi* 8.6 (*SVF* Antipater fr. 13).

82 Cicero, *On Appropriate Actions* 3.10 (fr. 35 van Straaten, fr. 94 Alesse, fr. A69 Vimercati), *Brutus* 114 (fr. 146 van Straaten, fr. 48 Alesse, fr. A40 Vimercati): *Panaeti auditor, prope perfectus in Stoicis.*

83 Cicero, *On the Orator* 1.75 (fr. 145 van Straaten, fr. 49 Alesse, fr. A49 Vimercati), cf. 1.45 (fr. 155 van Straaten, fr. 9 Alesse, fr. A48 Vimercati).

84 See further Klebs 1919, Kunkel 2001, no. 20, Garbarino frs. 161–76.

85 *nec vero scientia iuris maioribus suis Q. Aelius Tubero defuit, doctrina etiam superfuit.*

86 Cicero, *Brutus* 117: *mediocris in dicendo, doctissumus in disputando.*

87 Cicero, *On Ends* 4.23 (fr. 113 van Straaten, fr. 83 Alesse, fr. A87 Vimercati).

88 Cicero, *Lucullus* 145 (Crantor of Soli fr. 1 Mette; Panaetius fr. 137 van Straaten, fr. 89 Alesse, fr. A97 Vimercati).

89 Cicero, *Tusculan Disputations* 4.4 (fr. 47 van Straaten, fr. 88 Alesse, fr. A115 Vimercati).

Hecato. Unfortunately, the evidence about Hecato's whereabouts is limited: we thus simply do not know whether Tubero travelled up to Athens or whether Hecato met him in Rome. At any rate Hecato dedicated his book on casuistry to Tubero (Cicero, *On Appropriate Actions* 3.89, fr. 11 Gomoll).

The interest in casuistry among the philosophers turned out to be lasting. In later generations, this interest can obviously be found with Cicero himself, especially in his *On Appropriate Actions*. In Imperial times, cases are discussed by Roman Stoics, such as Seneca, especially in his *On Benefits*.

With regard to Cicero himself in his *On Appropriate Actions*: after he had given the first two cases discussed by Diogenes and Antipater, he continues with four other examples, offering his own solutions to them. In the cases discussed by Diogenes and Antipater, at 3.57, Cicero plays the roles of praetor and judge alike, applying the *formula* he had set out earlier in his third book, at 21: 'Concealment is unvirtuous if at the expense of another' (tr. Atkins),[90] thus siding in both cases with Antipater. In the other four examples, Cicero follows the same method. He first sets out the cases that originated in a legal context and then applies his own Stoically inspired *formula* to them. In the first of the four other examples, at 3.58, Cicero applies his *formula* to a case of fraud, in which the sellers not only conceal, but actually tell lies.[91] In the second of the four cases, at 62, he applies his *formula* with regard to the legal case of the sale of a farm that is worth more than the price asked. Quintus Mucius Scaevola would pay more than asked, which is 'what no one denies a good man would do, but they [the Stoics] do deny that a sage would' (tr. Atkins).[92] At 63 (fr. 10 Gomoll), Hecato is brought up as one of these Stoics. According to Hecato, in his books *On Appropriate Action*, a sage would take account of his personal wealth.[93] The sage should only refrain from what is not permitted. Applying his *formula*, Cicero disagrees with Hecaton. The third and fourth cases are yet again legal cases brought into the domain of philosophy: the third case, at 3.66, is about the sale of a 'condemned'

[90] *detrahere igitur alteri aliquid et hominem hominis incommodo suum commodum augere magis est contra naturam quam mors, quam paupertas, quam dolor, quam cetera, quae possunt aut corpori accidere aut rebus externis.*

[91] *quid de iis existimandum est, qui orationis vanitatem adhibuerunt?*

[92] *nemo est, qui hoc viri boni fuisse neget; sapientis negant.*

[93] *Hecatonem quidem Rhodium, discipulum Panaetii, video in iis libris, quos de officio scripsit Q. Tuberoni, dicere, sapientis esse nihil contra mores, leges, instituta facientem habere rationem rei familiaris.*

house; the fourth case, at 3.67, about the sale of a house with an undisclosed, but otherwise known servitude. Yet again Cicero judges these cases with the help of his *formula*, at 68: 'Trickery must be removed by the laws [as a lawyer should do] or by argument and insight [as a philosopher should]'[94] (tr. Atkins).

In Imperial times hard cases are discussed by Roman authors, such as Seneca. In the last three of the seven books of Seneca's *On Benefits*, in the words of Miriam Griffin, 'a series of dialectical exercises, answering hard questions and solving hard cases' can be found.[95] Since Seneca in these books often refers to Hecato,[96] it is likely that Seneca took his inspiration from Hecato's writings on casuistry.[97]

For the later Western tradition it is above all Cicero's *On Appropriate Actions* that has turned out to be influential. For the importance of Cicero's work as such, the formulation by Richard Tuck can be invoked: 'For fifteen hundred years, from the fourth century to the nineteenth, schoolchildren in Europe were exposed daily to two books. One was the Bible, and the other was the works of Cicero.'[98] With regard to his *On Appropriate Actions*, Nussbaum notes that it can be regarded as 'perhaps the most influential book in the Western tradition of political philosophy'.[99] With regard to casuistry, Jonsen and Toulmin refer to *On Appropriate Actions* as its 'cradle'.[100] As we have seen, though, however it may have served as a cradle in the later tradition, Cicero's *On Appropriate Actions* itself is already the result of a development which had started at least a century earlier. For the origins of casuistry in philosophical discourse we really have to look further – to the Roman jurists.

[94] *aliter leges, aliter philosophi tollunt astutias; leges, quatenus manu tenere possunt, philosophi, quatenus ratione et intellegentia.*

[95] Griffin 2013b, 120. Cf. Chaumartin 1985, 12, Fuhrmann 1997, 289.

[96] *On Benefits* 1.3, 2.18, 2.31, 3.18, 6.37; cf. *Letters* 5.7, 6.7, 9.6 (frs. 12–14 Gomoll).

[97] Cf. Sonntag 1913, 61–3.

[98] Tuck 1990, 43.

[99] Nussbaum 2000/2004/2019, 178/215/19.

[100] Jonsen and Toulmin 1988, 83.

CHAPTER 7

Property in philosophy

7.1 Introduction

The influence of Roman law on philosophy was not restricted to the method of casuistry: it also exerted its influence in matters of substance. In striking contrast to earlier thinkers, the Roman Stoics – Diogenes of Babylon, Antipater of Tarsus, but especially Panaetius of Rhodes and Hecato of Rhodes – made respect for private property a central tenet of their ethical thought, more in particular in relation to their thinking about justice. In this chapter I propose that these Roman Stoics did so under the influence of the Roman jurists. The relevance of this rethinking of justice cannot be easily underestimated: via Cicero's treatises, which would exert a major influence on liberal thinkers such as Locke and Kant, private property has become a pivotal notion in ethics in the broad, ancient meaning of the part of philosophy dealing with human matters, including politics.

Another matter of substance relating to property that would yet again have a major influence on the Western tradition, is rights. In Roman law the notion of 'rights' (*iura*) is used in a variety of senses: not only as property rights, that is rights derived from property, notably servitudes and usufruct, but also as entitlements, e.g. the right of the Roman citizen, the 'right to trade' (*ius commercii*), the 'right to marry' (*ius conubii*), and as 'powers' (*ius potestasque*), e.g. the power of the *paterfamilias* over his family or the power of the 'guardian' (*tutor*) over those who are not *sui iuris*, such as young persons, women, lunatics and those who cannot cope with money.[1] From the domain of civil law some of these different types of rights were already used by Cicero in his constitutional thought, especially in relation to his discussion of the *res publica* in his eponymous book.[2] Since Cicero's treatise was only rediscovered at the beginning of the nineteenth century, different from Roman law itself, it

[1] For succinct overviews see Heumann and Seckel 1914, *s.v. ius* b), Berger 1953, *s.v. ius*, cf. Garnsey 2007, 177–203.

[2] See Atkins 2013, 120–54.

could not play a role in the articulation of the different senses of the notion of rights from the late medieval and early modern period onwards.[3] In this chapter I will therefore rather focus on private property and show how the importance the Romans attached to private property was taken over by the 'Roman' Stoics in their thinking about justice.

Here another terminological remark needs to be made. In ancient Greek a specific term for private property did not come into being. In Greek thought a variety of words can thus refer to it: ousia is used, next to *ta idia*, 'private things',[4] *ta ema*, 'things mine', *ta oikeia*, 'possessions', *ktēmata*, 'things acquired', and *ploutos*, 'wealth'.[5] For the purposes of this chapter I will simply stick to the term private property, as it has remained common in philosophical discourse. I will thus leave aside the conceptual frameworks as developed in Roman law, such as the difference between legal entitlement and factual possession, or as developed in the common law tradition, with its distinction between the absolute right of property and the relative right of possession.[6] As I will argue in this chapter, the Roman Stoics were above all interested in rethinking the virtue of justice, in which private property would come to play a pivotal role.

I will proceed as follows. In section 7.2, I will briefly deal with the question of the relevance of private property in the ethical thought of the classical Greek and early Hellenistic thinkers, notably Socrates, Plato, Aristotle, Epicurus, the Cynics and the early Stoics. In section 7.3, I will offer a sketch of the relevance of private property in Roman law. This will give us the appropriate background to appreciate the novelty of the approach of the Stoics in Rome (section 7.4), in which property becomes a central topic in thinking about appropriate human conduct.

7.2 Greek philosophers about property

What relevance did the classical and early Hellenistic Greek philosophers assign to private property in ethics?[7] According to Socrates, at least as he

[3] For the articulation of the notion of rights in the late medieval and early modern period see Tuck 1979, Tierney 1997, Brett 1997.

[4] Macé 2012.

[5] Cf. Miller 1995, 311, to which Todd 1993, 241 can be added. In Phillips 2013, a source book on Athenian law, property is not dealt with separately.

[6] See Todd 1993, 241; accounts such as Lipsius 1905–1913, 674, Kränzlein 1963, MacDowell 1968, 133, start out from these later conceptual frameworks.

[7] General studies on the role of private property in ancient ethical thought and beyond include Hemelrijk 1925, Schlatter 1951, Pierson 2013, Garnsey 2007, Hoffmann 2009, Helmer 2016.

was depicted by Plato,[8] private property is not his main concern. A crucial account in this respect can be found in Plato's *Apology* 30a–b, where in front of the Athenian jurors Socrates, after having rebutted the false image on which his prosecutors relied, characterises himself in a positive manner,[9] describing his 'service to the god' of the Delphic oracle thus: 'I go about, doing nothing else but persuading both younger and older among you to concern yourselves not so much with your bodies or with money but rather with the best condition of your souls.'[10] It is virtue that counts, from which all other good things will follow: 'Virtue will not arise as a result of money, but as a result of virtue money and other things, all things personal and public, become good for human beings' (tr. Stokes, adapted).[11] For Socrates, private property is thus a secondary value at best.

For Plato's own thinking on private property the main sources are the *Republic* and the *Laws*.[12] In the *Republic*, the topic is discussed in relation to the main question posed in the dialogue, 'What is justice?', in so far as it concerns justice in the ideal city and in the citizen. Plato maintains that such a city is in need of a division of labour, which brings about three groups of people: those who rule it, those who protect it and those who produce and trade in it. Each group has its own virtue: moderation for those who produce and trade, courage for those who protect, and wisdom for those who rule. Justice is the overall virtue, as Plato formulates it in book 4 of the *Republic*:

> 433b: Well, it looks, my friend, as if in some way or other justice is this business of everyone dealing with his own matters.[13]
>
> 434c: The ability of the producing, protecting, and ruling classes to mind their own business, with each of them dealing with their own matters in the city – this will be justice, and will make the city just.[14] (tr. Griffith, adapted)

[8] On the problem of giving accounts of the 'historical' Socrates see Dorion 2011.

[9] For this contrast between the false and true Socrates see Reeve 1989, 4.

[10] οὐδὲν γὰρ ἄλλο πράττων ἐγὼ περιέρχομαι ἢ πείθων ὑμῶν καὶ νεωτέρους καὶ πρεσβυτέρους μήτε σωμάτων ἐπιμελεῖσθαι μήτε χρημάτων πρότερον μηδὲ οὕτω σφόδρα ὡς τῆς ψυχῆς ὅπως ὡς ἀρίστη ἔσται.

[11] οὐκ ἐκ χρημάτων ἀρετὴ γίγνεται, ἀλλ' ἐξ ἀρετῆς χρήματα καὶ τὰ ἄλλα ἀγαθὰ τοῖς ἀνθρώποις ἅπαντα καὶ ἰδίᾳ καὶ δημοσίᾳ.

[12] For modern studies on Plato on private property see – next to the general studies already mentioned in n. 7 – Hoffmann 2005, Schriefl 2013.

[13] τοῦτο τοίνυν, ἦν δ' ἐγώ, ὦ φίλε, κινδυνεύει τρόπον τινὰ γιγνόμενον ἡ δικαιοσύνη εἶναι, τὸ τὰ αὑτοῦ πράττειν.

[14] χρηματιστικοῦ, ἐπικουρικοῦ, φυλακικοῦ γένους οἰκειοπραγία, ἑκάστου τούτων τὸ αὑτοῦ πράττοντος ἐν πόλει, τοὐναντίον ἐκείνου δικαιοσύνη τ' ἂν εἴη καὶ τὴν πόλιν δικαίαν παρέχοι.

With regard to private property in this just city, Plato makes a distinction between those who rule and protect on the one hand and those who produce and trade on the other hand. As for those who rule and protect, they should hold things in common, they should not be allowed to call things their own:

416d: No one is to have any private property beyond what is absolutely essential;[15]

464c: The best regulated city is the one in which the greatest number of people use this phrase 'mine and not mine' in the same way about the same thing;[16]

543b: The housing [will be] common to all of them, and offering no private property to anyone.[17] (tr. Griffith)

The reason for this community of goods is that interests in things private deviate from the interests of the city as a whole and thus without private property (or private families for that matter) the interests of the city as a whole are best served. As for those who produce and trade, however, Plato does allow for the institution of private property; the division of labour upon which the just city is founded brings with it that 'these individuals should neither have another's things nor be deprived of their own'.[18] As one author put it recently, 'if a little reluctant', Plato allows for the institution of private property for the producers and traders in his ideal *polis*.[19] In Plato's account of the just city in the *Republic*, then, private property distracts the philosopher-kings from ruling and is otherwise an institution that is restricted to the lowest class in society: its role is thus limited and its value is low.

In the *Laws*, Plato offers another attempt to found an ideal city, this time a city that is led by the best laws rather than by the wisdom of its rulers. This wisdom – as Plato had already acknowledged in the *Republic* at 472c–4d and as he does again in the *Laws* at 739e – is virtually unattainable. In the *Laws* the three speakers from three different cities, Athens, Cnossus and Sparta, each with knowledge of their respective legal orders,

[15] οὐσίαν κεκτημένον μηδεμίαν μηδένα ἰδίαν, ἂν μὴ πᾶσα ἀνάγκη.

[16] ἐν ᾗτινι δὴ πόλει πλεῖστοι ἐπὶ τὸ αὐτὸ κατὰ ταὐτὰ τοῦτο λέγουσι τὸ ἐμὸν καὶ τὸ οὐκ ἐμόν, αὕτη ἄριστα διοικεῖται.

[17] οἰκήσεις [. . .] ἴδιον μὲν οὐδὲν οὐδενὶ ἐχούσας, κοινὰς δὲ πᾶσι.

[18] *Republic* 433e: ἕκαστοι μήτ' ἔχωσι τἀλλότρια μήτε τῶν αὑτῶν στέρωνται. The translation here is taken from Miller 1991, 228.

[19] Pierson 2013, 26; cf. Garnsey 2007, 6, who makes the point that the rulers and guardians cannot do without the producers and traders: 'These [communal] arrangements as materially dependent upon a private property regime.'

attempt to describe such an ideal city by finding the best available laws for it: 'So let us have a go at founding this – at first theoretical – city' (702e)[20] 'by drawing up laws from anywhere, if we think they are better' (702c).[21] In comparison with the *Republic,* in this 'second-best' (739e) city private property plays a more prominent, but still limited role. Three points can be made on this topic here. First, in comparison with the *Republic* in this city private property is a shared feature among all citizens, since communality of property would be asking too much from the citizens and the city (740a). Second, private property should be respected, as Plato states it at 913a: 'Nobody, as far as possible, is to lay a finger on my possessions [. . .] and I will observe the same rule [. . .] in regard to the property of others'[22] (tr. Griffith). Third, and most importantly here, limits are set to private property. The aim of the laws should make the people 'as happy as possible, and as far as possible friends with one another' (743c).[23] With regard to the three things that, according to Plato, any human being takes seriously, first, things of the soul, second, things of the body, and third money, the political system should value the things of the soul most highly, then those of the body, and only in third instance money or wealth (743e). In accordance with the aim of the laws, happiness and friendship, or – as it is put negatively at 744d – absence of civil war, then, there should be no harsh poverty nor any great wealth. The lawgiver should thus set a minimum as well as a maximum to what can be owned in the city (744e). Just as in the *Republic*, then, in the *Laws* the focus is on the happiness of the city: even though private property is now no longer simply condoned for the productive and commercial classes only, but accepted for all citizens, it still plays a subordinate role in the second-best ideal city, and as such is set severe limits.

Aristotle's writings as we know them, presumably only became available in the first half of the 1st century BCE. It is thus unlikely that these would have exerted influence upon the Romans in the late Republic (see Chapter 2, section 2.2). However, his published writings must have been available, and there is some evidence from which one might infer that Critolaus, head of the Lyceum in the 2nd century BCE, had some interest

[20] ἀτὰρ πειρώμεθα λόγῳ πρῶτον κατοικίζειν τὴν πόλιν.

[21] ἅμα δὲ καὶ νόμους τῶν τε αὐτόθι, εἴ τινες ἡμᾶς ἀρέσκουσιν, τίθεσθαι κελεύει, καὶ εἴ τινες ἑτέρωθεν, μηδὲν ὑπολογιζομένους τὸ ξενικὸν αὐτῶν, ἂν βελτίους φαίνωνται.

[22] μήτε οὖν τις τῶν ἐμῶν χρημάτων ἅπτοιτο εἰς δύναμιν, μηδ᾽ αὖ κινήσειεν μηδὲ τὸ βραχύτατον ἐμὲ μηδαμῇ μηδαμῶς πείθων· κατὰ ταὐτὰ δὲ ταῦτα καὶ περὶ τὰ τῶν ἄλλων ἐγὼ δρῴην.

[23] ὅπως ὡς εὐδαιμονέστατοι ἔσονται καὶ ὅτι μάλιστα ἀλλήλοις φίλοι.

in the topic. With regard to both thinkers, however, as far as it is possible to judge from the extant evidence, private property plays but a limited role.

Aristotle deals with private property in scattered remarks in the *Rhetoric*, *Ethics* and *Politics*.[24] Both in the *Rhetoric* as well as in the *Nicomachean Ethics* Aristotle discusses private property – the term is usually 'wealth' – in relation to happiness. In the *Rhetoric*, at 1.5, in line with the purpose of this treatise as a manual for those who want to speak well in public life, Aristotle lists common conceptions of happiness 'that everyone agrees about' and of which wealth is one of its parts, as follows: 'Good birth, good friends, and plenty of them, wealth, good children, and plenty of them, a good old age, and also physical virtues [. . .], reputation, honour, good fortune and virtue' (1.5 1361b16–20).[25] In the *Nicomachean Ethics*, Aristotle provides a more precise account of the relation between his own conception of happiness on the one hand and wealth on the other. In book 1, he rejects the conception in which happiness is identified with the wealthy life: if happiness is the highest good, and if wealth is but a means to something else, then wealth cannot be the highest good. In Aristotle's understanding, happiness is in the first place a life lived out of the virtuous dispositions that either are right reason (the 'intellectual' virtues) or go with the right use of reason with regard to the non-rational part of the soul (the 'ethical' virtues). Wealth belongs to the goods that Aristotle, at 1.8 1098b12, calls external, next to the goods of the soul, and those of the body. External goods include wealth, next to friends, power, good breeding, good children, noble looks – see 1.8 1099a35–b3. What then is the relation between happiness and these external goods? At 1.10 1101a14–16, Aristotle uses the phrase 'adequately supplied': 'That person is happy who is active in accordance with complete virtue and is adequately supplied with the external goods not for some chance period but for a complete life.'[26] How this phrase should be understood, whether these external goods are inclusive to happiness or whether they are dominant only, has been much discussed in recent scholarship.[27] Here it suffices to say that for Aristotle virtue is the most important part of happiness, with wealth at best one of the external goods that are part of the good life.

[24] See Miller 1995, chapter 9, cf. Miller 1991.

[25] εὐγένειαν, πολυφιλίαν, χρηστοφιλίαν, πλοῦτον, εὐτεκνίαν, πολυτεκνίαν, εὐγηρίαν· ἔτι τὰς τοῦ σώματος ἀρετάς [. . .], δόξαν, τιμήν, εὐτυχίαν, ἀρετήν.

[26] εὐδαίμονα τὸν κατ᾽ ἀρετὴν τελείαν ἐνεργοῦντα καὶ τοῖς ἐκτὸς ἀγαθοῖς ἱκανῶς κεχορηγημένον μὴ τὸν τυχόντα χρόνον ἀλλὰ τέλειον βίον.

[27] See Hardie 1965, cf. Szaif 2004.

In the *Politics*, the limited value Aristotle attaches to private property is made clear in two different contexts. First, in book 2, Aristotle already criticises Plato's proposal of the communalism of property among those who rule and those who guard the rulers in book 5 of the *Republic*. Whereas Aristotle, different from Plato, defends private property ('it is better for property to be private', 2.5 1263a38), he makes it subordinate to the virtue of generosity, at 2.5 1263b12: 'It is in the use made of property that generosity's work lies.'[28] Second, in book 7, chapters 9–10, in his account of the ideal city, Aristotle regards private property as the precondition for participating in the life of the *polis*.[29] The political therefore has priority over private property. If elsewhere in the *Politics* Aristotle discusses private property as relevant for the exercise of virtue, as 'a site for the practice of virtue',[30] the focus is on living well together in terms of virtue. As in the *Ethics*, also in the *Politics*, for Aristotle virtue comes first in importance; private property plays a limited role.

In Aristotle's school in the 2nd century, Critolaus of Phaselis, one of the three ambassadors sent by the Athenians to Rome (see Chapter 2, section 2.2), argued for an inclusive, but still subordinate place of bodily and external goods (presumably including private property) for the good life.[31] The evidence is patchy,[32] but inclusiveness can be derived from the doctrine that our ancient sources attribute to Critolaus: 'The end is completion according to the nature of a well-flowing life, indicating the triple completion made up of three kinds [of goods]',[33] whereas the subordination can be derived from the image of the scales, which is preserved by Cicero: 'The goods of the soul outweigh bodily and external goods to such an extent that it would require the earth and seas to equalize the scales'[34] (tr. Baltussen 2017, 94).

[28] ἐν τῇ γὰρ χρήσει τῶν κτημάτων τὸ τῆς ἐλευθεριότητος ἔργον ἐστίν. [29] Miller 1995, 327.

[30] Frank 2005, 70.

[31] Critolaus thus offers a clarification of the Aristotelian position, which – as we have seen in Chapter 2, section 2.2 – cannot have been based on Aristotle's texts as we have them. Inwood 2014 presents this clarification as an innovation, even a 'turning point' (51) in the 'ancient neo-Aristotelian' (6) tradition in ethics.

[32] Of the forty passages collected in Wehrli 1969b, five deal with ethical topics.

[33] Clement of Alexandria (*c.*150–211/216), *Miscellanies* 2.129.10, fr. 20 Wehrli, Peripatetics fr. 18H Sharples: Κριτόλαος δέ, ὁ καὶ αὐτὸς Περιπατητικός, τελειότητα ἔλεγεν κατὰ φύσιν εὐροοῦντος βίου, τὴν ἐκ τῶν τριῶν γενῶν συμπληρουμένην τριγενικὴν τελειότητα μηνύων; Stobaeus 2.46.10–12, fr. 19 Wehrli, Peripatetics fr. 18I Sharples: ὑπὸ δὲ τῶν νεωτέρων Περιπατητικῶν τῶν ἀπὸ Κριτολάου [the end is] 'τὸ ἐκ πάντων τῶν ἀγαθῶν συμπεπληρωμένον' (τοῦτο δὲ ἦν 'τὸ ἐκ τῶν τριῶν γενῶν').

[34] Cicero, *Tusculan Disputations* 5.51, fr. 21 Wehrli, Peripatetics fr. 18M Sharples: *libra illa Critolai, qui cum in alteram lancem animi bona imponat, in alteram corporis et externa, tantum propendere illam bonorum animi lancem putet, ut terram et maria deprimat.* On *deprimat* see Glucker 1992, 45–6.

With regard to Epicurean thought about private property, the extant evidence is limited.[35] Epicurus does not seem to have attached much value to it. According to Diogenes Laertius 10.120 (fr. 572 Usener), he recommended 'taking thought for his property and for the future'.[36] However, as 'taking thought' already suggests, this will not have meant that Epicurus recommended a life devoted to making money. Among later Epicureans, who usually closely adhered to the doctrines of their leader, whom they venerated as wise and divine,[37] we find similar and somewhat more elaborated accounts on private property. Philodemus of Gadara, in his *On Property Management* 17.6–40, rejected the kind of management that is aimed at making money, while endorsing the kind aimed at living an undisturbed life, 'sufficient for our needs' (ll. 19–20).[38] In a treatise, of which the title is lost, but which is now usually referred to as *On Choices and Avoidances*, at 21.17–20, Philodemus makes the comparable point that acquiring wealth is not what a good follower of Epicurus should be after: 'He distributes all that remains, such that only left remaining to him is what is necessary for life itself.'[39] Epicurus and his followers thus made property instrumental to their conception of pleasure as 'the beginning and end of the blessed life', with pleasure understood as 'freedom from pain in the body and from disturbance in the soul'.[40] The conclusion can thus be that the Epicureans had a limited, perhaps even 'minimal interest in property'.[41]

In their anti-conventional thinking, the Cynics outright rejected private property. They propagated – and indeed lived – their conception of the simple life, in which private property has no place. According to Diogenes Laertius 6.37 (cf. 6.72; both passages are assembled in fr. 353 Giannantoni), Diogenes of Sinope, who nicknamed himself the Cynic, 'the Doggish one', put it thus: 'All things belong the wise.' According to some modern scholars, the Cynics' denunciation of private property should even be regarded as the central characteristic of ancient Cynicism.[42]

[35] Overviews of Hellenistic thought on property, including that of the Epicureans, include Laurenti 1973, Natali 1995, Audring and Brodersen 2008.

[36] κτήσεως προνοήσεσθαι καὶ τοῦ μέλλοντος.

[37] See Sedley 1989, Brouwer 2014, 169–70.

[38] [πρ]ὸς τὴν χρεῖαν [ἀρ]κοῦν ἕκαστος ἡμῶν. For text and translation see Tsouna 2012, cf. Tsouna 2007, 163–94.

[39] με[τα]δίδωσιν, ὅταν τὸ πρὸς [τὸ] ζῆν αὐτὸ μόνον ὑπο[λείπ]ηται, πᾶν τὸ [λοιπὸ]ν. For text and translation see Indelli and Tsouna 1995.

[40] Epicurus, *Letter to Menoeceus* in Diogenes Laertius 10.128: τὴν ἡδονὴν ἀρχὴν καὶ τέλος λέγομεν εἶναι τοῦ μακαρίως ζῆν; 10.131: τὸ μήτε ἀλγεῖν κατὰ σῶμα μήτε ταράττεσθαι κατὰ ψυχήν.

[41] Long 1997, 17–18.

[42] Dawson 1992, 130–4, Desmond 2006, 16, Husson 2016. Others have emphasised their naturalism (or primitivism, see e.g. Lovejoy and Boas 1935, 117–52, Brouwer 2021) or their shamelessness (Sloterdijk 1983, Foucault 2001, Foucault 2016).

With regard to Crates of Thebes, Diogenes of Sinope's most important pupil, the rejection of private property is abundantly attested for. Three versions of Crates' rejection of private property are conveniently recorded by Diogenes Laertius, at 6.87–8 (fr. 4 Giannantoni). At 6.87, Crates is simply said to have turned his 'private property' (*ousia*) into money in order to distribute that among his fellow-citizens.[43] In the second version, also at 6.87, which Diogenes Laertius attributes to the historian Diocles of Magnesia (2nd or 1st century BCE), Diogenes of Sinope persuaded Crates to give up his property and throw his money into the sea.[44] In the third version, at 6.88, from the historian Demetrius of Magnesia (1st century BCE), Crates entrusted his money to a banker for his sons, asking him to give it to the people if they were to become philosophers, since then they would not need it.[45] Crates' aim in denunciating his property, so other sources have it, is freedom. Here are the accounts that survived in Origen and Epiphanius:

> Origen (*c.*184–*c.*253), *Commentary on Matthew* 15.15 (fr. 9 Giannantoni): They say that he gave all his property (*ousia*) to the people of Thebes, saying 'Crates on this day sets Crates free'.[46] (tr. Hard)
>
> Epiphanius (310/320–403), *On Faith* 3.9.32, p. 507.29–30 Holl (fr. 16 Giannantoni): Crates of Thebes in Boetia, who was a Cynic, too, used to say that poverty [literally the state of not having possessions] is the beginning of freedom.[47] (tr. Hard)

So, in their unconventional thinking, the Cynics showed the downside of the traditional value of private property: rather than financial independence they considered private property to be a burden that prevents one from enjoying the freedom that goes with living the simple life.

Just like the Greek thinkers brought up thus far, the early Stoics also discussed property in the context of happiness or the good life too. In their conception of happiness the Stoics offer an assessment of the value of private property that is more in line with the Cynics. This need not surprise us: Zeno of Citium, the founder of Stoicism, had Crates of

[43] ἐξαργυρισάμενόν τε τὴν οὐσίαν – καὶ γὰρ ἦν τῶν ἐπιφανῶν – ἀθροίσαντα πρὸς τὰ [ἑκατὸν] διακόσια τάλαντα, τοῖς πολίταις ἀνεῖναι ταῦτα.

[44] φησὶ δὲ Διοκλῆς πεῖσαι αὐτὸν Διογένην τὴν οὐσίαν μηλόβοτον ἀνεῖναι καὶ εἴ τι ἀργύριον εἴη, εἰς θάλατταν βαλεῖν.

[45] Δημήτριος ὁ Μάγνης τραπεζίτῃ τινὶ παρακαταθέσθαι τἀργύριον, συνθέμενον, εἰ μὲν οἱ παῖδες ἰδιῶται γενηθεῖεν, αὐτοῖς ἀποδοῦναι· εἰ δὲ φιλόσοφοι, τῷ δήμῳ διανεῖμαι· μηδενὸς γὰρ ἐκείνους δεήσεσθαι φιλοσοφοῦντας.

[46] φασὶν ἀποδόμενον πᾶσαν τὴν οὐσίαν τῷ Θηβαίων δήμῳ δεδωρῆσθαι, μετὰ τοῦ εἰρηκέναι ὅτι 'σήμερον ὁ Κράτης Κράτητα ἐλευθεροῖ'.

[47] Κράτης ἀπὸ Θηβῶν τῶν Βοιωτικῶν, καὶ αὐτὸς Κυνικός, ἔλεγεν ἐλευθερίαν εἶναι τὴν ἀκτημοσύνην.

Thebes as his first – perhaps most important – teacher (see e.g. Diogenes Laertius 7.2, cf. 6.105).

According to the early Stoics, happiness consists in living according to virtue. Different from Aristotle, they maintained that virtue is sufficient for happiness. According to the early Stoics, virtue is the stable disposition in which one's own rational nature is brought in accordance with the course of the universe, which is pervaded by reason as its guiding force. If human beings develop their rational nature to perfection, they, as Zeno formulated it, live 'a good flow of life'.[48] This means that, whereas according to Aristotle, virtue is a necessary, but not sufficient condition for happiness, according to the Stoics, virtue as a rational disposition as part of the rational guiding force is already sufficient for happiness. The Stoics themselves formulated it thus: virtue is the only good.[49]

If for happiness only virtue is needed, and if virtue is the only good, then the implication is that according to the Stoics for happiness private property is not needed, and that it is not to be reckoned among the things that can be called good. According to the Stoics, things commonly considered good (or bad) are at best 'indifferents'. See, for example, the beginning of the account on Stoic ethics, at Stobaeus 2.58.1–3 (*SVF* 1.190), which starts with Zeno's division into things good, bad and indifferent, and is followed by sets of examples: 'Examples of indifferent things: life and death; reputation and lack of reputation; hard labour and leisure; wealth and poverty; sickness and health, and things of this sort.'[50] In an anecdote, preserved by Diogenes Laertius (at 7.36, *SVF* 1.435), Zeno's favourite pupil Persaeus of Citium (*c.* 307/6–243 BCE) is challenged on his ability to live according to his teacher's doctrine that wealth is only an indifferent:

> When the Macedonian king Antigonus Gonatas, to whom Persaeus had been sent by Zeno as a tutor to his son, wanted to test Persaeus, he sent him the fake news that his estate had been plundered. When the king saw Persaeus' face turning pale, he said: 'Don't you see that wealth is not an indifferent?'[51]

At best, private property is what the Stoics called a 'preferred' indifferent, a doctrine that was also already formulated by Zeno: 'Among things that

48 Stobaeus 2.77.20–1, *SVF* 1.184, LS 63A: εὔροια τοῦ βίου.

49 See e.g. Diogenes Laertius 7.101 (*SVF* 3.30), Cicero, *On the Paradoxes of the Stoics*, no. 2.

50 ἀδιάφορα δὲ τὰ τοιαῦτα· ζωὴν θάνατον, δόξαν ἀδοξίαν, ἡδονὴν πόνον, πλοῦτον πενίαν, ὑγίειαν νόσον, καὶ τὰ τούτοις ὅμοια.

51 διάπειραν δέ ποτε βουληθεὶς λαβεῖν αὐτοῦ ὁ Ἀντίγονος ἐποίησεν αὐτῷ πλαστῶς ἀγγελῆναι ὡς εἴη τὰ χωρία αὐτοῦ πρὸς τῶν πολεμίων ἀφῃρημένα· καὶ σκυθρωπάσαντος, 'ὁρᾷς,' ἔφη, 'ὅτι οὐκ ἔστιν ὁ πλοῦτος ἀδιάφορον'.

have value, some have much, others little. Zeno was the first to call the former preferred, the latter dispreferred.'[52] For private property among those preferred indifferent the evidence can be found in Stobaeus 2.81.5–6 (*SVF* 3.136): 'Among [the preferred] external things are parents, children, a moderate amount of property, acceptance by other human beings.'[53]

If the Stoics speak of the wealth of the perfect human being, they do so in good Cynic fashion in terms that are 'paradoxical', that literally go 'against common sense'. A nice example is preserved by Cicero in his treatise *On the Paradoxes of the Stoics*. The sixth paradox is that only the sage is rich, in the sense of possessing true virtue, to which being rich in the common sense of the word (or being poor for that matter) does not make a difference: the sage declares himself to be rich, begging his bread from others.[54]

From an unfortunately rather compressed passage in book 3 of Cicero's *On Ends*, at 67 (*SVF* 3.371), some modern scholars have inferred that Chrysippus, the third head of the school, whom Cicero had just mentioned, would have made a concession to non-ideal human nature, allowing the institution of private property, after all.[55] In this passage, Cato the Younger, the main character in Cicero's third book, and brought up as spokesman for the Stoics, after having presented the doctrine that human beings are bound to each other by the law, declares:

> Now just as a theatre is communal, it can still rightly be said that the place which one occupies is one's own. So, too, in city or universe, though these are communal, it does not go against the law that to each belongs whatever is his.[56]

Here Cato seems to say that even if things are common to all, like the theatre in the comparison, things can still belong to someone, like the (better or worse) seat in a theatre, which one occupies.[57] Rather than a concession, the negative formulation of 'does not go against the law'

[52] Stobaeus 2.84.21–3, *SVF* 1.192, LS 58E: τὰ μὲν οὖν πολλὴν ἔχοντα ἀξίαν προηγμένα λέγεσθαι, τὰ δὲ πολλὴν ἀπαξίαν ἀποπροηγμένα, Ζήνωνος ταύτας τὰς ὀνομασίας θεμένου πρώτου τοῖς πράγμασι. Cf. Cicero, *Varro* 37, *SVF* 1.193, *On Ends* 3.51–3, *SVF* 1.194.

[53] τῶν δ' ἐκτὸς γονεῖς, τέκνα, κτῆσιν σύμμετρον, ἀποδοχὴν παρὰ ἀνθρώπων. Cf. Diogenes Laertius 7.106, *SVF* 3.127.

[54] See Brouwer 2014, 60 n. 27 for a list of further evidence for this Stoic commonplace.

[55] Annas 1989, 168, Lefèvre 2001, 123, Forschner 2018, 266. That is, if the passage deals with private property at all: Wacht 1982, 47 rightly remarks that the characteristic for calling the seat one's own is occupation rather than overall and absolute control (which one would connect with private property).

[56] *sed quem ad modum, theatrum cum commune sit, recte tamen dici potest eius esse eum locum, quem quisque occuparit, sic in urbe mundove communi non adversatur ius, quo minus suum quidque cuiusque sit.*

[57] See e.g. Schäfer 1934, 254, Long 1997, 24.

suggests that occupying a particular seat, or having (more or less) private property, is an indifferent – in line with the early Stoic evaluation of private property as an indifferent.

Let me sum up the background in classical Greek and Hellenistic thought against which the discussion of private property among the Roman Stoics in the late Republic can be judged. In Plato's *Apology* Socrates declares virtue rather than money to be the highest good. In the ideal city sketched in the *Republic*, Plato rejects private property for the ruling classes but allows it for the productive and commercial class. In his account of the no longer ideal, but best possible city in the *Laws*, Plato acknowledges that the abolition of private property is unrealistic; instead, he offers an account of property laws in such a manner that they contribute to the overall end of the good life of and the friendship among the citizens. While accepting private property, for Aristotle private property plays a subordinate role, too, both in his account of the good life in the *Ethics* or in his analysis of the communal life in the *Politics*. In the Hellenistic period Epicurus and his followers only show a limited interest in property, in as far as it contributes to or – perhaps better – does not deviate from the undisturbed life. The Cynics simply denunciate private property. As for the early Stoics, they follow the Cynics here and reject the value of property in relation to the good life. In order to live the good life only virtue is needed; if private property were to play a role at all, it is given the status of a preferred indifferent, but as such bears no relation to virtue or the good life.

7.3 Property in Roman law

Before moving on to the Roman Stoics, let us briefly look at the relevance of private property in Roman law. As in Greek, also in Latin the terminology (and the conceptual framework that goes with it) is still in development. For property we find 'thing' (*res*), 'being mine' (*meum esse*), and 'household (*familia*). From the 2nd century BCE onwards, the terms *dominium* and *proprietas* are also used.[58]

'Thing' and 'this is mine' are used in the earliest forms of dispute settlement in Rome, which have come down to us. This possibility of bringing a dispute before a judge, which had to be approved by the consul, later on by the praetor as the consul's deputy, was referred to as an 'action based on statute by oath with regard to a thing' (*legis actio sacramento in*

[58] See further Kaser 1956 [1942], 306, Kaser 1971, 401, Kaser, Knütel and Lohsse 2021, 180.

rem).[59] A Roman citizen could ask a judge to decide a dispute about property, claiming a thing as his own by using the words 'this thing is mine'.

'Household' (*familia*) had a broad meaning, and could not only be used to refer to the persons, but also to the things in it. Writing in the first half of the 2nd century BCE the playwright Terence offers an example of the latter in *The Self-Tormentor*, at 909: 'My household will barely last for ten days.'[60] In the 2nd century CE, Gaius *Teaching Manual* 2.102 also still uses it in order to refer to things, explaining household with 'estate' (*patrimonium*). The encompassing meaning can be found in what survived of the statute of the Twelve Tables, at 5.4–5, for which *Digest* 50.16.195.1, from Ulpian, *Edict* book 46 (fr. 1203 Lenel), is an important source. According to Ulpian, 'household' both refers to 'things', as in 'let the nearest descendant in line have the household' (*adgnatus proximus familiam habeto*), as well as to 'persons', as in the phrases 'from his family' (*ex ea familia*), 'in this family' (*in eam familiam*), which Ulpian explains as follows: 'It is agreed that the Statute [of the Twelve Tables] speaks of individual persons'. In the 2nd century BCE, surely connected to the rise of the 'large estates' (*latifundia*) outside Rome, in Italy and beyond, with a focus on 'property' (*res*), including living beings, such as 'semi-vocal' cattle and 'vocal' slaves,[61] 'household' develops a more restricted meaning, with a focus on the persons in it.

The importance of property in Roman law is best understood in relation to the 'head of the family' (*paterfamilias*), one of the cornerstones of Roman society. The head of the family enjoys *patria potestas*, an almost unrestricted power over his household, over the things as well as the persons in it. The 'cenre piece'[62] of the *patria potestas* was considered to be 'the power or right to decide over life and death of the family members' (*potestas* or *ius vitae necisque*),[63] surely extraordinary from a modern,

[59] See Gaius, *Teaching Manual* 4.16; cf. Kaser 1956 [1942], 6–16, Kaser 1971, 401, Kaser and Hackl 1996, 89–107.

[60] *decem dierum vix mi est familia.*

[61] This sober division between vocal and semi-vocal goes back to Varro, *Rural Matters* 1.17.1, who uses it in his systematic, tripartite account of the types of instruments needed on such a farm, including those living beings that can and cannot speak. See Lewis 2013 for further discussion. This tripartition would be used again and criticised – without explicit reference to Varro, though – by Marx in *Das Kapital* (at 146 n. 17 of the first edition from 1867 as printed in the Marx-Engels Gesamtausgabe of 1983).

[62] Kaser 1971, 60.

[63] Kaser, Knütel and Lohsse 2021, 418. The phrase occurs, e.g. in an oath that was used in order for someone to become part of a family in front of the Roman people, perhaps developed by Quintus Mucius Scaevola Pontifex. See Aulus Gellius, *Attic Nights* 5.19.4–9 (not referred to in Lenel; fr. 93

twenty-first-century point of view.[64] Included in this *patria potestas* was the full power over things, which would develop into the modern conception of property as the most encompassing right that one can have over a thing, and from which lesser rights, such as servitutes and usufruct, can be derived.[65] Unlike the power to decide over life and death, this power had at first no name, from at least the 2nd century BCE onwards *dominium* and *proprietas* are used.[66] As far as we can judge from the few extant sources (most through Justinian's *Digest*), in solving disputes the Roman judges and their jurists had, above all, to pay attention to the ways things could become someone else's property, not only during the lifetime of the *paterfamilias* (when the transfer of property could take place with or without ritual), but also after his death. The almost unrestricted nature of this power was unique in the ancient world: it stands in stark contrast to the far more limited powers that the heads of families enjoyed in the Greek cities or in the Etruscan world.[67]

The importance of property can further be derived from the first extant systematisations of Roman law. As we have already seen in Chapter 5, section 5.5, the jurists made property or 'things' (*res*) into one of their three main categories of Roman law, next to persons and obligations. As the second category of law, the law relating to things is by far the largest in Gaius' or Justinian's *Teaching Manual*.[68]

What is more, by the end of the second century, with the coming into being of the large estates in the countryside (Italy and beyond) on the one hand and sharply rising poverty in the expanding metropolis of Rome on the other hand, the distribution of property had become a major political issue too: the extreme wealth that the large estates made possible and the extreme poverty that existed in Rome made the Gracchi brothers demand their land reforms.[69] The issue would turn out to be the beginning of a full-blown civil war.

7.4 The Roman Stoics about property

For the topic of private property for the late 2nd century and early 1st century BCE Stoics, Cicero's *On Appropriate Actions* is an important

FSS = 19.6 only; for the attribution of 7–9 to Quintus Mucius Scaevola see Marotti in Schiavone 2016, 35; Stolfi in FSS, 387 n. 1032 is sceptical).

64 See e.g. Masi Doria 2011, 24, who characterises it as 'terribile'.

65 Kaser 1971, 119, Kaser, Knütel and Lohsse 2021, 179.

66 For 'having power' (*potestam habere*) as the characteristic of *dominium* see Gaius, *Teaching Manual* 1.54.

67 Wenger 1924, 1–24.

68 See e.g. Nicholas 1962, 98.

69 See Appian (first half of the second century CE), *Civil Wars* 1.7 (or *Roman History* 13.7, cf. McGing 2019, xvi–xvii), Plutarch, *Lives of the Gracchi* 8.2, cf. e.g. König 2012, 152–3.

source. The first book allows a tentative reconstruction of Panaetius' thought about private property, the third book offers further information for Diogenes of Babylon, Antipater of Tarsus, and Hecato of Rhodes on this topic.

For the first (and second) book of *On Appropriate Actions*, Cicero acknowledges in so many words that he used a work by Panaetius as his main underlying source.[70] At 1.6, Cicero states that he follows the Stoics, of whom he mentions Panaetius frequently at the beginning: at 1.7, Cicero mentions Panaetius in relation to the definition of an appropriate action, expressing his surprise that Panaetius did not give one, whereas at 1.9–10, Cicero writes about the three questions that according to Panaetius should be deliberated upon when deciding about whether an action is appropriate or not. First, one should consider whether a course of action is in accordance with virtue or not; second, whether it is beneficial or not; and third, what to do when an action that appears to be beneficial is in conflict with virtue. In his third book, at 7, Cicero returns to these three questions, declaring that Panaetius dealt with the first two questions in his first three books, but failed to deal with the third question in it (see also Chapter 6, section 6.4). Despite the emphasis on Panaetius' treatise, Cicero does not mention its title in his *On Appropriate Actions*. It survived in Cicero's correspondence, however: in the letter to his friend Atticus from 12 November 44 (no. 420 (16.11) Shackleton Bailey, fr. 34 van Straaten, fr. 92 Alesse, fr. A68 Vimercati), Cicero gives it in Greek: *The [Books] on the Appropriate Action* (*Ta peri tou kathēkontos*). Since Cicero furthermore writes that Panaetius' treatise is in three books, in which he only dealt with the first two questions, there can be no doubt that this is the title of the work he used as the underlying source for his own *On Appropriate Actions*.[71]

As we have seen in the previous chapters, Panaetius adapted Stoic doctrine, making it thus respectable among the Roman elite. He not only downplayed the Cynic elements in Stoicism,[72] he also mitigated the stern

[70] Despite his own acknowledgement, modern scholarship is divided on Cicero's dependence on Panaetius: Brunt 2013, 187–8 and Veillard 2014 take it at face value, arguing that Cicero followed Panaetius in the main; Lefèvre 2001 argues that Cicero would have moved away from Panaetius, especially in book 2 (see 83). Some scholars (e.g. De Ste. Croix 1981, 426, Wood 1988, 132) simply focus on Cicero, ignoring the question of Cicero's underlying sources altogether.

[71] Next to Cicero himself, further evidence for Panaetius as Cicero's source exists: Pliny the Elder, *Natural History*, Introduction 22 (fr. 41 van Straaten, fr. 99 Alesse, fr. A79 Vimercati), Aulus Gellius, *Attic Nights* 13.28 (fr. 116 van Straaten, fr. 87 Alesse, fr. A73 Vimercati), cf. Veillard 2014, 74–5.

[72] See Cicero, *On Appropriate Actions* 1.128 (cf. 148; fr. 73 Alesse, fr. C11 Vimercati), cf. Billerbeck 1979, 3–4, Mansfeld 1986, 347, Brouwer 2014, 116.

approach of the founders of the school[73] without rejecting their fundamental Stoic doctrines. He rather discussed the ethical doctrines of the early Stoics on a 'lower' level or in a 'second-rate way'. As Cicero puts it, in his treatise he thus aims at 'those who are doing splendidly as if they have in them images of virtue' (1.46),[74] or deals with 'such appropriate actions [. . .] said by them [i.e. Stoics like Panaetius] to be honourable in a second-rate way. [. . .] They are shared with the whole human race'.[75] This makes Cicero's *On Appropriate Actions*, or Panaetius' *The Books on the Appropriate Action* for that matter, not so much a treatise about perfect, but non-existent human beings, but rather a handbook aimed at ordinary human beings, who want to be instructed into how to live life as well as possible, comparable to the ideal of the *vir bonus* in the non-Stoic, ordinary sense of the word.

In the first book of Cicero's *On Appropriate Actions*, the main topic is Panaetius' first question about how to decide whether an action is virtuous or not. The starting point for answering this question on the level of the *vir bonus* is the subject of the four virtues, which are based on the four virtues of justice, wisdom, courage and moderation, which Plato had put centre stage in the *Republic*. For Plato, wisdom is insight into the order of things, on the basis of which the ruler must govern the city. For Panaetius, wisdom should not remain purely 'theoretical' either and should also be put into practice. Courage is replaced by 'greatness of spirit', and moderation by 'seemliness' (*to prepon* in Greek, *decorum* in Cicero's Latin translation). As for Plato's justice, this is referred to 'the most wide reaching virtue'. Since it is not given a specific name, modern scholars refer to it as the 'social virtue'.[76] The social virtue is subdivided into 'justice' and 'beneficence', at 1.20 (fr. 105 van Straaten, fr. 69 Alesse, fr. B10 Vimercati):

> The most wide-reaching [virtue] is the reason by which the fellowship of men with one another, and the communal life, are held together. There are two parts of this: justice, the most illustrious of the virtues, on account of which men are called 'good'; and of the beneficence connected with it, which may be either kindness or liberality.[77] (tr. Atkins)

[73] See Cicero, *On Ends* 4.79 (fr. 55 van Straaten, fr. 79 Alesse, fr. A95 Vimercati).

[74] *vivitur non cum perfectis hominibus planeque sapientibus, sed cum iis, in quibus praeclare agitur, si sunt simulacra virtutis.*

[75] *haec igitur officia* [. . .] *quasi secunda quaedam honesta esse dicunt, non sapientium modo propria, sed cum omni hominum genere communia.*

[76] See Miriam Griffin's introduction in Atkins and Griffin 1991, xlviii, Dyck, 106.

[77] *de tribus autem reliquis latissime patet ea ratio, qua societas hominum inter ipsos et vitae quasi communitas continetur; cuius partes duae: iustitia, in qua virtutis splendor est maximus, ex qua viri*

From each of these virtues appropriate actions are derived, for which a reasonable justification can be given. In the section on wisdom (18–19) only two appropriate actions are given (and immediately thereafer illustrated): 'Do not take things for granted too easily' and 'Do not devote excessive attention to abstruse and difficult matters.' The sections on the appropriate actions to be derived from the other three virtues are more substantial, and occupy the remainder of the book, sections 20–151.

The next section deals with the appropriate actions to be derived from justice as part of the social virtue. This is how the section starts, still at 1.20 (fr. 105 van Straaten, fr. 69 Alesse, fr. B10 Vimercati):

> Of justice, the first task is that no man should harm another unless he has been provoked by injustice; the next that one should treat common goods as common and private ones as one's own [*sua*].[78] (tr. Atkins)

Among the two main tasks to be derived from justice, then, respect for property is brought up. The passage continues with an account of the origins of private property, which the modern editors of the passages on Panaetius no longer include in their editions (the actual examples of Cicero's home town or to the place where he had one of his villas are indeed surely not by Panaetius), where Cicero continues to discuss the origins of private property:

> Now no things are private by nature, but rather by long occupation (as when men moved into some empty property in the past), or by victory (when they acquired it in war), or by law, by treaty, by agreement, or by lot. The result is that the land of Arpinum is said to belong to the Arpinates, and that of Tusculum to the Tusculani. The distribution of private property is of a similar kind. Consequently, since what becomes each man's own comes from what had in nature been common, each man should hold on what has fallen to him; if anyone else should seek any of it for himself, he will be violating the law of human fellowship.[79] (tr. Atkins)

As is made clear in the first sentence of the passage, the origins of private property are not to be found in nature; private property is rather an

boni nominantur, et huic coniuncta beneficentia, quam eandem vel benignitatem vel liberalitatem appellari licet.

[78] *sed iustitiae primum munus est, ut ne cui quis noceat, nisi lacessitus iniuria, deinde ut communibus pro communibus utatur, privatis ut suis.*

[79] *sunt autem privata nulla natura, sed aut vetere occupatione, ut qui quondam in vacua venerunt, aut victoria, ut qui bello potiti sunt, aut lege, pactione, condicione, sorte; ex quo fit, ut ager Arpinas Arpinatium dicatur, Tusculanus Tusculanorum; similisque est privatarum possessionum discriptio. ex quo, quia suum cuiusque fit eorum, quae natura fuerant communia, quod cuique optigit, id quisque teneat; e quo si quis <quaevis> sibi appetet, violabit ius humanae societatis.*

institution that is the result of an historical development. As is repeated at the beginning of the final sentence, in the original state of nature things are common, in a negative sense, as Pufendorf would later characterise it.[80] The ways in which property can become one's own are given in-between the first and last sentence, together with examples of things that have become private, both in the spheres of groups of peoples as well as of individuals.[81]

The comparison with the theatre in *On Ends* 3.67, already discussed and quoted in n. 56, has also been understood as dealing with the origins of private property. The theatre is communal, the seats can become private: all things are communal, but can become private.[82] The main difference between *On Ends* 3.67 and *On Appropriate Actions* 1.21 surely lies in the importance attached to private property: whereas in *On Ends* the seat interpreted as private property is an indifferent that has to be accepted, in *On Appropriate Actions* respect for property has become one of the main tasks that go with justice.

The stance on private property as developed by Panaetius is thus rather different from the one held by the early Stoics: for Panaetius respect for property becomes one of the main appropriate actions that go with being just.[83] How can this remarkable difference best be explained?[84] As we have seen, for the primacy of respect for property Panaetius had no Greek predecessors that he could rely on. Here the Roman background presents itself. First, Panaetius offers a more practical, down-to-earth approach, moving away from the elusive ideal of the early Stoic sage towards a more attainable ideal, comparable to that of the Roman *vir bonus*. Second, he was also well acquainted with the Roman upper class, especially with Publius Cornelius Scipio Aemilianus Africanus and those connected with him. Third, he was interested in Roman topics, also legal ones (see *On Laws* 3.13–14, Panaetius fr. 48 and 61 van Straaten, fr. 103 Alesse, fr. A103 Vimercati, where Panaetius is mentioned together with Diogenes of Babylon as interested in the more practical topic of magistrates[85]). Fourth, he read Latin, such as Appius Claudius Caecus' collection of maxims,

[80] Garnsey 2007, 114–16 brings Pufendorf's notion of a negative community into play here, from his *On the Law of Nature and Nations* (1672), at 4.4.2: in a negative community the resources of the world were initially nobody's with private property rights coming in through first acquisition, as opposed to a positive community, where the resources belong to all.

[81] See Wacht 1982, 34–5. [82] See Garnsey 2007, 116–17. [83] See e.g. Vimercati 2004, 176.

[84] The question was put forcefully by Hadot 1970, 167: 'Comment il était possible [. . .] d'accorder une telle importance au maintien de la propriété privée?' Her answer was that such respect could only be justified in combination with the virtue of benificence.

[85] Marcus: *sed huius loci de magistratibus sunt propria quaedam, a Theophrasto primum, deinde a Diogene Stoico quaesita subtilius.* Atticus: *ain tandem? etiam a Stoicis ista tractata sunt?* Marcus: *non sane, nisi ab eo quem modo nominavi et postea a magno homine et in primis erudito, Panaetio.*

written around 300.[86] Fifth, the focus on private property is typically Roman, based on the *paterfamilias* as a core institution in Roman society, with the unrestricted power of the father over his household, including persons and things. Even though given the state of the extant evidence we cannot be sure, given these factors, Panaetius' focus on private property is best explained as accommodating in his more down-to-earth ethics a specific Roman value.

If this conclusion is indeed correct, then perhaps even the standard manners along which property can be acquired in Roman law, occupation, victory, law, treaty, agreement or lot, mentioned at 1.21, should already be attributed to Panaetius rather than to Cicero himself.[87]

Moreover, among the Roman Stoics, Panaetius was not alone in his interest in and justification of private property. Already his predecessors Diogenes of Babylon and Antipater of Tarsus, and also his pupil Hecato of Rhodes had dealt with the topic. Diogenes and Antipater discussed cases about the transfer of property, and in particular debated the question: which information ought the seller supply to the buyer? Should the seller think about his own interests, or should he also take the interests of the buyer into account? As we have seen in Chapter 6 on casuistry, Diogenes maintained that the seller ought to take his own interests into account, whereas Antipater maintained that the seller ought also to think of the interests of the buyer.[88] Hecato apparently sided with Diogenes. For Hecato this has to be inferred from a slightly different case, discussed by Cicero, *On Appropriate Actions* 3.62, about whether the buyer ought to pay a higher price if the price asked by the seller was too low. According to Cicero, *On Appropriate Actions* 3.63 (fr. 10 Gomoll), Hecato, in his books on appropriate action addressed to Quintus Aelius Tubero, argued that the capacities and resources of individuals are the riches of the city and hence that a wise man ought to think of his own interests (the Latin used here is *res familiaris*), and in doing so would contribute to his children, his friends and his political community.[89] Just as with Diogenes of Babylon (see Chapter 6, section 6.4), the invisible hand springs yet again to mind.

Further Stoic interest in property is attested for Panaetius' contemporary Gaius Blossius of Cumae, the house friend of the Mucii and a student of

[86] Cicero, *Tusculan Disputations* 4.4 (fr. 47 van Straaten, fr. 88 Alesse, fr. A115 Vimercati).

[87] See Brunt 2013, 229. For Cicero as the source see Lefèvre 2001, 123.

[88] See Cicero, *On Appropriate Actions* 3.51–5, 3.91.

[89] *Hecatonem quidem Rhodium, discipulum Panaetii, video in iis libris, quos de officio scripsit Q. Tuberoni, dicere, sapientis esse nihil contra mores, leges, instituta facientem habere rationem rei familiaris.*

Antipater, and also the driving force behind Tiberius Gracchus' proposals for land reform.[90]

In the modern literature, scholars have sometimes reckoned Publius Cornelius Scipio Aemilianus Africanus as among those who opposed these reforms, with Panaetius as his adviser.[91] However, there are several problems with this opposition between the progressive Gracchus and Blossius on the one hand and the conservative Scipio and Panaetius on the other hand. First, in the sources Africanus is not mentioned as the leader of the conservatives, who according to Plutarch, *Lives of the Gracchi* 19, rather gathered around Publius Cornelius Scipio Nasica Serapion (consul in 138 BCE).[92] Second, Scipio is usually presented as a somewhat more moderate force, as for example in the first book of Cicero, *On the res publica*.[93] Third, there is neither explicit evidence of Panaetius advising Scipio in this respect, nor of Panaetius as taking a conservative stance. It is more likely that Panaetius entertained a more moderate opinion about the land reforms, which can perhaps be inferred from Cicero's *On Appropriate Actions* 2.79–82. There, the Spartan leaders Lysander and Agis as well as the Gracchi are made responsible for the unrest that followed upon their disrespect for existing private property arrangements. They are compared with Aratus of Sicyon (271–213 BCE), who gained control over Sicyon in 251 after it had been ruled by the tyrant Niocles for fifty years. Aratus is confronted not only with the claims of the earlier owners, who as exiles had their property confiscated by Niocles, but also with the interests of the present owners. Aratus is praised for finding a way out of this problem by securing a loan that enables him to compensate the first owners in order to maintain social harmony. Aratus thus avoided doing harm to anyone and showed respect for existing property arrangements. Panaetius may well have been Cicero's source here,[94] for at least two reasons. First, Aratus acted in accordance with the two main tasks that followed from justice set out in 1.20. Second, the two examples are part of the Stoic tradition: Sphaerus of Borysthenes (*c.*285–*c.*210 BCE), a pupil of Cleanthes, Zeno's successor as head of the school, was involved with the Spartans,[95] whereas

[90] See above Chapter 6, section 6.5. [91] Hadot 1970, 113. [92] Alesse 1997, 171.

[93] Becker 1964, 128. Cf. Barlow 2018, who argues for Scipio as possessing the four cardinal virtues in the Panaetian understanding.

[94] Pohlenz 1934a, 118 (unfortunately in national-socialist newspeak: 'Dieser Mann [sc. Aratus] [. . .] erschien Panaitios [. . .] als idealer Führer'), Erskine 1990, 160–1; cf. Alesse 1997, 169–70. Barlow 2012, 235–6, deals with the Aratus example, too, but as evidence for Cicero on private property only.

[95] For Sphaerus and Cleomenes see Plutarch, *Lives of Agis and Cleomenes* (the Greek counterpart of the Roman *Lives of the Gracchi*), at 23.2–6 (*SVF* 1.622), 33.4 (*SVF* 1.623). Sphaerus' interest in matters

Persaeus of Citium, Zeno's favourite pupil, helped Aratus in gaining control over Sicyon.[96] According to Cicero or Panaetius, then, land reforms are possible as long as sufficient compensation is offered. If Panaetius indeed held this moderate position, the passage thus provides further evidence for Panaetius' interest in private property, also in the context of Roman politics.[97]

7.5 Conclusion and outlook

In Cicero's *On Appropriate Actions* we find Greek philosophers interacting with the Romans. Unlike the earlier Greek philosophers, these Roman Stoics, such as Panaetius and Hecato, considered private property to be of overriding importance in relation to the good life, in line with the importance attached to private property by the Romans or their jurists. The Roman Stoics argued that respecting private property arrangements is one of the key features of justice. In a paper that deals with Cicero on private property, Tiziana Chiusi posed the question whether Cicero would have been influenced by Greek thinkers on this topic. Her answer was that Cicero would not have been, in the sense that Cicero would not have given up the typically Roman interest in private property.[98] She is surely right in the sense that Cicero did not abandon this interest. However, as for the influence of the Greek philosophers, Cicero could already rely on the Roman Stoics, who had integrated the Roman focus on private property into their thinking about justice and the good life.

As for its influence: in sixteenth- and seventeenth-century philosophy, the Roman Stoics' perspective on the re-evaluation of private property as transmitted by Cicero in his *On Appropriate Actions* became mainstream. Two examples should suffice here: Grotius and Locke. Grotius (1583–1645) picked it up in terms of laws of nature, Locke (1632–1704) in terms of inalienable rights. Grotius' account can be found in chapter 5, section 32, of his *The Free Sea* (*Mare liberum*), which is in fact part of a larger work that remained unpublished during Grotius' lifetime,

Spartan can further be derived from the titles of two treatises, *On the Spartan Constitution* and *On Lycurgus and Socrates*, which survived in the catalogue in Diogenes Laertius, at 7.178 (*SVF* 1.620).

96 For Persaeus and Aratus see Pausanias 2.8.4, 7.8.3 (*SVF* 1.442), Plutarch, *Life of Aratus* 18.1, 23.5 (*SVF* 1.443).

97 Perhaps even Critolaus' clarification of the Aristotelian position on private property as an external good as part of happiness (see above, section 7.2) can be understood as an attempt to gain support among the Roman elite.

98 Chiusi 2005, 71: 'Nach unserer Betrachtung läßt sich dies nicht bejahen, mindestens nicht in dem Sinne, daß er dafür römisches Gedankengut aufgegeben hätte.'

that is *On the Right of Booty* (*De iure praedae*), where the account can be found in chapter 2, section 2.[99] Just as in Cicero's *On Appropriate Actions*, Grotius' starting point is also that there is no private property by nature. Grotius then formulates four 'laws of natural law' (*leges iuris naturalis*). The first law is that all human beings strive for self-preservation and that they are entitled to do so. This brings with it the second law, that they are entitled to the external goods useful to that end. Here Grotius' justification of 'private property' comes in. These first two laws are supplemented with the two appropriate actions that go back to Cicero's account in *On Appropriate Actions* 1.20–1. Cicero's first main appropriate action becomes Grotius' third law: no one should inflict injury upon someone else. Cicero's second appropriate action becomes Grotius' fourth law: 'No one should seize possession of that which has been taken into possession of another.'[100] Once property arrangements have come into existence, they ought to be respected. In the dedication of the *Mare liberum*, Grotius offers a succinct account of the justification of private property, again clearly reminiscent of Cicero's *On Appropriate Actions*:

> Now, as there are some things, which every man enjoys in common with all other men, and as there are other things, which are distinctly his and belong to no one else, just so has nature willed that some of the things which she has created for the use of mankind remain common to all, and that others through the industry and labour of each man become his own. Laws moreover were given to cover both cases so that all men might use common property without prejudice to anyone else, and in respect to other things so that each man being content with what he himself owns might refrain from laying his hands on the property of others.[101] (tr. Magoffin)

Locke's account is surely more familiar.[102] In his influential *Second Treatise on Government*, in the fifth chapter on property, Locke's starting point is that land is held in common (section 26), but that use can make its one's own (section 31): '*As much land* as a man tills, plants, improves, cultivates, and can use the product of, so much is his *property*.' This property should be respected as such by others. Here, for Locke, the origins of the political

[99] For a more elaborate discussion see Straumann 2015, 170–206.

[100] *ne quis occupet altera occupata.*

[101] *sicut autem in ipso homine alia sunt quae habet cum omnibus communia, alia quibus ab altero quisque distinguitur, ita earum rerum quas in usum hominis produxisset natura alias eam manere communes, alias cuiusque industria ac labore proprias fieri voluisse, de utrisque autem datas leges, ut communibus quidem sine detrimento omnium omnes uterentur, de ceteris autem quod cuique contigisset eo contentus abstineret alieno.*

[102] Cf. Pierson 2013, 21, who characterises Locke '(alongside Marx) as the most widely discussed writer on the provenance of property in the English speaking world.'

community can be found, for which he simply could follow Cicero's *On Appropriate Actions* 2.73: 'Political communities and citizenships were constituted especially so that human beings could hold on to what was theirs.'[103]

[103] *hanc enim ob causam maxime, ut sua tenerentur, res publicae civitatesque constitutae sunt.* For a discussion of the Ciceronian background to Locke's account see Long 1997, for a critical discussion of Locke's account as such (without reference to Cicero, let alone Panaetius) see Pierson 2013, 208–45.

CHAPTER 8

Law and philosophy after 50 BCE

8.1 Further interaction

In the late Roman Republic, in the relatively short period between 150 and 50 BCE, the interaction between law and philosophy proved to be especially productive. The Roman jurists were influenced by the Hellenistic philosophers in that they started to study law as a science, as a system of rules, to be divided in the categories of notably persons and property. Philosophers were influenced jurists in the sense that they got interested in casuistry and in discussing the importance of property for the good life.

In the Imperial period, after Augustus had become sole ruler over Rome and its empire, restoring the *libertas* of its people and the *res publica* in name only, the interaction between jurists and philosophers lost its intensity. The disciplines of law and philosophy developed largely autonomously again, with only a few exceptions.

With regard to law: the jurists, now from 'ordinary' backgrounds, continued to give advice on how to solve the legal disputes among citizens, but now often on the basis a formally granted (and hence imperially controlled) *ius respondendi*.[1] With the help of the methods and abstract notions introduced in the late Republic, these jurists developed their legal doctrines further: as Schiavone put it, starting out from the categorical framework developed in the Republic they laid bare a 'metaphysics of social relations'.[2]

With regard to philosophy, the main schools had now all become dogmatic: under the guidance of Antiochus of Ascalon, Plato's Academy had completely discarded its sceptical outlook. In this Imperial, authoritarian era a similar more inward-looking tendency can be discerned towards the interpretation of the texts and the systematisation of the

[1] For the *ius respondendi* under Imperial control see Magdelain 2015 [1950], 105–16.
[2] Schiavone 2012, 202/2017, 196.

doctrines from the founders of the schools, which were now considered to be 'authorities', especially within the Academy and the Lyceum. Platonists came to consider Plato as someone who had revealed the truth: they considered it their task to set out his doctrines in teaching manuals and make clear what he had actually said, often using the hitherto unknown form of a commentary.[3] In the 1st century CE the Academic Eudorus of Alexandria presumably did both: he wrote a *Division of Philosophical Discourse* as well as commented on Plato's *Timaeus*.[4] Aristotelians started to study the newly published corpus of Aristotle's lecture notes, with Aspasius' *Commentary on the Nicomachean Ethics* as a first extant example of the many commentaries that were to follow.[5]

The interaction between law and philosophy became piecemeal. Whereas in the late Republic some jurists had expressed their allegiance to one of the philosophical schools (as we have seen, most of them to the Stoics, others to Philo's Academy), in the Imperial period jurists just pick and choose. Among legal historians, this is sometimes referred to as eclecticism.[6]

The scattered examples of the influence of philosophy on law are perhaps best presented from the point of view of its different parts: logic, physics and ethics. In logic, jurists may have become acquainted with Aristotle's predicate logic and his conception of science,[7] whereas Proculus and Salvius Julianus applied the propositional logic that the Stoics had developed in their legal arguments.[8]

In ethics, Aristotle's conception of justice appears to have been taken over. In the law of obligations, the third part of private law, next to the law of persons and property, Gaius' division between voluntary contract and involuntary delict in his *Teaching Manual* 3.88, on which the remainder of

[3] Bonazzi 2015, 81.

[4] For the evidence on his teaching manual, see the summary by Arius Didymus, presumably Augustus' 'court philosopher', in Stobaeus 2.42.7–5.6 (Eudorus of Alexandria fr. 1 Mazzarelli, Platonists fr. 18A Boys-Stones), for his commentary on Plato's *Timaeus* see Plutarch, *On the Generation of the Soul in the Timaeus* 1012d–3d (Eudorus of Alexandria fr. 6 Mazzarelli, Platonists fr. 8Q Boys-Stones).

[5] According to Barnes 1999, 3–4, it was probably written shortly after 131 CE: at 106.5–6 Aspasius refers to the temple of Olympian Zeus, by then just, but finally completed at the orders of Emperor Hadrian.

[6] Giltay 2016, 193. Among the ancient thinkers themselves, only Potamo of Alexandria considered himself to be an eclectic, see Hatzimichali 2011; for the question of 'eclecticism' in ancient philosophy see Dillon and Long 1988.

[7] It is here only that the influential accounts by Villey 1951, repeated in his 2003 [1975], 105–6, or Wieacker 1988, 622–7, on the usefulness of Aristotle's logic for law, would fit in.

[8] Proculus (presumably 1st century CE, see Kunkel 2001 no. 11), *Letters*, book 2 in *Digest* 50.16.124, Salvius Julianus, *Ambiguities* in a single book in *Digest* 24.5.13. Cf. Miquel 1970, Armgardt 2008.

the third book is built,[9] may have been inspired by Aristotle's succinct analysis of corrective justice in *Nicomachean Ethics* 1131a1–9. According to Aristotle, corrective justice plays a rectifying part in the transactions between human beings, 'of which there are two parts: voluntary transactions, such as sale, purchase, loan etc., and involuntary transactions, such as theft, adultery etc.'.[10] Similarly, according to Gaius, who avoids the use of the term 'justice' (let alone corrective justice),[11] obligations can either arise out of a contract or out of a delict: in the former the obligations arise voluntarily, in the latter the obligation arises involuntarily.[12]

Again in ethics (or ethics combined with physics, as a Stoic might argue), the discussions on the nature of law drew the interest of at least some jurists. As already discussed in relation to the notion of 'rule' in Chapter 4, section 4.3, the early Stoics, from Zeno of Citium onwards, used 'law' (*nomos*) as one of the many names that they gave to the active principle within nature that shapes the world, each name bringing out a different aspect of this principle.[13] As we have seen, in Chrysippus' definition of law as 'king of all human and divine matters', law brings out the aspect that the active principle is the standard of just and unjust, ordering rational animals on what they should do. According to the early Stoics, neither are rational beings usually able to perfect their reason in such a manner that they are always able to live according to this standard (with Socrates towards the end of his life as a rare exception), nor are actual statutes and constitutions always in accordance with this standard. As already discussed in Chapter 4, section 4.4, with the Roman Stoics, like Panaetius, a shift in focus occurs: without discarding the early Stoics' stance altogether, they are prepared to lower the standard from perfect reason to reasonable justification. According to these Roman Stoics, precepts for which a reasonable justification can be given are good enough.

In his *On Laws*, Cicero showed clear interested in the 'Roman' Stoic understanding of the 'law of nature' as a set of precepts with a reasonable

[9] Contract is discussed in 3.89–181, delict in 3.182–225.

[10] τούτου δὲ μέρη δύο· τῶν γὰρ συναλλαγμάτων τὰ μὲν ἑκούσιά ἐστι τὰ δ' ἀκούσια, ἑκούσια μὲν τὰ τοιάδε οἷον πρᾶσις ὠνὴ [. . .], τῶν δ' ἀκουσίων [. . .] οἷον κλοπὴ μοιχεία [. . .]. Cf. Winkel 1985, 68–76, Winkel 2000–2001.

[11] See Finkenauer 2014, 11 about the rare use of terms like 'justice' or 'just' among the Roman jurists: 'Es war die Sache der römischen Juristen nicht, eine allgemeine Theorie der Gerechtigkeit aufzustellen.' Since Finkenauer restricts his overview to the explicit use of these terms, he does not discuss the Gaius passage.

[12] *nunc transeamus ad obligationes, quarum summa divisio in duas species diducitur: omnis enim obligatio vel ex contractu nascitur vel ex delicto.*

[13] Diogenes Laertius 7.135 (*SVF* 1.102, 2.580).

justification, connecting it with actual Roman statutes. In book 1, at 18, Cicero brings up the Stoic definition of law as 'highest reason, rooted in nature, which commands things that must be done and prohibits the opposite'.[14] In books 2 and 3 he connects it with Roman statutes in the field of religion and magistrates respectively.[15] In Imperial times, the jurists themselves, notably Gaius and Ulpian, became interested in the theoretical foundations of law.[16] In the introductory lines of his *Teaching Manual*, at 1.1, Gaius made a distinction between the law specific for a particular community and the law common to all peoples, of which, Gaius maintained, the latter is based on natural reason. Roman law would thus be based partly on what the Romans had decided themselves and partly on natural reason.[17] The practical implications of this distinction in law were limited, if only because generally speaking the jurists, different from Cicero, did not assign the highest authority to natural law: if natural law and positive law were in conflict, they made positive law prevail.[18] By the beginning of the 3rd century CE, with Ulpian, this may well have changed, in the sense that natural law did have practical implications. According to Ulpian, in his *Teaching Manual* in *Digest* 1.1.1.3, 'natural law is the law that nature has taught all animals',[19] a formulation that reappears in Justinian's *Teaching Manual*, at 1.2. Ulpian, as Emperor Caracalla's chief legal advisor, may have used it in order to justify or even bring about the *Constitutio Antoniana*, in which Caracalla granted citizenship to (almost) all inhabitants of the Empire.[20]

In the other direction, that of law to philosophy, the Roman notion of freedom appears to have been taken over. The conception of freedom of 'doing what one pleases', in the expression of Florentinus, an otherwise unknown author of a voluminous teaching manual in 12 books living in the 2nd century CE, was one of the cornerstones of Roman social life and provided the basis for modern conceptions of freedom. The definition, which was taken over by Justinian, *Teaching Manual* 1.3.1, can be found

[14] *lex est ratio summa, insita in natura, quae iubet ea quae facienda sunt, prohibetque contraria.*

[15] See esp. Atkins 2013, 155–85, Schiavone 2012/2017, 285–306 at 297/275–96 at 287.

[16] This influence is even acknowledged by Watson 1995b, 164, who otherwise defends law as an autonomous discipline (see above chapter 1, n. 21).

[17] *quod vero naturalis ratio inter omnes homines constituit, id apud omnes populos peraeque custoditur vocaturque ius gentium, quasi quo iure omnes gentes utuntur. populus itaque Romanus partim suo proprio, partim communi omnium hominum iure utitur.*

[18] See Johnston 2000, 621, Atkins 2013, 225.

[19] *ius naturale est, quod natura omnia animalia docuit.*

[20] On Ulpian see Honoré 2002. For the *Constitutio* and its philosophical background see Brouwer 2015, 75–6.

in book 9 of Florentinus' *Teaching Manual* in *Digest* 1.5.4 pr. (fr. 25 Lenel): 'Freedom is one's natural ability of doing what one pleases, as long as the law or some other force does not prevent him'[21] (tr. De Ste. Croix). The standard example for this unrestricted power is the *patria potestas*, which we already encountered in Chapter 7, section 3. This power is the 'unrestricted rule of the father within his own home', including the *ius vitae necisque*, the right of the father over life and death of the family members.[22] According to Gaius, *Teaching Manual* 1.55, this institution is unique in the world: 'We have in our power our children, the offspring of a Roman law marriage. This right is one which only citizens have (there are virtually no peoples who have such powers over their sons as we have over ours).'[23] This understanding of freedom may have attracted the attention of philosophers, perhaps already that of Epictetus in the early Imperial age,[24] and given rise to the modern conception of freedom as 'doing what one pleases'.[25]

8.2 Rethinking the present

In this final section, I return to the impact of the late Republican interaction between jurists and philosophers by giving a brief overview of its influence on law and philosophy as well by offering some suggestions as to how this account offers the opportunity to reconsider the results of the interaction.

We have seen that the interaction had profound effects on the Western tradition. In law, in the late 2nd and early 1st century BCE, the jurists became acquainted with the Stoic definitions of science and applied the Stoic methods of dialectic to their legal output. In doing so, they produced systematic accounts of the cases judged within the *ius civile*. This change in the study of law in Roman times was brought to another dimension in the Byzantine era, when Emperor Justinian declared his 'own' systematic account of law, in fact an adaptation by his civil servants of Gaius' second century *Teaching Manual*, to be law itself. This systematic account would become the model for the legal codes on the European continent, including the French and German civil codes (see Chapter 3). As for rules, the

[21] *libertas est naturalis facultas eius quod cuique facere libet, nisi si quid vi aut iure prohibetur.*
[22] For a list of the implied rights see Sachers 1954.
[23] *in potestate nostra sunt liberi nostri, quos iustis nuptiis procreavimus. quod ius proprium civium Romanorum est (fere enim nulli alii sunt homines, qui talem in filios suos habent potestatem, qualem nos habemus).*
[24] Frede 2011. [25] Atkins 2018, 37–52, cf. Brouwer 2020a, 43–4.

Roman jurists may at first have restricted their use in the study of law as a mnemotechnic device, as a reminder of the *ratio* in the underlying case. In the modern codes the rules have come to be understood as the descriptions of the relations between and within the categories of the system, with no reference whatsoever to the facts in which the rules had their origins (see Chapter 4). Already in later Roman law the notion of person came to be applied to all human beings, while allowing for subdivisions, and was thus considered to be an ideal starting point for a taxonomy in law. It became one of the three general categories of the law that deals with the disputes of citizens among each other. Via the systematisations of Gaius and Justinian, this notion also has become a cardinal notion in contemporary substantive law, giving its name to one of three main fields within private law,[26] next to the law of property rights and the law of obligations, and as laid down in national codes (see Chapter 5).

In philosophy, Roman legal casuistry would attract the attention of the Roman Stoics. Owing to the success of Cicero's *On Appropriate Actions* in modern times, this casuistry may even have served as the cradle for the moral theories that no longer focus on the good life and the virtuous dispositions out of which the good life can be lived, but on actions: these theories thus enable the moral agent to evaluate whether an act is good or bad, or right or wrong. Like Cicero or Panaetius, in his *Groundwork* Kant developed a moral theory according to which acts have to be assessed from their starting point; different from Cicero and Panaetius, the starting point for Kant is no longer human reason within nature, but human reason as an independent faculty, with the help of which the moral agent can answer the question: 'Can I want my prospective course of action to be universalised?' With a similar focus on actions as such, but otherwise clearly different from Cicero and Panaetius, in his *Introduction to the Principles of Morals and Legislation* (1780) Jeremy Bentham developed a theory according to which acts have to be assessed in terms of their expected results only; that is, benefit or utility.

With regard to private property, the Roman Stoics' interest in the subject taken over from the Roman jurists gained momentum in the sixteenth and seventeenth centuries, when the centrality of private

[26] Civil law is once again ambiguous: next to, first, the law dealing with disputes of citizens among themselves, it can be used with regard to; second, law that is developed on the basis of the interpretation of statute (*ius civile* in the strict sense); third, law developed on the basis of the power of the praetor (*ius civile* in the broad sense); fourth, to Roman law in general; and fifth, to the law that has been developed on the basis of Roman law in the later, continental European civil law tradition (as opposed to the English law-based common law tradition).

property in relation to justice was taken over by thinkers like Grotius and Locke. Grotius does so in terms of laws of nature, Locke in terms of natural rights. Discussions about justice would henceforward be dominated by private property, as they still are today (see Chapter 7).

Second, the interaction allows for a rethinking of the roads taken, of promoting awareness of alternative approaches, both in law as well as in philosophy.[27] In law, with regard to resolving disputes, in the European continental civil law tradition, and in the jurisdictions that are based on that tradition, legal disputes have come to be solved by applying the relevant, abstract rules from the systematic code to the case. The Aristotelian practical syllogism is the model here, with the relevant article from the code serving as the major proposition, the facts as the minor, from which a conclusion ought to follow. The *jurisprudence* from the French Supreme Court offers the best instances thereof. It still formulates its judgment in the form of one single sentence, with (usually only a reference to) the article from the code as the major, with a summary of the facts as the minor, to be followed by a conclusion.[28] Given the often abstract nature of the rules, the general formulations in the major may sometimes need to be explained by the judges. Here, liberal methods of interpretation have been developed in order to explain the abstract notions. Continental lawyers have thus come to understand codifications as the culmination of a development, only to be followed by a further continental European unification of these different codes.

Here the question can be posed as to whether the ever further developing systematisation of law itself has served the overall aim of the resolution of disputes. Are disputes best solved by relying on a system of abstract rules that are no longer understood in connection with the dispute from which they were derived? Does the gain of simplicity here outweigh the application of the abstracted rule which, especially with the liberal methods of interpretation, may bring about unanticipated results? As in Roman law, finding the best solution embedded in the case itself, as one to be followed in later similar cases, might offer a viable alternative. Already the awareness thereof may be helpful in cooperating with jurisdictions comparable to that of the Romans, especially those within the case law-based common

[27] Here a parallel with a recent discussion of norms may be helpful: Möllers 2015, 13–14 understands norms as 'positiv markierte Möglichkeiten [. . .], die sich verwirklichen sollen'. Of course, the results of the interaction discussed here are no longer possibilities. Here, from hindsight, the question is put: should these results, now 'positiv markiert', be taken for granted?

[28] A judgment looks in principle like this: 'Vu l'article . . . (*major*), en attendu que . . . (*minor*), casse . . . (*conclusion*).'

law tradition. In this tradition, developed in England since Norman times, disputes are resolved by the courts by finding the solutions in the cases, such that they are in accordance with the best solutions in earlier decisions. Within European institutions, like the European Union or the European Court of Human Rights, both products of the continental legal tradition, the English legal tradition fits in uneasily.[29]

In philosophy, the interaction resulted in a focus on actions rather than virtues. It has thus contributed to the development of moral theories that enable the evaluation of the goodness of actions, while moving away from the ancient focus on the good life. Rethinking this movement away from the good life has already led to a renewed interest in virtues, in the form of either virtue ethics or the capability approach,[30] which their advocates usually associate with Aristotle. As should be clear by now, Aristotle's ethics is part of a much broader ancient tradition of thinking about the good life. In this tradition the relevance of private property for the good life was at best considered limited. Under the influence of the Roman jurists, as picked up by the Roman Stoics, it has become of overriding importance. Here again the interaction between the Roman jurists on the hand and the Hellenistic philosophers on the other hand offers ample opportunity to rethink the present and to shape the future.

[29] See further Brouwer 2018.

[30] Anscombe 1958 is usually regarded as the beginning of Neo-Aristotelian virtue ethics, Sen 1984 and Nussbaum 1988 of the capability approach.

Bibliography

Abbreviated references

CAG: *Commentaria in Aristotelem Graeca* (1882–1909) Berlin.
FRHist.: Cornell, T.J. (ed.) (2013) *The Fragments of the Roman Historians*. Oxford.
FDS: Hülser, K. (1987–1988) *Fragmente der Dialektik der Stoiker*. Stuttgart.
FIRA: Riccobono, S. and others (1968–1972 [1940–1941]) *Fontes iuris Romani Antejustiniani*. Florence.
FSS: Ferrary, J.-L., A. Schiavone and A. Stolfi (2018) *Quintus Mucius Scaevola. Opera*. Rome.
Garbarino: Garbarino, G. (1973) *Roma e la filosofia greca dalle origini alla fine del II secolo A.C.* Turin.
Giannantoni: Giannantoni, G. (1990) *Socratis et Socraticorum reliquiae*. Naples.
Lenel: Lenel, O. (1889) *Palingenesia iuris civilis*. Leipzig.
LS: Long, A.A. and D.N. Sedley (1987) *The Hellenistic Philosophers*. Cambridge.
LSJ: Liddell, H.G., R. Scott and H.S. Jones (1996) *A Greek-English Lexicon. With a Revised Supplement*. Oxford.
RE: Wissowa, G., W. Kroll and K. Mittelhaus (eds) (1893–1980) *Paulys Realencyclopädie der classischen Altertumswissenschaft*. Stuttgart.
SVF: Arnim, H. von (1903–1905) *Stoicorum veterum fragmenta* 1–3. Leipzig.

Primary literature

Aelian, *Historical Miscellany*: Wilson, N.G. (ed., tr.) (1997) *Aelian. Historical Miscellany*. Cambridge (Mass.)
Aelius, *Fragments*: Bottiglieri, A. (2019) 'Sextus Aelius', in Bottiglieri, A., A Manzo, F. Nasti and G. Viarengo *Antiquissima iuris sapientia*. Rome: 297–321.
Anaximenes of Lampsacos [?], *Rhetoric to Alexander*: Fuhrmann, M. (ed.) (2000) *Anaximenes. Ars rhetorica quae vulgo fertur Aristotelis ad Alexandrum*, 2nd ed. Munich.
Appian, *Civil Wars*: Mendelssohn, L. and P. Viereck (eds) (1905) *Appiani Historia Romana* 2, 2nd ed.. Leipzig.
Arcesilaus, *Fragments*: Mette, H.J. (1984) 'Zwei Akademiker heute: Krantor von Soloi und Arkesilaus von Pitane', *Lustrum* 26: 7–94, and Vezzoli, S. (2016) *Arcesilao di Pitane*. Turnhout.

Aristophanes of Byzantium: Nauck, A. (1848) *Aristophanis Byzantii grammatici Alexandrini fragmenta.* Halle, and Slater, W.J. (1986) *Aristophanis Byzantii fragmenta*, Berlin.

Aristotle, *On the Heaven*: Moraux, P. (ed.) (1965) *Aristote. Du ciel.* Paris.

Metaphysics: Ross, W.D. (ed.) (1924) *Aristotle's Metaphysics.* Oxford.

Nicomachean Ethics: Susemihl, F. and O. Apelt (eds) (1912) *Aristotelis Ethica Nicomachea*, 3rd ed. Leipzig.

Physics: Ross, W.D. (ed.) (1936) *Aristotle's Physics.* Oxford.

Politics: Dreizehnter, A. (ed.) (1970) *Aristoteles' Politik.* Munich.

Rhetoric: Kassel, R. (ed.) (1976) *Aristotelis Ars rhetorica.* Berlin.

On the Soul: Siwek, P. (ed.) (1965) *Aristotelis De anima Graece et Latine.*

Topics: Brunschwig, J. (ed., tr.) (1967–2007) *Aristote. Topiques.* Paris.

Fragments: Gigon, O. (1987) *Aristotelis opera volumen tertium: librorum deperditorum fragmenta.* Berlin.

[Aristotle], *Constitution of Athens*: Chambers, M. (ed.) (1994) *Aristoteles. ΑΘΗΝΑΙΩΝ ΠΟΛΙΤΕΙΑ*, 2nd ed. Stuttgart.

Aspasius, *Commentary on Aristotle's Nicomachean Ethics*: Heylbut, G. (ed.) (1889) *Aspasii in Ethica Nicomacheia quae supersunt commentaria.* CAG 19.1. Berlin.

Athenaeus: Olson, S.D. (ed., tr.) (2006–2012) *Athenaeus. The Learned Banqueters.* Cambridge (Mass.), and, for books 8–15, Olson, S.D. (ed.) (2019–2020) *Athenaeus Naucratites Deipnosophistae.* Berlin.

Augustine, *On Christian Doctrine*: Martin, J. (ed.) (1982) *Sancti Aurelii Augustini De doctrina christiana, De vera religione.* Turnhout.

On the City of God: Dombart, B. and A. Kalb (eds.) (1955) *Sancti Aurelii Augustini De civitate dei.* Turnhout.

[Augustine], *On Rhetoric*: Halm, C. (ed.) (1863) *Rhetores Latini minores.* Leipzig: 135–51.

Carneades, *Fragments*: Mette, H.J. (1985) 'Weitere Akademiker heute (Fortsetzung von Lustr. 26, 7-94): Von Lakydes bis zu Kleitomachos', *Lustrum* 27: 39–148.

Cato the Elder, *Fragments*: see Jordan, H. (ed.) (1840) *Catonis quae exstant.* Leipzig, and Malcovati, H. (1976) *Oratorum Romanorum fragmenta liberae rei publicae*, 4th ed., Turin: 12–97.

Charisius, *Science of Grammar*: Barwick, K. and F. Kühnert (eds) (1964 [1925]), *Charisius. Ars grammatica*, 2nd ed. Leipzig.

Cicero, *On Appropriate Actions*: Winterbottom, M. (ed.) (1994) *M. Tulli Ciceronis De officiis.* Oxford.

Brutus: Jahn, O., Kroll, W. and B. Kytzler (eds.), *Cicero. Brutus*, 6th ed., Berlin 1962, and Douglas, A.E. (ed.) (1966) *M. Tulli Ciceronis Brutus.* Oxford.

In Defence of Cluentius: in Clark, A.C. (ed.) (1905), *M. Tulli Ciceronis orationes* 1. Oxford.

On Divination: Pease, A.S. (ed.) (1955 [1920–1923]), *M. Tulli Ciceronis De divinatione*, 2nd ed. Darmstadt.

On Ends: Schiche, T. (ed.) (1915) *M. Tulli Ciceronis De finibus bonorum et malorum.* Leipzig.

On Friendship: in Powell, J.G.F. (ed.) (2006) *M. Tulli Ciceronis De re publica, De legibus, Cato maior de senectute, Laelius de amicitia*. Oxford: 317–65.
On Invention: Bornecque, H. (ed., tr.) (1932) *Cicéron. De l'invention*. Paris.
On Laws: in Powell, J.G.F. (ed.) (2006) *M. Tulli Ciceronis De re publica, De legibus, Cato maior de senectute, Laelius de amicitia*. Oxford: 155–266.
Letters to Atticus: Shackleton Bailey, D.R. (ed., tr.) (1999) *Cicero. Letters to Atticus*. Cambridge (Mass.).
Letters to Friends: Shackleton Bailey, D.R. (ed., tr.) (2001) *Cicero. Letters to Friends*. Cambridge (Mass.).
Lucullus: Schäublin, C. (ed., tr.) (1995) *Cicero. Akademische Abhandlungen. Lucullus*. Hamburg.
In Defence of Murena: in Clark, A.C. (ed.) (1905) *M. Tulli Ciceronis orationes* 1. Oxford.
On Old Age: in Powell, J.G.F. (ed.) (2006) *M. Tulli Ciceronis De re publica, De legibus, Cato maior de senectute, Laelius de amicitia*. Oxford: 267–315.
On the Nature of the Gods: Pease, A.S. (ed.) (1955–1958) *M. Tulli Ciceronis De natura deorum*. Cambridge (Mass.).
Orator: Westman, R. (ed.) (1980) *Cicero. Orator*. Leipzig.
On the Orator: Wilkins, A.S. (ed.) (1902) *M. Tullius Cicero. De Oratore*. Oxford.
On the Paradoxes of the Stoics: Molager, J. (ed., tr.) (1971) *Cicéron. Les paradoxes des Stoïciens*. Paris.
On the res publica: in Powell, J.G.F. (ed.) (2006) *M. Tulli Ciceronis De re publica, De legibus, Cato maior de senectute, Laelius de amicitia*. Oxford: 1–154.
Topics: Reinhardt, T. (ed.) (2003) *Cicero's Topica*. Oxford.
Tusculan Disputations 1–2: Pohlenz, M. (ed.) (1918) *M. Tulli Ciceronis scripta quae manserunt omnia* 44: *Tusculanae disputationes*. Leipzig.
Varro: in Plasberg, O. (ed.) (1922) *Cicero: Academicorum reliquiae cum Lucullo*. Leipzig: 1–25.
Fragments on philosophy: Garbarino, I. (1984) *M. Tulli Ciceronis fragmenta ex libris philosophicis, ex aliis libris deperditis, ex scriptis incertis*. Turin.

Clement of Alexandria, *Miscellanies* 1–6: Stählin, O. and L. Früchtel (eds) (1960) *Clemens Alexandrinus* 2: *Stromata Buch* 1–6, 3rd ed. Berlin.

Coruncanius, *Fragments*: Viarengo, G. (2019) 'Tiberius Corunicianus' in Bottiglieri, A., A Manzo, F. Nasti and G. Viarengo *Antiquissima iuris sapientia*. Rome: 167–89.

Crantor of Soli, *Fragments*: Mette, H.J. (1984) 'Zwei Akademiker heute: Krantor von Soloi und Arkesilaus von Pitane', *Lustrum* 26: 7–43.

Crates of Mallus, *Fragments*: Broggiato, M. (2001) *Cratete di Mallo. I frammenti*. La Spezia.

Crates of Thebes, *Fragments*: in Giannantoni (1990), vol. 2, 523–75.

Critolaus of Phaselis, *Fragments*: Wehrli, F. (1969b) *Hieronymos von Rhodos. Kritolaos und seine Schüler. Rückblick: Der Peripatos in vorchristlicher Zeit. Register*, 2nd ed. Basel.

David, *Introduction*: in Busse, A. (ed.) (1904) *Davidis Prolegomena philosophiae et In Porphyrii isagogen commentarium*. CAG 18.2. Berlin: 1–79.

Digest: in Mommsen, T. (ed.) (1911) *Corpus iuris civilis* 1, 12th ed. Berlin.
Diogenes of Sinope, *Fragments*: in Giannantoni (1990), vol. 2, 227–509.
Diogenes Laertius: Dorandi, T. (ed.) (2013) *Diogenes Laertius. Lives of Eminent Philosophers*. Cambridge.
Diomedes, *Science of Grammar*: in Keil, H. (ed.) (1857) *Grammatici Latini* 1. Leipzig: 297–590.
Dionysius of Halicarnassus, *Roman Antiquities*: Jacoby, C. (ed.) (1885–1925) *Dionysi Halicarnasensis Antiquitatum Romanarum quae supersunt*. Leipzig.
Dionysius Thrax, *The Science of Grammar*: Pecorella, G.B. (ed.) (1962) *Dionisio Trace. ΤΕΧΝΕ ΓΡΑΜΜΑΤΙΚΗ*. Bologna.
[Dionysius Thrax] *Scholia on Dionysius Thrax:* Hilgard, A. (ed.) (1901) *Scholia in Dionysii Thracis Artem grammaticam*. Grammatici graeci 1.3. Leipzig.
Epicurus, *Fragments*: Usener, H. (1887) *Epicurea*. Leipzig.
Epiphanius, *On Faith*: in Holl, K. and J. Dummer (eds) (1985) *Epiphanius 3: Panarion haer. 65–80, De fide*, 2nd ed. Berlin: 496–526.
Eudorus of Alexandria, *Fragments*: Mazzarelli, C. (1985) 'Raccolta e interpretazione delle testimonianze e dei frammenti del medioplatonico Eudoro di Alessandria', *Rivista di filosofia neoscolastica* 77: 197–209, 535–55.
Eusebius of Casarea, *Preparation for the Gospel*: Mras, K. (ed.) (1954) *Eusebius Werke 8: Die Praeparatio evangelica*. Berlin.
Eustathius of Thessalonica, *Commentary on the Odyssey*: Stallbaum, J.G. (ed.) (1826) *Eustathii Archiepiscopi Thessalonicensis Commentarii ad Homeri Odysseam* 2. Leipzig.
Gaius, *Teaching Manual*: Seckel, E. and B. Kübler (eds) (1939) *Gai Institutiones*, 8th ed. Leipzig.
Gellius, *Attic Nights*: Holford-Strevens, L. (ed.) (2020) *Auli Gellii Noctes Atticae libri*. Oxford.
Hecato, *Fragments*: Gomoll, H. (1933) *Der stoische Philosoph Hekaton*. Leipzig-Borsdorf.
Hermagoras of Temnos, *Fragments*: Matthes, D. (1962) *Hermagorae Temnitae testimonia et fragmenta*. Leipzig, and Woerther, F. (2012) *Hermagoras. Fragments et témoignages*. Paris.
[Hippolytus of Rome?], *Refutation of All Heresies*: Litwa, M.D. (ed., tr.) (2016) *Refutation of all heresies*. Atlanta.
Isidorus of Sevilla, *Etymology*: Lindsay, W.M. (ed.) (1911) *Isidori Hispalensis episcopi Etymologiarum sive originum libri xx*. Oxford.
Justinian, *Digest*, see *Digest*.
Teaching Manual: in Mommsen, T. (ed.), *Corpus iuris civilis* 1, 12th edn, Berlin.
Juvenal, *Satires*: in Clausen, W.V. (ed.) (1992) *A. Persi Flacci et D. Iuni Iuvenalis Saturae*. Oxford.
Lactantius, *Divine Teaching Manual*: Brandt, S. (ed.) (1890) *L. Caeli Firmiani Lactanti opera omnia* 1. Vienna.
Livy: Livy's work is quoted from the OCT editions.
Marius Victorinus, *Science of Grammar*: Mariotti, I. (ed.) (1967) *Marii Victorini Ars grammatica*. Florence.

Olympiodorus, *Commentary on the Gorgias*: Westerink, L.G. (ed.) (1970) *Olympiodori in Platonis Gorgiam commentaria*. Berlin.

Origen, *Commentary on Matthew*: Klostermann, E. (ed.) (1935–1941) *Origenes. Matthäuserklärung*. Berlin.

Panaetius, *Fragments*: Straaten, M. van (1962) *Panaetii Rhodii fragmenta*, 3rd ed. Leiden, Alesse, F. (1997) *Panezio di Rodi. Testimonianze*. Naples, and Vimercati, E. (2002) *Panezio. Testimonianze e frammenti*. Milan.

Pausanias: Spiro, F. (ed.) (1903) *Pausaniae Graeciae descriptio*. Leipzig.

Peripatetics, *Fragments*: Sharples, R.W. (2010) *Peripatetic Philosophy 200 BC to AD 200*, Cambridge.

Philodemus of Gadara, *History of the Stoics*: Dorandi, T. (ed., tr.) (1994) *Philodemus. Storia dei filosofi*. Leiden.

On Property Management: Tsouna, V. (ed., tr.) (2012) *Philodemus. On Property Management*. Atlanta (Ga.).

On the Stoics: Dorandi, T. (ed., tr.) (1982) 'Filodemo. *Gli Stoici* (PHerc. 155 e 339)', *Cronache ercolanesi* 12: 92–133.

[On Choices and Avoidances]: Indelli, G. and V. Tsouna (eds, tr.) (1995) *[Philodemus]. [On Choices and avoidances]*. Naples.

Plato: Plato's dialogues are quoted from the Oxford Classical Texts (OCT) editions.

Platonists, *Fragments*: Boys-Stones, G. (2017) *Platonist Philosophy 80 BC to 250 AD*, Cambridge, and Dörrie, H. and M. Baltes (1987–1996) *Der Platonismus in der Antike*, Stuttgart.

Pliny the Elder, *Natural History*: Mayhoff, C. (ed.) (1899–1909) *C. Plini Secundi Naturalis historiae libri xxxvii*. Leipzig.

Pliny the Younger, *Letters*: Mynors, R.A.B. (ed.) (1966) *C. Plini Caecili Secundi epistularum libri decem*. Oxford.

Plutarch, *Life of Aemilius Paullus*: in Ziegler, K. (ed.) (1993) *Plutarchus. Vitae parallelae* 2.1, 2nd ed. with corr. H. Gärtner. Stuttgart: 184–222.

Lives of Agis and Cleomenes: in Ziegler, K. (ed.) (1996) *Plutarchus. Vitae parallelae* 3.1, 2nd ed. with corr. H. Gärtner. Stuttgart: 352–415.

Life of Aratus: in Ziegler, K. (ed.) (1996) *Plutarchus. Vitae parallelae* 3.1, 2nd ed. with corr. H. Gärtner. Stuttgart: 264–317.

Life of Cato the Elder: in Ziegler, K. (ed.) (2000) *Plutarchus. Vitae parallelae* 1.1, 5th ed. with corr. H. Gärtner. Munich: 287–423.

Lives of the Gracchi: in Ziegler, K. (ed.) (1996) *Plutarchus. Vitae parallelae* 3.1, 2nd ed. with corr. H. Gärtner. Stuttgart: 416–63.

Life of Pyrrhus: in Ziegler, K. (ed.) (1996) *Plutarchus. Vitae parallelae* 3.1, 2nd ed. with corr. H. Gärtner. Stuttgart: 153–203.

Life of Sulla: in Ziegler, K. (ed.) (1973) *Plutarchus. Vitae parallelae* 3.2, 2nd ed. Leipzig: 131–93.

On the Generation of the Soul in the Timaeus: in Cherniss, H. (ed.) (1976) *Plutarch. Moralia* 13.1, Cambridge (Mass.): 131–345.

Political Instructions: in Hubert, C., M. Pohlenz and M. Drexler (eds) (1971) *Plutarchi moralia* 5.1. Berlin: 58–126.

Sayings of the Romans: in Nachstädt, W., W. Sieveking and J.B. Titchener (eds) (1971) *Plutarchi moralia* 2. Berlin: 70–109.

Pollux of Naucratis, *Thesaurus*: Bethe, E. (ed.) (1900–1937) *Pollucis Onomasticon*. Leipzig.

Polybius, *Histories*: Dindorf, L. and T. Büttner-Wobst (eds) (1889–1905) *Polybios. Historiae*. Leipzig.

Pomponius, *Handbook*: see *Digest* (at. 1.2.2).

Posidonius, *Fragments*: Edelstein, L. and I.G. Kidd (eds) (1972) *Posidonius* 1. *The Fragments*. Cambridge.

Rutilius Rufus, *Fragments*: in *FRHist*. no. 21.

Seneca the Elder, *Controversies*: Winterbottom, M. (ed., tr.) (1974) *The Elder Seneca*. Cambridge (Mass.).

Seneca, *On Benefits*: in Hosius, C. (ed.) (1914) *L. Annaei Senecae de beneficiis libri VII de clementia libri II*. Leipzig.

On Clemency: Malaspina, E. (ed.) (2016) *L. Annaeus Seneca. De clementia libri duo*. Berlin.

Letter(s): Reynolds, L.D. (ed.) (1965) *L. Annaei Senecae ad Luculium epistulae morales*. Oxford.

Sextus Empiricus, *Against the Professors* 1–6: Mutschmann, H. and I. Mau. (eds) (1954) *Sexti Empirici opera* 3: *Adversus mathematicos libros* 1–6, 2nd ed. Berlin.

Against the Professors 7–11: Mutschmann, H. (ed.) (1914) *Sexti Empirici opera* 2: *Adversus dogmaticos libros quinque (Adv. Mathem.* 7–11*)*. Berlin.

Outlines of Pyrrhonism: Mutschmann, H. and I. Mau (eds) (1958) *Sexti Empirici opera* 1: *ΠΥΡΡΩΝΕΙΩΝ ΥΠΟΤΥΠΩΣΕΩΝ*, 2nd ed. Berlin.

Stobaeus: Wachsmuth, C. and O. Hense (eds) (1884–1923) *Ioannis Stobaei anthologium*. Berlin.

Strabo: Radt, S. (ed., tr.) (2002–2011) *Strabons Geographika*. Göttingen.

Suetonius, *Caesar*: Ihm, M. (ed.) (1907) *C. Suetoni Tranquilli De vita Caesarum libri*. Leipzig.

On the Teachers of Grammar and Rhetoric: Kaster, R. (ed., tr.) (1995) *C. Suetonius Tranquilius. De grammaticis et rhetoribus*. Oxford.

Suidas: Adler, A. (ed.) (1928–1938) *Suidae lexicon*. Leipzig.

Tacitus, *Yearbooks*: Borzsák, S. (ed.) (1992) *Cornelii Taciti libri qui supersunt* 1*: Ab excessu Divi Augusti libri I–VI*. Leipzig.

Terence, *The Eunuch*: in Barsby, J. (ed., tr.) (2001) *Terence* 1. Cambridge (Mass.): 305–443.

The Self-Tormentor: in Barsby, J. (ed., tr.) (2001) *Terence* 1. Cambridge (Mass.): 171–303.

Thespis: Pickard-Cambridge, A.W. and T.B.L. Webster (1962), *Dithyramb*. Oxford, and Snell, B., 'Thespis' (1971) in his *Tragicorum Graecorum fragmenta* 1, Göttingen: 61–7.

Timon of Phlius, *Fragments*: Di Marco, M. (1989) *Timone di Fliunte. Silli*. Rome, and Lloyd-Jones, H. and P. Parsons (1983) *Supplementum Hellenisticum*, Berlin: 369–95.

Varro, *Rural Matters*: Flach, D. (ed., tr.) (2006) *Marcus Terentius Varro. Gespräche über die Landwirtschaft*. Darmstadt.
On the Latin Language: De Melo, W.D.C. (ed., tr.) (2019) *Varro: De lingua Latina*. Oxford.
Velleius Paterculus, *Roman History*: Watt, W.S. (ed.) (1998) *Vellei Paterculi Historiarum ad M. Vinicium consulem libri duo*, 2nd ed. Leipzig.
Xenocrates, *Fragments*: Isnardi Parente, M. and T. Dorandi (2012) *Senocrate e Ermodoro. Testimonianze e frammenti*. Pisa.

Secondary literature (including translations of the primary sources)

Abel, K. (1987) '100 Jahre Hekaton-Forschung', *Würzburger Jahrbücher für die Altertumswissenschaft NF* 13: 101–20.
Alesse, F. (1997) *Panezio di Rodi. Testimonianze*. Naples.
(2017) 'Filosofia stoica e classe dirigente romana nel II secolo a.C. Panezio, Blossio, gli Scipioni', in *Philosophari*, ed. P. Vesperini. Paris: 77–88.
Alexander, M.C. (1990) *Trials in the Late Roman Republic, 149 BC to 50 BC*. Toronto.
Algra, K.A. (1997) 'Chrysippus, Carneades, Cicero. The ethical divisiones in Cicero's *Lucullus*', in *Assent and Argument*, eds B. Inwood and J. Mansfeld. Leiden: 107–39.
Altheim, F. (1929) 'Persona', *Archiv für Religionswissenschaft* 27: 35–52.
Althoff, J. and D. Zeller (2006) *Die Worte der sieben Weisen*. Darmstadt.
Ankum, H. (1974) 'Towards a rehabilitation of Pomponius', in *Daube noster*, ed. A. Watson. Edinburgh: 1–14.
Annas, J. (1989) 'Cicero on Stoic moral philosophy and private property', in *Philosophia togata* 1, eds. M. Griffin and J. Barnes. Oxford: 151–73.
(2007) 'Carneades' classification of ethical theories', in *Pyrrhonists, Patricians, Platonizers*, eds A.M. Ioppolo and D.N. Sedley. Naples: 187–223.
Anscombe, G.E. (1958) 'Modern moral philosophy', *Philosophy* 33: 1-19.
Arangio-Ruiz, V. (1970 [1938]) 'La règle de droit et la loi dans l'antiquité classique', reprinted in his *Rariora*. Rome: 231–69.
Archi, G.G. (1970) 'Interpretatio legis – interpretatio iuris – interpretatio legum', *Zeitschrift der Savigny-Stiftung. Romanistische Abteilung* 87: 1–49.
Armgardt, M. (2008) 'Zur Bedingungsdogmatik im klassischen römischen Recht und zu ihren Grundlagen in der stoischen Logik', *Tijdschrift voor Rechtsgeschiedenis* 76: 219–35.
Arnim, H. von (1898) *Leben und Werke des Dio von Prusa mit einer Einleitung: Sophistik, Rhetorik, Philosophie in ihrem Kampf um die Jugendbildung*. Berlin.
Asmis, E. (1984) *Epicurus' Scientific Method*. Ithaca (NY).
Astin, A.E. (1967) *Scipio Aemilianus*. Oxford.
(1978) *Cato the Censor*. Oxford.

Atkins, E.M. (tr.) and M. Griffin (ed.) (1991) *Cicero. On Duties*. Cambridge.
Atkins, E.M. (2000) 'Cicero', in *The Cambridge History of Greek and Roman Political Thought*, eds C. Rowe and M. Schofield. Cambridge: 477–516.
Atkins, J.W. (2013) *Cicero on Politics and the Limits of Reason*. Cambridge.
(2015) 'Zeno's *Republic*, Plato's *Laws*, and the early development of Stoic natural law theory', *Polis* 32: 166–90.
(2018) *Roman Political Thought*. Cambridge.
Audring, G. and K. Brodersen (2008) *Quellen zur Wirtschaftstheorie der griechischen Antike*. Darmstadt.
Austin, J. (1995 [1832]) *The Province of Jurisprudence Determined*, ed. S. Rumble. Cambridge.
Ax, W. (1996) 'Pragmatic morphology: Varro's defence of analogy in Book 9 of his *De lingua Latina*', in *Ancient Grammar: Content and Context*, ed. P. Swiggers and A. Wouters. Leuven: 105–19.
Babusiaux, U. (2015) *Wege zur Rechtsgeschichte: Römisches Erbrecht*. Vienna.
Backhaus, R. (2006) 'Ethik und Recht in Cicero, de officiis 3.12.50ff.', in *Humaniora*, eds B.-R. Kern and others. Berlin: 3–23.
Bakker, F.A. (2016) *Epicurean Metereology*. Leiden.
Baltussen, H. (2016) *The Peripatetics*. Abingdon.
Baraz, Y. (2012) *A Written Republic*. Princeton.
Barlow, J.J. (2012) 'Cicero on property and the state', in *Cicero's Practical Philosophy*, ed. W. Nicgorski. Notre Dame (Ind.): 212–41.
(2018) 'Scipio Aemilianus and Greek ethics', *Classical Quarterly* 64: 112–27.
Barnes, J. (2015 [1986]) 'Is rhetoric an art?', reprinted in Barnes (2015), 80–105.
(1999) 'An introduction to Aspasius', in *Aspasius: the Earliest Extant Commentary on Aristotle's Ethics*, eds A. Alberti and R.W. Sharples. Berlin: 1–50, reprinted in Barnes (2011), 212–60.
(1997) 'Roman Aristotle,' in *Philosophia togata* 2, eds J. Barnes and M. Griffin. Oxford: 1–69, reprinted in Barnes (2015), 359–406.
(2011) *Essays in Ancient Philosophy* 1. Oxford.
(2015) *Essays in Ancient Philosophy* 4. Oxford.
Barnes J. and M. Griffin (eds) (1989) *Philosophia togata* 1. Oxford.
Baronowski, D.W. (2011) *Polybius and Roman Imperialism*. London.
Barsby, J. (tr.) (2001) *Terence* 1. Cambridge (Mass.).
Barta, H. (2010) *'Graeca non leguntur'?* Wiesbaden.
Bauman, R.A. (1983) *Lawyers in Roman Republican Politics*. Munich.
(1985) *Lawyers in Roman Transitional Politics*. Munich.
(1989) *Lawyers and Politics in the Early Roman Empire*. Munich.
(1996) *Crime and Punishment in Ancient Rome*, London.
Beard, M., and M. Crawford (1999) *Rome in the Late Republic*, 2nd ed. London.
Becker, J.C. (1964) 'The influence of Roman Stoicism upon the Gracchi economic land reforms', *La parola del passato* 19: 125–34.
Behrends, O. (1976) *Die Wissenschaftslehre im Zivilrecht des Q. Mucius Scaevola pontifex*. Göttingen.

(1978) 'Institutionelles und prinzipielles Denken im römischen Privatrecht', *Zeitschrift der Savigny-Stiftung für Rechtsgeschichte. Romanistische Abteilung* 95: 187–231, reprinted in Behrends (2004), 15–50.
(1980a) 'Prinzipat und Sklavenrecht', in *Rechtsentwicklung und Rechtswissenschaft*, ed. U. Immenga. Göttingen: 53–88, reprinted in Behrends (2004), 417–55.
(1980b) 'Tiberius Gracchus und die Juristen seiner Zeit – die römische Jurisprudenz gegenüber der Staatskrise des Jahres 133 v. Chr.', in *Das Profil des Juristen in der europäischen Tradition*, eds K. Luig and D. Liebs. Ebelsbach: 25–121.
(1982) *Die fraus legis*. Göttingen.
(2004) *Institut und Prinzip*. Göttingen.
(2008) 'Die geistige Mitte des römischen Rechts. Die Kulturanthropologie der skeptischen Akademie', *Zeitschrift für Rechtsgeschichte der Savigny-Stiftung. Romanistische Abteilung* 125: 25–107.
Benelli, E. (ed.) (2009) *Thesaurus linguae Etruscae 1: Indice lessicale*, 2nd ed. Pisa.
Benferhat, Y. (2005) *Ciues Epicurei*. Brussels.
Beresford, A. (tr.) (2020) *Aristotle. The Nicomachean Ethics*. London.
Berger, A. (1932) 'Tabulae duodecim', *RE* 4A: cols. 1900–49.
(1940) 'Tabulae duodecim', *RE* Suppl. 7: cols. 1275–6.
(1953) *Encyclopedic Dictionary of Law*. Philadelphia (Pa).
Berthold, R.M. (1984) *Rhodes in the Hellenistic Age*. Ithaca (NY).
Bett, R. (tr.) (2005) *Sextus Empiricus. Against the Logicians*. Cambridge.
Bettini, M. (2012) *Vertere. Un'antropologia della traduzione nella cultura antica*. Turin.
Bichlin, R. (1991) 'Über die Geschichte des Hellenismus-Begriffs in der deutschen Historiographie. Leitende Gedanken, Probleme, Perspektiven', in *Hellenismos*, ed. S. Said. Leiden: 363–86.
Bieber, M. (1930) 'Maske', *RE* 14: cols. 2070–120.
Billerbeck, M. (1979) *Der Kyniker Demetrius*. Leiden.
Blank, D. (2005) 'Varro's anti-analogist', in *Language and Learning*, eds D. Frede and B. Inwood. Cambridge: 210–38.
Bleicken, J. (1995) *Die Verfassung der römischen Republik*, 8th ed. Paderborn.
Blom, H. van der (2016) *Oratory and Political Career in the Late Roman Republic*. Cambridge.
Blumenthal, F. von and R. Düll (1937) 'Persona', *RE* 19: cols. 1036–41.
Bod, R. (2013) *A New History of the Humanities*, tr. L. Richards. Oxford.
Boeri, M.D. (2013) 'Natural law and world-order in Stoicism', in *Nature and the Best Life*, ed. G. Rosi. Hildesheim: 183–223.
Boeri, M.D. and R. Salles (2014) *Los filósofos estoicos*. Sankt Augustin.
Bollansée, J. (1999) *Hermippus of Smyrna and His Biographical Writings*. Leuven.
Bona, F. (1973) 'Sulla fonte di Cicero, De oratore 1,56, 239–240 e sulla chronologia dei 'Decem libelli' di P. Mucio Scevola', *Studia et documenta historiae et iuris* 39: 425–80.

Bonazzi, M. (2015) *Il platonismo*. Turin.
Bonfante, G. and L. Bonfante (2003) *The Etruscan Language*, 2nd ed. Manchester.
Boyle, A.J. (2006) *An Introduction to Roman Tragedy*. London.
Boys-Stones, G. (2017) *Platonist Philosophy 80 BC to 250 AD*. Cambridge.
Bremer, F.P. (1898) *Iurisprudentiae Antehadrianae quae supersunt* 2.1. Leipzig.
Brennan, T.C. (2000) *The Praetorship in the Roman Republic*. New York.
Bretone, M. (1971) 'Publius Mucius et Brutus Manilius qui fundaverunt ius civile', in *La critica del testo*, ed. B. Pardisi. Florence: 103–16.
(1982 [1970]) *Tecniche e ideologie dei giuristi romani*, 2nd ed. Bari.
(2008) *Ius controversum nella giurisprudenza classica*. Rome.
Brett, A.S. (1997) *Liberty, Right and Nature*. Cambridge.
Breyer, G. (1993) *Etruskisches Sprachgut im Lateinischen unter Ausschluss des spezifisch onomastischen Bereiches*. Leuven.
Brittain, C. (2001) *Philo of Larissa*. Oxford.
(tr.) (2006) *Cicero. On Academic Scepticism*. Indianapolis (Ind.).
Broggiato, M. (2001) *Cratete di Mallo. I frammenti*. La Spezia.
(2014) *Filologia e interpretazione a Pergamo*. Rome.
Broggini, G. (1959) 'Ius lexque esto', in *Ius et lex*, eds E. Isele, V. Schwander and G. Broggini. Basel: 23–44.
Brouwer, R. (2008) 'On the ancient background of Grotius's notion of natural law', *Grotiana* 29: 1–24.
(2011a) 'On law and equity: the Stoic view', *Zeitschrift der Savigny-Stiftung für Rechtsgeschichte. Romanistische Abteilung* 128: 17–38.
(2011b) 'Polybius on Stoic *tyche*', *Greek, Roman, and Byzantine Studies* 51: 111–32.
(2012) 'Musil's search for ethics', *Monatshefte* 104: 511–26.
(2014) *The Stoic Sage*. Cambridge.
(2015) 'Ulpian's appeal to nature: Roman law as universal law', *Tijdschrift voor Rechtsgeschiedenis* 83: 60–76.
(2017) '"Richer than the Greeks": Cicero's constitutional thought in *Republic* 1', in *Ciceros Staatsdenken*, ed. O. Höffe. Berlin: 33–46.
(2018) 'On the meaning of 'system' in the Common and Civil Law traditions: two approaches to legal unity', *Utrecht Journal for International and European Law*, 45–55.
(2019) 'Funerals, faces and Hellenistic philosophy: on the origins of the concept of person in Rome', in *Persons*, ed. A. Lolordo. New York: 19–45.
(2020a) 'Divine and human will in Imperial Stoicism', in *Fate, Providence, and Free Will*, eds R. Brouwer and E. Vimercati. Leiden: 31–48.
(2020b) 'Socratic ethics and ignorance in the Stoa', in *The Routledge Handbook of Hellenistic Philosophy*, ed. K. Arenson. New York: 107–118.
(2021) 'Cynic origins of natural law?', in *State and Nature in Antiquity*, eds P. Adamson and C. Rapp. Berlin: 159–80.
(unpublished) 'Rhetoric, philosophy and law in the late Roman Republic' (paper presented at the conference 'Rhetoric of Philosophers' at the Czech Academy of Sciences, March 2020).

Brouwer, R. and E. Vimercati (eds) (2020) *Fate, Providence, and Free Will*. Leiden.

Brown, P.G.M. (2014) 'The beginnings of Roman comedy', in *The Oxford Handbook of Greek and Roman Comedy*, eds M. Fontaine and A.C. Scafuro. Oxford: 401–8.

Brunschwig, J. (1995 [1977]) 'Épicure et le problème du "langage privé"', reprinted in his *Études sur les philosophies hellénistiques*. Paris: 43–68.

(1995 [1988]) 'Le problème de l'heritage conceptuel dans le scepticisme: Sextus Empiricus et la notion de κριτήριον', reprinted in his *Études sur les philosophies hellénistiques*. Paris: 289–319.

Brunt, P.A. (2013) *Studies in Stoicism*, eds M. Griffin and A. Samuels. Oxford.

Bryen, A.Z. (2014) 'Law in many pieces', *Classical Philology* 109: 346–65.

Burkert, W. (1960) 'Platon oder Pythagoras. Zum Ursprung des Wortes "Philosophie"', *Hermes* 88: 159–77.

Cairns, J.W. and P.J. Du Plessis (eds) (2010) *The Creation of the ius commune*. Edinburgh.

Camporeale, G. (2003 [2000]) *Die Etrusker*, tr. H. Schareika. Düsseldorf.

Canfora, L. (1989 [1987]) *The Vanished Library*, tr. M. Ryle. London.

Cannata, C.A. (1997) *Per una storia della scienza giuridica europea* I. Turin.

Capogrossi Colognesi, L. (2014 [2009]). *Law and Power in the Making of the Roman Commonwealth*, tr. L. Kopp. Cambridge.

Carcaterra, A. (1966) *Le definizioni dei giuristi romani*. Naples.

Cardauns, B. (2001) *M. Terentius Varro*. Heidelberg.

Cascione, C. (2018) 'Il contesto storico della legislazione decemvirale', in *XII Tabulae*, ed. M.F. Cursi. Naples: 1–30.

Castner, C.J. (1988) *Prosopography of Roman Epicureans*. Frankfurt am Main.

Catana, L. (2008) *The Historiographical Concept 'System of Philosophy'*. Leiden.

Cavarzere, A. (2000) *Oratoria a Roma*. Rome.

Cavazza, F. (1981) *Studio su Varrone etimologo e grammatico*. Florence.

Cerami, P. (1998) 'Il sistema ofiliano', in *La codificazione del diritto dall'antico al moderno*. Naples: 83–119.

Chaumartin, F.-R. (1985) *Le De Beneficiis de Seneque, sa signification philosophique, politique et sociale*. Paris.

Chiusi, T.J. (2005) 'Strukturen des römischen Eigentums im Spiegel rhetorisch-philosophischer Texte Ciceros', in *Was ist Eigentum?*, eds A. Eckl and B. Ludwig. Munich: 59–72.

Christes, J. (1975) *Bildung und Gesellschaft*. Darmstadt.

Chroust, A.-H. (1962) 'The miraculous disappearance and recovery of the corpus aristotelicum', *Classica et mediaevalia* 23: 50–67.

Clarke, M.L. (1971) *Higher Education in the Ancient World*. London.

Cohn, L. (1896) 'Aristophanes aus Byzanz', *RE* 2: cols. 994–1005.

Corbino, A. (2014) 'Caso, diritto e regula. Limiti della funzione normativa del caso deciso nella visione romana', *Revue internationale des droits de l'antiquité* 61: 47–82.

Cornell, T.J. (1995) *The Beginnings of Rome*. London.

Crawford, M.H. (ed.) (1996) *Roman Statutes*. London.
Crivelli, P. (2010) 'The Stoics on definitions', in *Definition in Greek Philosophy*, ed. D. Charles. Oxford: 359–423.
Crönert, W. (1906) *Kolotes und Menedemos*. Leipzig.
Cursi, M.F. (ed.) (2018) *XII Tabulae*. Naples.
Dancy, J. (2004) *Ethics without Principles*, Oxford.
(2017) 'Moral particularism', *Stanford Encyclopedia of Philosophy* (online).
Dawson, D. (1992) *Cities of the Gods*. New York.
De Ste. Croix, G.E.M. (1980) *The Class Struggle in the Ancient Greek World*. London.
Desbordes, F. (1995) 'Les débuts de la grammaire à Rome', *Laelius* 15: 125–37.
(1990) *Idées romains sur l'écriture*. Lille.
Desmond, W.D. (2006) *The Greek Praise of Poverty*. Notre Dame (Ind.).
Dickey, E. (2007) *Ancient Greek Scholarship*. New York.
Dillon, J. (2016) 'The reception of Aristotle in Antiochus and Cicero', in *Brill's Companion to the Reception of Aristotle in Antiquity*, ed. A. Falcon. Leiden: 183–201.
Dillon, J.M. and A.A. Long (eds) (1988) *The Question of 'Eclecticism'*. Berkeley.
Dillon, S. (2006) *Ancient Greek Portrait Sculpture*. Cambridge.
Domingo, R. (2018) *Roman Law*. London.
Dominik, W. (2017) 'The development of Roman rhetoric', in *The Oxford Handbook of Rhetorical Studies*, ed. M.J. MacDonald. Oxford: 159–72.
Dorion, L.-A. (2011) 'The rise and fall of the Socratic problem', in *The Cambridge Companion to Socrates*, ed. D.R. Morrison. Cambridge: 1–23.
Dörrie, H. and M. Baltes (1996) *Der Platonismus in der Antike* 4. Stuttgart.
Dovring, F. and others (eds) (1965 [1951]), *Hugo de Groot. Inleidinge tot de Hollandsche rechts-geleerdheid*, 2nd ed. Leiden.
Droysen, J.G. (1836) *Geschichte des Hellenismus*. Hamburg.
Du Plessis, P. (ed.) (2016) *Cicero and the Law*. Edinburgh.
Du Plessis, P. (2020) *Burkowski's Textbook on Roman Law*, 6th ed. Oxford.
Du Plessis, P., C. Ando and K. Tuori (eds) (2016) *The Oxford Handbook of Roman Law and Society*. Oxford.
Dudley, D. (1937) *A History of Cynicism*. London.
(1941) 'Blossius of Cumae', *Journal of Roman Studies* 31: 94–9.
Düll, R. (1995) *Das Zwölftafelgesetz*, 7th ed. Munich.
Düring, I. (1968) 'Aristotle's use of examples in the *Topics*', in *Aristotle on Dialectic*, ed. G.E.L. Owen, Oxford: 202–29.
Dworkin, R. (1977) *Taking Rights Seriously*. Cambridge (Mass.).
Dyck, A.R. (1996) *A Commentary on Cicero, De officiis*. Ann Arbor (Mich.).
Engberg-Pedersen, T. (1990) 'Stoic philosophy and the concept of the person', in *The Person and the Human Mind*, ed. C. Gill. Oxford: 109–35.
Engberg-Pedersen, T. (ed.) (2017) *From Stoicism to Platonism*. Cambridge.
Erskine, A. (1990) *The Hellenistic Stoa*. London.
(2010) *Roman Imperialism*. Edinburgh.
(2012) 'Polybius among the Romans: life in the Cyclops' cave', in *Imperialism, Cultural Politics and Polybius*, eds C. Smith and L.M. Yarrow. Oxford: 17–31.

Fantham, E. (1997) 'The contexts and occasions of Roman rhetoric', in *Roman Eloquence*, ed. W. Dominik. London: 111–28.

(2004) *The Roman World of Cicero's De oratore*. Oxford.

Faro, S. (2010) 'La maschera è il volto', *Atti dell' accademia Romanistica Costantiniana* 17: 629–48.

Feeney, D. (2005) 'The beginnings of a literature in Latin', *Journal of Roman Studies* 95: 226–40.

(2016) *Beyond Greek*. Cambridge (Mass.).

Ferguson, W.S. (1911) *Hellenistic Athens*. London.

Ferrary, J.-L. (2003) 'La législation romaine dans les livres 21 à 45 de Tite-Live', in *Laurea internationalis*, ed. T. Hantos. Wiesbaden: 107–42.

(2007) 'Les philosophes grecs à Rome (155–86 av J.-C.)', in *Pyrrhonists, Patricians, Platonizers*, eds A.-M. Ioppolo and D.N. Sedley. Naples: 17–46.

(2014 [1988]) *Philhellénisme et impérialisme*, 2nd ed. Rome.

Ferrary, J.-L., A. Schiavone and A. Stolfi (2018) *Quintus Mucius Scaevola. Opera*. Rome.

Festa, N. (1932–1935) *I frammenti degli Stoici antichi*. Bari.

Fink, J. (1952) 'Analogie und Anomalie in der Sprache. Zu Varro De lingua Latina 9, 1', *Hermes* 80: 377–9.

Finkenauer, T. (2012) '[Review of] Barta 2010', *Sehepunkte* 12 nr. 12 (online).

(2014) 'Die römischen Juristen und Gerechtigkeit', in *Recht und Gerechtigkeit*, ed. O. Höffe. Freiburg i. B.: 11–46.

(2015) 'Le 'regulae iuris' come strumenti mnemotecnici', *Index* 43: 15–21.

Fiori, R. (2011) *Bonus vir. Politica filosofia retorica e diritto nel De officiis di Cicerone*. Naples.

(2013) 'Il vir bonus tra filosofia greca e tradizioni romani nel *De officiis* di Cicerone', in *Vir bonus*, ed. A. Lovato. Bari: 19–39.

(2014) 'The *vir bonus* in Cicero's *De officiis*: Greek philosophy and Roman legal science', in *Aequum ius*. Moscow: 187–202.

Flach, D. (2004) *Das Zwölftafelgesetz*. Darmstadt.

Flower, H.I. (1996) *Ancestor Masks and Aristocratic Power*. Oxford.

(2010) *Roman Republics*. Princeton.

(2014) 'Spectacle and political culture in the Roman Republic', in *The Cambridge Companion to the Roman Republic*, ed. H. Flower, 2nd ed. Cambridge: 377–98.

Fögen, M.T. (2002) *Rechtsgeschichten*. Göttingen.

Forschner, M. (2001) 'Der Begriff der Person in der Stoa', in *Person*, ed. D. Sturma. Paderborn: 37–57.

(2018) *Die Philosophie der Stoa*. Darmstadt.

Fott, D. (tr.) (2014) *Marcus Tullius Cicero. On the Republic and On the Laws*. Ithaca (NY).

Foucault, M. (2016) *Discours et verité précédé de La parrêsia*, eds H.-P. Fruchaud and D. Lorenzini. Paris.

(2001) *Fearless Speech*, tr. J. Pearson. Los Angeles.

Frank, J. (2005) *A Democracy of Distinction*. Chicago.

Frede, M. (1974) *Die stoische Logik*. Göttingen.
(1978) 'Principles of Stoic grammar', in *The Stoics*, ed. J.M. Rist. Berkeley: 27–75, reprinted in Frede (1987), 301–37.
(1987) *Essays in Ancient Philosophy*. Minneapolis (Minn.).
(2011) *A Free Will*. Berkeley.
Friedländer, P. (1909) 'Persona', *Glotta* 2: 164–8.
Frier, B.W. (1985) *The Rise of the Roman Jurists*. Princeton.
Fuhrer, T. and M. Hose (2017) *Das antike Drama*. Munich.
Fuhrmann, M. (1960) *Das systematische Lehrbuch*. Göttingen.
(1997) *Seneca und Kaiser Nero*. Berlin.
Garbarino, G. (1973) *Roma e la filosofia greca dalle origini alla fine del II secolo A.C.* Turin.
(1984) *M. Tulli Ciceronis fragmenta ex libris philosophicis, ex aliis libris deperditis, ex scriptis incertis*. Turin.
(2003) *Philosophorum Romanorum fragmenta usque ad L. Annaei Senecae aetatem*. Bologna.
Garber, D. (2016) 'Why the scientific revolution wasn't a scientific revolution and why it matters', in *Kuhn's Structure of Scientific Revolutions at Fifty*, eds R.J. Richards and L. Daston. Chicago: 115–48.
Garcea, A. (2012) *Caesar's De analogia*. Oxford.
Garnsey, P. (2007) *Thinking about Property*. Cambridge.
(2017) 'Property and its limits: historical analysis', in *La propriété et ses limites/Der Eigentum und seine Grenzen*, eds B. Winiger and others. Stuttgart: 12–38.
Garnsey, P. and C. Whittaker (eds) (1978) *Imperialism in the Ancient World*. Cambridge.
Giglio, F. (2018) 'The jurist's mind' (unpublished inaugural lecture at the University of Surrey, October 2018).
Gigon, O. (1987) *Aristotelis opera volumen tertium: librorum deperditorum fragmenta*. Berlin.
Gill, C. (1988) 'Personhood and personality: the four-*personae* theory in Cicero, *De officiis* 1', *Oxford Studies in Ancient Philosophy* 6: 169–99.
(2009) 'Ancient concepts of personal identity', in *The Oxford Handbook of Hellenic Studies*, eds G. Boys-Stones and others. Oxford: 260–70.
Giltay, J. (2016) 'Greek philosophy and classical Roman law', in *The Oxford Handbook of Roman Law and Society*, eds P. du Plessis, C. Ando and K. Tuori. Oxford: 188–99.
Glare, P.G.W. (2012) *Oxford Latin Dictionary*, 2nd ed. Oxford.
Glenn, H.P. (2014) *Legal Traditions in the World*, 5th ed. Oxford.
Glucker, J. (1988) 'Cicero's philosophical affiliations', in *The Question of "Eclecticism"*, eds J.M. Dillon and A.A. Long. Berkeley: 34–69.
(1992) 'Critolaus' scale and Philo', *Classical Quarterly* 42: 142–6.
Gomoll, H. (1933) *Der stoische Philosoph Hekaton*. Borsdorf-Leipzig.
Gottschalk, H.B. (1987) 'Aristotelian philosophy in the Roman world from the time of Cicero to the end of the second century AD', in *Aufstieg und Niedergang der römischen Welt 2.36.2*, ed. W. Haase. Berlin: 1079–174.

Goulet-Cazé, M.-O. (1993) 'Le mouvement cynique et les Romains: attraction et repulsion', in *Le cynisme ancien et ses prolongements*, eds M.-O. Goulet-Cazé and R. Goulet. Paris: 241–58.
Graver, M. (2002) *Cicero on the Emotions*, Chicago.
(2007) *Stoicism and Emotion*. Chicago.
Green, P. (tr.) (1974) *Juvenal. Sixteen Satires*, 2nd ed, Harmondsworth.
Griffin, M. (2015) *Aristotle's Categories in the Early Roman Empire*. Oxford.
Griffin, M. (2008) '*Iure plectimur*. The Roman critique of Roman imperialism', in *East & West*, eds T.C. Brennan and H.I. Flower. Cambridge (Mass.): 85–110.
(2013a) 'Latin philosophy and Roman law', in *Politeia in Greek and Roman Philosophy*, eds V. Harte and M. Lane. Cambridge: 96–116.
(2013b) *Seneca on Society*. Oxford.
(2017) 'Dignity in Roman and Stoic thought', in *Dignity*, ed. R. Debes. New York: 47–65.
Griffin, M. and J. Barnes (eds) (1997) *Philosophia togata* 2. Oxford.
Griffith, T. (tr.) (2000) *Plato. The Republic*, ed. G.R.F. Ferrari. Cambridge.
(tr.) (2016) *Plato. The Laws*, ed. M. Schofield. Cambridge.
Grimal, P. (1975) *Le siècle des Scipions*. Paris.
Grotius, H. (1618) *Mare liberum* [Eng.: *The Free Sea*]. Leiden.
Introduction to the Study of the Law of Holland: see Dovring and others (1965) and Lee (1953).
On the Right of Booty: Hamaker, H.G. (ed.) (1868) *Hugonis Grotii De jure praedae commentarius*. The Hague.
Guarino, A. (1969) 'Noterelle Pomponiane', *Labeo* 15: 102–7.
(1981) *La coerenza di Publio Mucio*. Naples.
Gudeman, A. (1934) *Aristoteles. ΠΕΡΙ ΠΟΙΗΤΙΚΗΣ*. Berlin.
Guibal, M.-P. (1937) *De l'influence de la philosophie sur le droit romain et la jurisprudence de l'époque classique*. Paris.
Gwynn, A. (1926) *Roman Education from Cicero to Quintilian*. Oxford.
Habicht, C. (1990) *Cicero the Politician*. Baltimore (MD).
Habinek, T. (2005) *Ancient Rhetoric and Oratory*. Oxford.
Hadot, I. (1970) 'Tradition stoïcienne et idées politiques au temps des Gracques', *Revue des études latines* 48: 133–79.
Hadot, P. (2002) *Exercises spirituels et philosophie antique*, 4th ed. Paris.
Hager, P. (1998) 'System', in *Historisches Wörterbuch der Philosophie* 10, eds J. Ritter and K. Gründer. Basel: cols. 824–5.
Hahm, D.E. (2007) 'Critolaus and late Hellenistic Peripatetic philosophy', in *Pyrrhonists, Patricians, Platonizers*, eds A.-M. Ioppolo and D.N. Sedley. Naples: 47–101.
Hard, R. (2012) *Diogenes the Cynic*. Oxford.
Hardie, W.F.R. (1965) 'The final good in Aristotle's ethics', *Philosophy* 40: 277–95.
Harries, J. (2006) *Cicero and the Jurists*. London.
(2007) *Law and Crime in the Roman World*. Cambridge.
Hart, H.L.A (2012 [1961]) *The Concept of Law*. 3rd ed. Oxford.

Hatzimichali, M. (2011) *Potamo of Alexandria and the Emergence of Eclecticism in Late Hellenistic Philosophy*. Cambridge.

(2013) 'The texts of Plato and Aristotle in the first century BC', in *Aristotle, Plato and Pythagoreanism in the First Century BC*, ed. M. Schofield. Cambridge: 1–27.

(2016) 'Andronicus of Rhodes and the construction of the Aristotelian corpus', in *Brill's Companion to the Reception of Aristotle in Antiquity*, ed. A. Falcon. Leiden: 81–100.

Haynes, S. (1963) 'Ludiones etruriae', in *Festschrift Harald Keller*. Darmstadt: 13–21.

Helmer, É. (ed.) (2016) *Richesse et pauvreté chez les philosophes de l'antiquité*. Paris.

Hemelrijk, J. (1925) *Penia en ploutos*. Amsterdam.

Hendrickson, G.L. (1933) 'The *Memoirs* of Rutilius Rufus', *Classical Philology* 28: 153–75.

Heumann, H.G. and G. Seckel (1914) *Handlexikon zu den Quellen des römischen Rechts*, 9th ed. Jena.

Hodge, H.G. (tr.) (1927) *Cicero. The Speeches: Pro lege Manilia, Pro Caecina, Pro Cluentio, Pro Rabirio perduellionis*. Cambridge (Mass.).

Höffe, O. (2017) 'De re publica III: Über Ungerechtigkeit und Gerechtigkeit', in *Ciceros Staatsphilosophie*, ed. O. Höffe. Berlin: 73–89.

Hoetink, H.R. (1955) 'Les notions anachroniques dans l'historiographie du droit', *Tijdschrift voor Rechtsgeschiedenis* 23: 1–20.

Hoffmann, T.S. (2005) 'Die Güter, das Gute und die Frage des rechten Maßes: Platon und das Eigentum', in *Was ist Eigentum?*, eds A. Eckl and B. Ludwig. Munich: 29–42.

(2009) *Wirtschaftsphilosophie*. Wiesbaden.

Honoré, T. (1962) *Gaius*. Oxford.

(1973) 'Legal reasoning in Rome and today', *Cambrian Law Review* 4: 58–67.

(2002) *Ulpian*, 2nd ed. Oxford.

Horn, C. (2018) 'Anknüpfung an die Schultradition', in *Die Philosophie der Kaiserzeit und der Spätantike*, eds C. Riedweg, C. Horn and D. Wyrwa. Basel: 15–18.

Howe, H.M. (1951) 'Amafinius, Lucretius and Cicero', *American Journal of Philology* 72: 57–62.

Humm, M. (2005) *Appius Claudius Caecus*. Rome.

(2014) 'Numa and Pythagoras: the life and death of a myth', in *The Roman Historical Tradition*, eds J.H. Richardson and F. Santangelo. Oxford: 35–52.

(2017) 'La philosophie grecque et les réformes d'Appius Claudius Caecus', in *Philosophari*, ed. P. Vesperini. Paris: 13–75.

(2018) *La République romaine et son empire*. Paris.

Humfress, C. (2015) 'Telling stories about (Roman) law', in *Legalism: Rules and Categories*, eds P. Dresch and J. Scheele. Oxford: 79–104.

Huss, W. (1988) *Geschichte der Karthager*. Munich.

Husson, S. (2016) 'Peut-on être riche et cynique?', in *Richesse et pauvreté chez les philosophes de l'antiquité*, ed. É. Helmer. Paris: 125–46.

Ibbetson, D. (2015) 'Sources of law from the Republic to the Dominate', in *The Cambridge Companion to Roman Law*, ed. D. Johnston. Cambridge: 25–44.

Indelli, G. and V. Tsouna (eds, tr.) (1995) *[Philodemus]. [On Choices and avoidances]*. Naples.

Inwood, B. (2014) *Ethics after Aristotle*. Cambridge (Mass.).

Inwood, B. and L.P. Gerson (2008) *The Stoics Reader*. Indianapolis (Ind.).

Ioppolo, A.M. (1980) *Aristone di Chio e lo Stoicismo antico*. Naples.

Ioro, M. and R. Reisenzein (eds) (2010) *Regel, Norm, Gesetz*. Frankfurt am Main.

Isnardi Parente, M. (1966) *Techne*. Florence.

Jannot, J.-R. (1993) 'Phersu, phersuna, persona. À propos du masque étrusque', in *Spectacles sportifs et scèniques dans le monde étrusco-italique*. Rome: 281–320.

Jörs, P. (1888) *Römische Rechtswissenschaft zur Zeit der Republik* 1*: Bis auf die Catonen*. Berlin.

Johnston, D. (2000) 'The jurists' in *The Cambridge History of Greek and Roman Political Thought*, eds C. Rowe and M. Schofield. Cambridge: 616–34.

Jolowicz, H.F. and B. Nicholas (1972) *Historical Introduction to the Study of Roman Law*, 3rd ed. Cambridge.

Jones, A.H.M. (1972) *The Criminal Courts of the Roman Republic and Principate*, 3rd ed. Oxford.

Jones, G. (ed.) (1973) *The Sovereignty of the Law. Selections from Blackstone's Commentaries on the Laws of England*. London.

Jonsen, A.R. and S. Toulmin (1988) *The Abuse of Casuistry*. Berkeley.

Kacprzak, A. (2016) 'Rhetoric and Roman law', in *The Oxford Handbook of Roman Law and Society*, eds P. du Plessis, C. Ando and K. Tuori. Oxford: 200–13.

Kant, I. (1911 [1785]), *Grundlegung zur Metaphysik der Sitten* [Eng.: *Groundwork of the Metaphysics of Morals*], Akademie-Ausgabe [Ak.] 4. Berlin: 385–483.

Karamanolis, G.E. (2006) *Plato and Aristotle in Agreement?* Oxford.

Kaser, M. (1956) *Eigentum und Besitz im älteren Römischen Recht*, 2nd ed. Cologne.

(1971) *Das römische Privatrecht* 1, 2nd ed. Munich.

(1986 [1978]) 'Zur Problematik der römischen Rechtsquellenlehre', in his *Römische Rechtsquellen und angewandte Juristenmethode*. Vienna: 8–41.

Kaser, M. and K. Hackl (1996) *Das römische Zivilprozessrecht*. Munich.

Kaser, M., R. Knütel and S. Lohsse (2021) *Römisches Privatrecht*, 22nd ed. Munich.

Kaster, K.A. (tr.) (2020) *Cicero. Brutus and Orator*. New York.

Kasulke, C.T. (2005) *Fronto, Marc Aurel und kein Konflikt zwischen Rhetorik und Philosophie im 2. Jh. n. Chr.* Munich.

Kelly, J.M. (1979) 'Gaius noster: substructures of Western social thought', *American Historical Review* 84: 619–48.

Kemp, A. (1987) 'The *Tekhnē Grammatikē* of Dionysius Thrax: English translation with introduction and notes', in *The History of Linguistics in the Classical Period*, ed. D.J. Taylor. Amsterdam: 169–90.

Kennedy, G. (1963) *The Art of Persuasion in Greece*. Princeton.
(1972) *The Art of Rhetoric in the Roman World*. Princeton.
(1994) *A New History of Classical Rhetoric*. Princeton.
Kerferd, G.B. (1972–1973) 'The search for personal identity in Stoic thought', *Bulletin of the John Rylands University Library of Manchester* 55: 177–96.
Kierdorf, W. (1980) *Laudatio funebris*. Meisenheim am Glan.
Klebs, E. (1919) 'Aelius 155', *RE* 1: cols. 535–7.
König, I. (2012) *Die römische Republik*, 2nd ed. Stuttgart.
Kränzlein, A. (1963) *Eigentum und Besitz im griechischen Recht des fünften und vierten Jahrhunderts*. Berlin.
Krauskopf, I. (1985) 'Phersu', in *Dizionario della civiltà etrusca*, ed. M. Cristofani. Florence: 218–19.
Kroll, W. (1940) 'Rhetorik', *RE* 7A: cols. 1039–1138.
Krüger, P. (1912) *Geschichte der Quellen und Litteratur des römischen Rechts*, 2nd ed. Leipzig.
Kunkel, W. (1962) *Untersuchungen zur Entwicklung des römischen Kriminalrechtsverfahrens in vorsullanischer Zeit*. Munich.
(2001) *Die römischen Juristen*. Cologne.
Kunkel, W. and R. Wittmann (1995) *Die Magistratur*. Munich.
La Greca, F. (2016) *Tiberio Gracco e Blossio di Cuma*. Ogliastro Cilento.
La Pira, G. (1935a) 'La genesi del sistema nella giurisprudenza romana [1]', in *Studi in onore di Filippo Virgilii*. Siena: 159–82.
(1934) 'La genesi del sistema nella giurisprudenza romana 2: L'arte sistematrice', *Bullettino dell istituto di diritto romano* N.S. 1: 336–55.
(1935b) 'La genesi del sistema nella giurisprudenza romana 3: Il metodo', *Studia et documenta historiae et iuris* 1: 319–48.
(1936–1937) 'La genesi del sistema nella giurisprudenza romana 4: Il concetto di scienza e gli strumenti della costruzione scientifica', *Bullettino dell istituto di diritto romano* N.S. 3: 131–59.
Lanni, A. (2016) *Law and Order in Ancient Athens*. Cambridge.
Laurenti, R. (1973) *Filodemo e il pensiero economico degli Epicuri*. Milan.
Law, V. (2003) *The History of Linguistics in Europe: From Plato to 1600*. Cambridge.
Lee, R.W. (tr.) (1953) *Hugo Grotius. The Jurisprudence of Holland*, 2nd ed. Oxford.
Leeman, A.D. (1963) *Orationis ratio*. Amsterdam.
Lefebvre, R. (2004) 'Règle et critère chez Épicure', *Revue des études grecques* 117: 82–103.
Lefèvre, E. (2001) *Panaitios' und Ciceros Pflichtenlehre*. Wiesbaden.
Lenel, O. (1889) *Palingenesia iuris civilis*. Leipzig.
Leonardis, I. (2019) *Varrone. Unus scilicet antiquorum hominum*. Bari.
Lesky, A. (1956) *Die tragische Dichtung der Hellenen*. Göttingen.
(1971) *Geschichte der griechischen Literatur*, 3rd ed. Bern.
Lévi-Strauss, C. (1962) *La pensée sauvage*. Paris.
Lewis, C.T. and C. Short (1879) *A Latin Dictionary*. Oxford.

Lewis, J.P. (2013) 'Did Varro think that slaves were talking tools?', *Mnemosyne* 66: 634–48.

Liebersohn, Y.Z. (2010) *The Dispute Concerning Rhetoric in Hellenistic Thought*, Göttingen.

Liebs, D. (1997) 'Jurisprudenz', in *Die Literatur des Umbruchs von der römischen zur christlichen Literatur*, ed. K. Sallmann. Munich: 83–217.

(2002) 'Die vorklassischen juristischen Fachschriften', in *Die archaische Literatur*, ed. W. Suerbaum. Munich: 560–80.

Lipsius, J. (1905–1913) *Das attische Recht und Rechtsverfahren*. Leipzig.

Lloyd-Jones, H. and P. Parsons (1983) *Supplementum Hellenisticum*. Berlin.

Locke, J., *Second Treatise on Government*: in Laslett, P. (ed.) (1988) *John Locke. Two Treatises of Government*. Cambridge: 265–428.

Long, A.A. (1978) 'Dialectic and the Stoic sage', in *The Stoics*, ed. J.M. Rist. Berkeley: 101–24.

(1991) 'The harmonics of Stoic virtue', *Oxford Studies in Ancient Philosophy*. Supplement, 97–116, reprinted in Long (1996), 202–33.

(1996) *Stoic Studies*. Cambridge.

(1997) 'Stoic philosophers on persons, property-ownership and community', in *Aristotle and After*, ed. R. Sorabji. London: 13–31.

Long, A.A. and D.N. Sedley (1987) *The Hellenistic Philosophers*. Cambridge.

Lovejoy, A. and G. Boas (1935) *Primitivism and Related Ideas in Antiquity*. Baltimore (MD).

Lübtow, U. von (1944) 'Cicero und die Methode der römischen Jurisprudenz', in *Festschrift Wenger*. Munich: 224–35.

Luschnat, O. (1958) 'Das Problem des ethischen Fortschritts in der alten Stoa', *Philologus* 102: 178–214.

MacDowell, D.M. (1968) *The Law in Classical Athens*. London.

Macé, A. (ed.) (2012) *Choses privées et chose publique en Grèce ancienne*. Grenoble.

Machek, D. (2016) 'Using our selves: an interpretation of the Stoic four-*personae* theory in Cicero's De officiis I', *Apeiron* 49: 163–92.

Macrae, D. (2017) '"The laws of the rites and of the priests": Varro and late Republican Roman sacral jurisprudence', *Bulletin of the Institute of Classical Studies* 60: 34–48.

Magdelain, A. (2015) 'Ius respondendi' [1950] in his *Jus imperium auctoritas*, 2nd ed, Rome: 103–52.

Malcovati, H. (1976) *Oratorum Romanorum fragmenta liberae rei publicae*, 4th ed. Turin.

Mansfeld, J. (1983) '*Techne*: a new fragment of Chrysippus', *Greek, Roman and Byzantine studies* 24: 57–65.

(1986) 'Diogenes Laertius on Stoic philosophy', *Elenchos* 7: 295–382.

Mantovani, D. (1999) *Le formule del processo privato romano*, 2nd ed. Padua.

(2009) 'Cicerone e il doppio ritratto di Tuberone il vecchio. Sul liber de iure civile in artem redigendo', *Studia et documenta historiae et iuris* 75: 113–30.

(2018a [2012]) *Legum multitudo*, tr. U. Babusieux. Berlin.

(2018b) *Les juristes écrivains de la Rome antique*. Paris.

Manzoni, G.E. (tr.) (2019) *Cicerone. Opere di retorica*. Brescia.
Manuwald, G. (2011) *Roman Republican Theatre*. Cambridge.
(tr.) (2019) *Fragmentary Republican Latin: Oratory*. Cambridge (Mass.).
Marincola, J. (2017) *On Writing History*, London.
Mariotti, I. (ed.) (1967) *Marii Victorini Ars grammatica*. Florence.
Marx, K., *Das Kapital* 1 (1983 [1867]). Marx-Engels-Gesamtausagabe [MEGA] 2.5. Berlin.
Masi Doria, C. (2011) 'Principii e regole. Valori e razionalità come forme del discorso giuridico', in *Tra retorica e diritto*, ed. A. Lovato. Bari: 19–41.
Maso, S. (2012) *Filosofia a Roma*. Rome.
Matthaios, S. (1999) *Untersuchungen zur Grammatik Aristarchs*. Göttingen.
(2001) 'Das Wortartensystem der Alexandriner: Skizze seiner Entwicklungsgeschichte und Nachwirkung', *Göttinger Beiträge zur Sprachwissenschaft* 5: 65–94.
May, J.M. and J. Wisse (tr.) (2001) *Cicero. On the Ideal Orator*. New York.
Mazzarelli, C. (1985) 'Raccolta e interpretazione delle testimonianze e dei frammenti del medioplatonico Eudoro di Alessandria', *Rivista di filosofia neoscolastica* 77: 197–209, 535–55.
McConnell, S. (2014) *Philosophical Life in Cicero's Letters*. Cambridge.
McElduff, S. (2013) *Roman Theories of Translation*. London.
McGing, B. (2010) *Polybius' Histories*. New York.
(2019) 'Introduction', in *Appian. Roman History* 1, tr. B. McGing. Cambridge (Mass.): ix–xxxv.
McKnight, E. (2017) 'Offences against the res publica: the role of public interest arguments in Cicero's forensic speeches', *The Hague Journal of the Rule of Law* 9: 237–63.
Mette, H.J. (1954) *Ius civile in artem redactum*. Göttingen.
(1984) 'Zwei Akademiker heute: Krantor von Soloi und Arkesilaus von Pitane', *Lustrum* 26: 7–94.
(1985) 'Weitere Akademiker heute (Fortsetzung von Lustr. 26, 7-94): Von Lakydes bis zu Kleitomachos', *Lustrum* 27: 39–148.
Metzger, E. (2015) 'Roman litigation', in *The Cambridge Companion to Roman Law*, ed. D. Johnston. Cambridge: 272–98.
Miglietta, M. (2010) 'Servius respondit'. *Studi intorno a metodo e interpretazione nella scuola giuridica serviana – Prolegomena I*. Trento.
Miller, F.D. (1991) 'Aristotle on property rights', in *Essays in Ancient Greek Philosophy 4: Aristotle's Ethics*, eds J.P. Anton and A. Preus. New York: 227–61.
(1995) *Nature, Justice, and Rights in Aristotle's Politics*. Oxford.
Mitchell, R.E. (1990) *Patricians and Plebeians*. Ithaca (NY).
Miquel, J. (1970) 'Stoische Logik und römische Jurisprudenz', *Zeitschrift der Savigny-Stiftung für Rechtsgeschichte* 87: 85–122.
Moatti, C. (1997) *La raison de Rome*. Paris.
(2015) *The Birth of Critical Thinking in Rome*, tr. J. Lloyd of Moatti (1997). Cambridge.

(2018) *Res publica*. Paris.
Möllers, C. (2015) *Die Möglichkeit der Normen*, Berlin.
Momigliano, A. (1941) '[Review of] Farrington, B. (1939) *Science and Politics in the Ancient World*. London', *Journal of Roman studies* 31: 149–57.
(1971) *Alien Wisdom*. Cambridge.
Mommsen, T. (1887) *Römisches Staatsrecht* 2.1, 3rd ed. Berlin.
Montana, F. (2015) 'Hellenistic scholarship', in *Brill's Companion to Ancient Greek Scholarship*, eds F. Montanari, S. Matthaios and A. Rengakos. Leiden: 60–183.
Moore, C. (2020) *Calling Philosophers Names*. Princeton.
Moore, G.E. (1993 [1903]) *Principia ethica*, ed. T. Baldwin. Cambridge.
Moraux, P. (1973) *Der Aristotelismus bei den Griechen 1: Die Renaissance des Aristotelismus im 1. Jahrhundert v. Chr.* Berlin.
Morford, M. (2002) *The Roman Philosophers*. London.
Mousourakis, G. (2007) *A Legal History of Rome*. London.
Mühll, P. von der (1976 [1963]) 'Zwei alte Stoiker: Zuname und Herkunft', in his *Ausgewählte kleine Schriften*. Basel: 359–70.
Mygind, B. (1999) 'Intellectuals in Rhodes', in *Hellenistic Rhodes*, eds V. Gabrielsen and others. Aarhus: 247–93.
Nagy, A. (2017) 'Author and actor. Plotinus and the Stoics on the autonomy of action', *Rivista di filosofia neo-scolastica* 109: 109–30.
Natali, C. (1995) '*Oikonomia* in Hellenistic political thought', in *Justice and Generosity*, eds A. Laks and M. Schofield. Cambridge: 95–128.
Natali, C. and C. Viano (eds) (2014) *Aitia* 2. Louvain-la-Neuve.
Nédoncelle, M. (1948) 'Prosopon et persona dans l'antiquité classique', *Revue des sciences religieuses* 22: 277–99.
Neuhausen, K.A. (2008) 'Kato v. Karneades in Rom (155 v. Chr.): Grenzen des tolerablen Streits zwischen Protagonisten römischer Politik und griechischer Philosophie im Hellenismus', in *Streitkultur*, eds U. Baumann, W. Steiner and A. Becke. Bonn: 31–78.
Neuhauser, W. (1958) *Patronus und orator*. Innsbruck.
Nicholas, B. (1962) *An Introduction to Roman Law*. Oxford.
Nielsen, K.M. (2012) 'The *Nicomachean Ethics* in Hellenistic philosophy', in *The Reception of Aristotle's Ethics*, ed. J. Miller. Cambridge: 5–30.
Nörr, D. (1972a) *Divisio et partitio. Bemerkungen zur römischen Rechtsquellenlehre und zur antiken Wissenschaftstheorie*. Berlin, reprinted in Nörr (2003), 775–850.
(1972b) 'Spruchregel und Generalisierung', *Zeitschrift der Savigny-Stiftung für Rechtsgeschichte. Romanistische Abteilung* 89: 18–93, reprinted in Nörr (2003), 705–74.
(1976) 'Pomponius oder "Zum Geschichtsverständnis der römischen Juristen"', in *Aufstieg und Niedergang der römischen Welt* 2.15, eds H. Temporini and W. Haase. Berlin: 497-604, reprinted in Nörr (2003), 985–1092.
(2003) *Historiae iuris antiqui*. Goldbach.

Nussbaum, M.C. (1986) *The Fragility of Goodness*. Cambridge.
(1988) 'Nature, functioning and capability: Aristotle on political distribution', *Oxford Studies in Ancient Philosophy*. Supplementary Volume, 145–84.
(2000) 'Duties of justice, duties of material aid: Cicero's problematic legacy', *Journal of Political Philosophy* 8: 176–206, reprinted with revisions in Strange and Zapko (2004), 214–49 and in Nussbaum (2019), 18–63.
(2019) *The Cosmopolitan Tradition*. Cambridge (Mass.).
Overgaard, S., P. Gilbert and S. Burwood (2013) *An Introduction to Metaphilosophy*. Cambridge.
Pallottino, M. (ed.) (1968) *Testimonia linguae Etruscae*, 2nd ed. Florence.
Papke, R. (1988) *Caesars 'De analogia'*. Eichstätt.
Paricio, J. (2012) '[Review of] Ribas Alba, J., *Persona*, Granada 2012', *Annali del seminario giuridico dell' università degli studi di Palermo* 55: 443–62.
Pearson, A.C. (1891) *The Fragments of Zeno and Cleanthes*. London.
Pernot, L. (2000) *La rhétorique dans l'Antiquité*, Paris.
Pezzini, G. (2017) 'Caesar the linguist: the debate about the Latin language', in *The Cambridge Companion to the Writings of Julius Caesar*, eds L. Grillo and C.B. Krebs. Cambridge: 173–92.
Phillips, D.D. (2013) *The Law of Ancient Athens*. Ann Arbor (Mich.).
Pickard-Cambridge, A.W. and T.B.L. Webster. (1962) *Dithyramb*. Oxford.
Pierson, C. (2013) *Just Property* 1. Oxford.
Pitcher, L. (2009) *Writing Ancient History*, London.
Pohlenz, M. (1934a) *Antikes Führertum*. Leipzig.
(1934b) 'Cicero de officiis III', *Nachrichten von der Gesellschaft der Wissenschaften zu Göttingen. Philologisch-historische Klasse* I 1: 1–40, reprinted in Pohlenz (1965), 253–91.
(1949) 'Panaetius 5)', *RE* 9: cols. 418–40.
(1965) *Kleine Schriften* 1. Hildesheim.
Pólay, E. (1965a) 'Der Kodifizierungsplan des Julius Caesar', *Iura* 16: 27–51.
(1965b) 'Der Kodifizierungsplan des Pomponius', *Acta antiqua academicae scientiarum Hungaricae* 13: 85–95.
(1968) 'Zur Geschichte der Rechtswissenschaft im republikanischen Rom', in *Gesellschaft und Recht im griechisch-römischen Altertum*, eds M.N. Andreev and others. Berlin: 150–92.
Pöschl, V. (1989) *Der Begriff der Würde im antiken Rom und später*. Heidelberg.
Powell, J.F.G. (2013) 'The embassy of the three philosophers to Rome in 155 BC', in *Hellenistic Oratory: Continuity and Change*, eds C. Kremmydas and K. Tempest. Oxford: 219–47.
Primavesi, O. (2007) 'Ein Blick in den Stollen von Skepsis: vier Kapitel zur frühen Überlieferung des *Corpus Aristotelicum*', *Philologus* 151: 51–77.
Primavesi, O. and C. Rapp (2016) *Aristoteles*. Munich.
Pufendorf, S. von (1672) *De iure naturae et gentium* [Eng.: *On the Law of Nature and Nations*]. Lund.
Pugsley, D. (1993) 'On compiling Justinian's *Digest* 3: The Florentine index', *Journal of Legal History* 14: 94–105, reprinted in Pugsley (1995), 41–52.

(1994) 'Gaius or Pomponius', *Revue de l'histoire des droits de l'antiquité* 41 (online), reprinted in Pugsley (1995), 83–97.
(1995) *Justinian's Digest and the Compilers*. Exeter.
Puhle, A. (1987) *Persona. Zur Ethik des Panaitios*. Frankfurt am Main.
Quadrato, R. (1986) 'La persona in Gaio', *Iura* 37: 1–33.
Ramis Barceló, R. (2013) 'Notas sobre la historia del concepto de persona', *Index* 41: 305–12.
Raubitscheck, A.E. (1949) 'Phaidros and his Roman pupils', *Journal of the American School at Athens* 18: 96–103.
Rawson, E. (1978) 'The introduction of logical organisation in Roman prose literature', *Papers of the British School at Rome* 46: 12–34, reprinted in Rawson (1991), 324–51.
(1985) *Intellectual Life in the Late Roman Republic*. London.
(1991) *Roman Culture and Society*. Oxford.
Reeve, C.D.C. (1989) *Socrates in the Apology*. Indianapolis (Ind.).
Reinhardt, T. (2000) 'Rhetoric in the fourth Academy', *Classical Quarterly* 50: 531–47.
(2003) *Cicero's Topica*. Oxford.
Rheinfelder, H. (1928) *Das Wort 'persona'*. Halle.
Ribas Alba, J.M. (2012) *Persona desde el derecho romano a la teología cristiana*. Granada.
(2014) 'El concepto de persona: culminación de la antropolgía jurídica romana', in *Persona, derecho y poder en perspectiva histórica*, eds B. Perinán and M. Guerrero. Granada: 1–15.
Riesenweber, T. (2019) 'Rhetorische Theorie in Rom: Von den rhetores Latini bis zu Seneca d. Ä.', in *Handbuch Antike Rhetorik*, eds M. Erler and C. Tornau. Berlin: 383–418.
Riggsby, A. (2016) 'Public and private criminal law', in *The Oxford Handbook of Roman Law and Society*, eds P. du Plessis, C. Ando and K. Tuori. Oxford: 310–21.
Rist, J.M. (2020) *What Is a Person?* Cambridge.
Rix, H. (1995) 'Il latino e l'etrusco', *Eutopia* 4: 73–88.
Rohde, E. (1870) *De Julii Pollucis in apparatu scaenico enarrando fontibus*. Leipzig.
Rolfe, J.C. (tr.) (1927) *Aulus Gellius. Attic Nights*. Cambridge (Mass.).
Roller, D. (2018) *A Historical and Topographical Guide to the Geography of Strabo*. Cambridge.
Roskam, G. (2007) *Live unnoticed (ΛΑΘΕ ΒΙΩΣΑΣ)*. Leiden.
Rotondi, G. (1922a) 'L'indice fiorentino delle Pandette e l'ipotesi del Bluhme', in his *Scritti giuridici* 1, Milan: 298–339.
(1922b) *Leges publicae populi Romani*. Milan.
Ruschenbusch, E. (1963) 'Die Zwölftafeln und die römische Gesandtschaft nach Athen', *Historia* 12: 250–3.
Russo, F. (2005) 'Genealogie numaiche e tradizioni pitagoriche', *Rivista di cultura classica e medioevale* 47: 265–90.

Sacchi, O. (2008) '*Phersu*/persona? Contributo per un'etimologia di *prosōpon*,' *Ius antiquum* 22: 26–41.
(2010) 'Persona e diritto romano. Elementi per un'archeologia giuridica del concetto', *Atti dell'accademia Romanistica Costantiniana* 17: 1189–263.
Sachers, E. (1954) '*potestas patria*', *RE* 22: cols. 1046–175.
Sandbach, F.H. (1985) *Aristotle and the Stoics*, Cambridge.
Sanio, F.D. (1845) *Rechtshistorische Abhandlungen und Studien*, Königsberg.
Saunders, C. (1911) 'The introduction of masks on the Roman stage', *American Journal of Philology* 32: 58–73.
Scarano Ussani, V. (1997) *L'ars dei giuristi*. Turin.
Schadewaldt, W. (1973) 'Humanitas Romana', in *Aufstieg und Niedergang der römischen Welt* 1.4, ed. H. Temporini. Berlin: 52–61.
Schäfer, M. (1934) *Ein frühmittelstoisches System der Ethik bei Cicero*. Munich.
Schauer, F. (1991) *Playing by the Rules*. Oxford.
Schefold, K. (1943) *Die Bildnisse der antiken Dichter, Redner und Denker*. Basel.
Schenkeveld, D. (1997) 'Philosophical prose', in *Handbook of Classical Rhetoric in the Hellenistic Period 330 B.C.–400 A.D.*, ed. J.E. Porter. Leiden: 195–337.
Scherillo, G. (1952) 'Note critiche: 3. Quinti Mucii ὅρων liber singularis', *Iura* 1: 180–90.
(1953) 'Il sistema civilistico', in *Festschrift Arangio-Ruiz* 4. Naples: 445–67.
Schiavone, A. (1974) 'Quinto Mucio teologo', *Labeo* 20: 315–61.
(1976) *Nascita della giurisprudenza*. Rome.
(1992) *Giuristi e nobili nella Roma repubblicana*. Rome.
(2012) *The Invention of Law in the West*, tr. J. Carden and A. Shugaar of Schiavone (2005). Cambridge (Mass.).
(2017 [2005]) *Ius. L'invenzione del diritto in Occidente*, 2nd ed. Turin
Schiavone, A. (ed.) (2016) *Storia giuridica di Roma*. Turin.
Schiesaro, A. (2007) 'Didaxis, rhetoric and the law in Lucretius', in *Classical Constructions*, ed. S.J. Heyworth. Oxford: 63–90.
Schiller, A.A. (1978) *Roman Law*. The Hague.
Schlatter, R. (1951) *Private Property*. London.
Schmekel, A. (1892) *Die Philosophie der mittleren Stoa in ihrem geschichtlichen Zusammenhange*. Berlin.
Schmidlin, B. (1970) *Die römischen Rechtsregeln*. Cologne.
(1976) 'Horoi, pithana, und regulae. Zum Einfluß der Rhetorik und Dialektik auf die juristische Regelbildung', in *Aufstieg und Niedergang der römischen Welt* 2.15, ed. W. Haase. Berlin: 101–30.
Schofield, M. (1995) 'Cicero's definition of the *res publica*', in *Cicero the Philosopher*, ed. J.G.F. Powell. Oxford: 63–83.
(1999a) 'Morality and the law: the case of Diogenes of Babylon', in his *Saving the City*. London: 160–77.
(1999b [1991]) *The Stoic Idea of the City*, 2nd ed. Chicago.

(2012) 'The fourth virtue', in *Cicero's Practical Philosophy*, ed. W. Nicgorski. Notre Dame (Ind.): 43–57.

(2013) 'Cosmopolitanism, imperialism, and justice in Cicero's *Republic* and *Laws*', *Journal of Intellectual History and Political Thought* 2: 5–34.

(2018) 'Philosophers and politics in Diogenes Laertius', in *Diogenes Laertius. Lives of the Eminent Philosophers*, tr. P. Mensch. New York: 570–4.

Schofield, M., M. Burnyeat and J. Barnes (eds) (1980) *Doubt and Dogmatism*. Oxford.

Scholz, P. (2015) *Der Hellenismus*. Munich.

Schriefl, A. (2013) *Platons Kritik an Geld und Reichtum*. Berlin.

Schulz, F. (1936) *Principles of Roman Law*, translated from a text revised and enlarged by the author by M. Wolff. Oxford.

(1946) *History of Roman Legal Science*, abbreviated translation by F. de Zulueta of Schulz (1961). Oxford.

(1961) *Geschichte der römischen Rechtswissenschaft*. Weimar.

Schütrumpf, E. (ed.) (2008) *Heraclides of Pontus*. New Brunswick (NJ).

Schwartz, A. (1951) 'Das strittige Recht der römischen Juristen', in *Festschrift Fritz Schulz* 2, eds H. Niedermeyer and W. Flume. Weimar: 201–25.

Sedley, D. (1989) 'Philosophical allegiance in the Greco-Roman world', in *Philosophia togata*, eds M. Griffin and J. Barnes. Oxford: 97–119.

(1997) 'The ethics of Brutus and Cassius', *Journal of Roman studies* 87: 41–53.

(2003) 'The school from Zeno to Arius Didymus', in *The Cambridge Companion to the Stoics*, ed. B. Inwood. Cambridge: 7–32.

(2009) 'Epicureanism in Rome', in *The Cambridge Companion to Epicureanism*, ed. J. Warren. Cambridge: 29–45.

Sellars, J., (2007) 'Stoic cosmopolitanism and Zeno's Republic', *History of Political Thought* 28: 1–29.

(2009) *The Art of Living*, 2nd ed. London.

Sen, A. (1984) 'Rights and capabilities', in his *Resources, Values and Development*. Cambridge (Mass.): 307–24.

Senn, F. (1927) *De la justice et du droit*. Paris.

Sensen, S. (2009) 'Kant's conception of dignity', *Kant-Studien* 100: 309–31.

(2011) 'Human dignity in historical perspective', *European Journal of Political Theory* 10: 71–91.

Settis, S. and C. Gasparri (eds) (2020) *I marmi Torlonia*. Rome.

Shapin, S. (1996) *The Scientific Revolution*. Chicago.

Sharples, R.W. (2008) 'Habent sua fata libelli: Aristotle's *Categories* in the first century BC', *Acta antiqua academiae scientiarum Hungaricae* 48: 273–87.

(2010) *Peripatetic Philosophy 200 BC to AD 200*. Cambridge.

Shields, C. (2014) *Aristotle*, 2nd ed. London.

Sinko, T. (1903) *De Romanorum viro bono*. Krakow.

Sloterdijk, P. (1983) *Kritik der zynischen Vernunft*. Frankfurt am Main.

Smith, C. (2018) 'Varro and the contours of Roman antiquarianism', *Latomus* 77: 1090–118.

Smith, J.E.H. (2016) *The Philosopher*. Princeton.

Smith, R. (1997) *Aristotle. Topics. Book I and VIII*. Oxford.
Smuts, F. (1958) 'Stoïcynse invloed op Tiberius Gracchus', *Acta classica* 1: 106–16.
Sonnabend, H. (1996) *Die Freundschaften der Gelehrten und die zwischenstaatliche Politik im klassischen und Hellenistischen Griechenland*. Hildesheim.
Sonntag, M. (1913) *L. Annaei Senecae De beneficiis libri explicantur*. Leipzig.
Sparshott, F.E. (1978) 'Zeno on art: anatomy of a definition', in *The Stoics*, ed. J. Rist. Berkeley: 273–90.
Stanojević, O. (1977) 'Gaius and Pomponius', *Revue de l'histoire des droits de l'antiquité* 44 (online).
(1989) *Gaius noster*. Amsterdam.
Steel, C. (2006) *Roman Oratory*. Cambridge.
Stein, P. (1962) 'The Digest title, De diversis regulis iuris antiqui and the general principles of law', in *Essays in Jurisprudence in Honour of Roscoe Pound*, ed. R.A. Newman. Westport (Conn.): 1–20.
(1966) *Regulae iuris*. Edinburgh.
(1967) 'Justice Cardozo, Marcus Terentius Varro and the Roman juristic process', *Irish Jurist* 2: 367–74.
(1969) *Roman Law and English Jurisprudence Yesterday and Today*. Cambridge.
(1971) 'The relations between grammar and law in the Early Principate: the beginnings of analogy', in *La critica del testo* 2. Florence: 757–69.
(1978) 'The place of Servius Sulpicius Rufus in the development of Roman legal science', in *Festschrift Wieacker*. Göttingen: 175–84.
Steinbauer, D.H. (1999) *Neues Handbuch des Etruskischen*. St. Katharinen.
Steingräber, S. (1985) *Etruskische Wandmalerei*. Stuttgart.
Stephens, W.O. (ed.) (2006) *The Person. Readings in Human Nature*. Upper Saddle River (NJ).
Stokes, M.C. (1997) *Plato. Apology*. Warminster.
Strange, S. and J. Zapko (eds) (2004) *Stoicism: Traditions and Transformations*. Cambridge.
Straumann, B. (2015) *Roman Law in the State of Nature*. Cambridge.
(2016) *Crisis and Constitutionalism. Roman Political Thought from the Fall of the Republic to the Age of Revolution*. New York.
Striker, G. (1996 [1974]) 'κριτήριον τῆς αληθείας', reprinted, translated by B. Smith, in her *Essays on Hellenistic Epistemology and Ethics*. New York: 22–76.
Stroup, S.C. (2007) 'Greek rhetoric meets Rome: expansion, resistance, and acculturation', in *A Companion to Roman Rhetoric*, eds W. Dominik and J. Hall. Malden: 23–37.
Stroux, J. (1926) *Summum ius, summa iniuria*. Leipzig, reprinted in Stroux (1949), 1–66.
(1934) 'Griechische Einflüsse auf die Entwicklung der römischen Rechtswissenschaft gegen Ende der republikanischen Zeit', in *Atti del congresso internazionale di diritto romano* 1. Pavia: 111–32, reprinted in Stroux (1949), 81–107.
(1949) *Römische Rechtswissenschaft und Rhetorik*. Potsdam.

Suerbaum, W. (ed.) (2002) *Die archaische Literatur*. Munich.
Sunstein, C. (1996) *Legal Reasoning and Political Conflict*. New York.
Sutton, E.W. and H. Rackham (tr.) (1942) *Cicero. On the Orator*. Cambridge (Mass.).
Syme, R. (1939) *The Roman Revolution*. Oxford.
Szaif, J. (2004) 'Naturbegriff und Güterlehre in der Ethik des Aristoteles', in *Was ist das fuer den Menschen Gute?*, eds J. Szaif and M. Lutz-Bachmann. Berlin: 54–100.
Talamanca, M. (1977) *Lo schema 'genus-species' nelle sistematiche dei giuristi romani*. Accademia nazionale dei Lincei 374. Rome.
(1981) 'Costruzione giuridica e struttura social fino a Quinto Mucio', in *Modelli etici, diritto e trasformazioni sociali*, eds A. Giardina and A. Schiavone. Rome: 15–39.
(2009) 'L'oratore, il giurista, il diritto nel *De oratore*', *Ciceroniana* 13: 29–100.
Taylor, D.J. (2015) 'The new Varro and the structure of his *De Lingua Latina*', in *Varro varius*, ed. D. Butterfield. Cambridge: 19–32.
Tellegen-Couperus, O.E. (1991) 'C. Aquilius Gallus dans le discours *Pro Caecina* de Cicéron', *Tijdschrift voor Rechtsgeschiedenis* 59: 37–46.
Tellegen-Couperus, O.E. and J.W. Tellegen (2013) '*Artes urbanae*: Roman law and rhetoric', in *New Frontiers*, ed. P. Du Plessis. Edinburgh: 31–50.
Thamin, R. (1884) *Un problème moral dans l'antiquité*. Paris.
Thomas, P. (2016) 'A Barzunesque view of Cicero', in Du Plessis (2016), 11–25.
Thomas, Y. (2011 [1986]) 'Idées romaines sur l'origine et la transmission du droit', reprinted in Thomas (2011), 69–84.
(2011) *Les opérations du droit*. Paris.
Thonemann, P. (2016) *The Hellenistic Age*. Oxford.
Tièche, E. (1933) *Thespis*. Leipzig.
Tieleman, T. (2007) 'Panaetius' place in the history of Stoicism with special reference to his moral psychology', in *Pyrrhonists, Patricians, Platonizers*, eds A.-M. Ioppolo and D.N. Sedley. Naples: 103–42.
Tierney, B. (1997) *The Idea of Natural Rights*. Grand Rapids (Mich.).
Todd, S.C. (1993) *The Shape of Athenian Law*. Oxford.
Toher, M. (1986) 'The Tenth Table and the conflict of the orders', in *Social Struggles in Archaic Rome*, ed. K. Raaflaub. Berkeley: 301–26.
Tondo, S. (1979) 'Note esegetiche sulla giurisprudenza romana', *Iura* 30: 34–77.
Tornau, C. (2018) 'Rhetorik', *Reallexikon für Antike und Christentum* 29: 1–94.
Trendelenburg, A. (1908) 'Zur Geschichte des Wortes Person', *Kant-Studien* 13: 1–17.
(1910), 'A contribution to the history of the word person', tr. C.H. Haessler of Trendelenburg (1908), *Monist* 20: 336–63.
Tsouna, V. (2007) *The Ethics of Philodemus*. Oxford.
(tr.) (2012) *Philodemus. On Property Management*. Atlanta (Ga.).

Tuck, R. (1979) *Natural Rights Theories*. Cambridge.
(1990) 'Humanism and political thought', in *The Impact of Humanism on Western Europe*, eds A. Goodman and A. MacKay. New York: 43–65.
Tuori, K. (2004) 'The myth of Quintus Mucius Scaevola: founding father of legal science?', *Tijdschrift voor Rechtsgeschiedenis* 72: 243–62.
(2007) *Ancient Roman Lawyers and Modern Legal Ideals*. Frankfurt am Main.
Tutrone, F. (2013) 'Libraries and intellectual debate in the late Republic: The case of the Aristotelian corpus,' in *Ancient Libraries*, eds J. König, K. Oikonomopoulou and G. Woolf. Cambridge: 152–66.
Twining, W. and D. Miers (2010) *How to do Things with Rules*, 5th ed. Cambridge.
Usener, H. (1887) *Epicurea*. Leipzig.
Varvaro, M. (2014) *Der Glücksstern Niebuhrs und die Institutionen des Gaius*. Heidelberg.
Veillard, C. (2000) 'Hécaton de Rhodes', in *Dictionnaire des philosophes antiques* 3, ed. R. Goulet. Paris: 526–7.
(2008) 'Hécaton de Rhodes et la transformation de l'éthique stoïcienne', diss. Aix-en-Provence 2008 [unfortunately not accessible to me].
(2014) 'Comment définir son dévoir? Les enseignements du plan suivi par Panétius dans son *Peri kathekontos*', *Philosophie antique* 14: 71–109.
(2015) *Les Stoïciens 2: Le stoïcisme intermédiaire*. Paris.
Vesperini, P. (2012) *La philosophia et ses pratiques d'Ennius à Cicéron*. Rome.
Viehweg, T. (1974) *Topik und Jurisprudenz*. 5th ed. Munich.
Villey, M. (1945) *Recherches sur la littérature didactique du droit romain*. Paris.
(1951) 'Logique d'Aristote et droit romain', *Revue historique de droit français et étranger* 4.28: 309–28.
(2003 [1975]) *La formation de la pensée juridique moderne*, ed. S. Rials. Paris.
Vimercati, E. (2002) *Panezio. Testimonianze e frammenti*. Milan.
(2004) *Il mediostoicismo di Panezio*. Milan.
Visconti, C.L. (1884–1885) *I monumenti del Museo Torlonia*. Rome.
Vlastos, G. (1983) 'The Socratic elenchus', *Oxford Studies in Ancient Philosophy* 1: 27–74, reprinted in Vlastos (1994), 1–37.
(1991) *Socrates. Ironist and Moral Philosopher*. Cambridge.
(1994) *Socratic Studies*. Cambridge.
Vogt, K. (2008) *Law, Reason, and the Cosmic City*. New York.
Wacht, M. (1982) 'Privateigentum bei Cicero und Ambrosius', *Jahrbuch für Antike und Christentum* 25: 28–64.
Walbank, F. (1979) *A Historical Commentary on Polybius* 3. Oxford.
Waldstein, W. and M. Rainer (2014) *Römische Rechtsgeschichte*, 11th ed. Munich.
Wallace, R.E. (2008) *Zikh Rasna. A Manual of the Etruscan Language and Inscriptions*. Ann Arbor (Mich.).
Walter, U. (2017) 'Legislation in the Roman Republic: setting rules or just political communication?', in *La norme sous la République romaine et le Haut-Empire*, eds T. Itgenshorst and P. Le Doze. Bordeaux: 533–40.

Wardy, R. (1996) *The Birth of Rhetoric*. London.
Waterfield, R. (tr.) (2010) *Polybius. The Histories*. Oxford.
Waterfield, R. (2014) *Taken at the Flood*. Oxford.
Watson, A. (1974) *Lawmaking in the Later Roman Republic*. Oxford.
(1995a) 'From legal transplants to legal formants', *American Journal of Comparative Law* 43: 469–76.
(1995b) *The Spirit of the Laws*, Athens (Ga.).
Watson, A. (ed.) (1998) *The Digest of Justinian*, 2nd ed. Philadelphia (Penn.).
Wegehaupt, H. (1932) *Die Bedeutung und Anwendung von dignitas in den Schriften der republikanischen Zeit*. Breslau.
Wehrli, F. (1969a) *Herakleides Pontikos*, 2nd ed. Basel.
(1969b) *Hieronymos von Rhodos. Kritolaos und seine Schüler. Rückblick: Der Peripatos in vorchristlicher Zeit. Register*, 2nd ed. Basel.
Wenger, L. (1924) 'Hausgewalt und Staatsgewalt im römischen Altertum', in *Miscellanea Francesco Ehrle*. Rome: 1–24.
(1953) *Die Quellen des römischen Rechts*. Vienna.
Wieacker, F. (1944) *Vom römischen Recht*. Leipzig.
(1950) '[Review of] Stroux 1949', *Gnomon* 22: 253–8.
(1953) 'Griechische Wurzeln des Institutionensystems', *Zeitschrift der Savigny-Stiftung für Rechtsgeschichte. Romanistische Abteilung* 70: 93–126.
(1961) *Vom römischen Recht. Zehn Versuche*, 2nd ed. Stuttgart.
(1967) *Privatrechtsgeschichte der Neuzeit*. Göttingen.
(1969) 'Über das Verhältnis der römischen Fachjurisprudenz zur griechisch-hellenistischen Theorie', *Iura* 20: 448–77.
(1970) 'Die römischen Juristen in der politischen Gesellschaft des zweiten vorchristlichen Jahrhunderts', in *Sein und Werden im Recht*, eds W.G. Becker und L. Schnorr von Carolsfeld. Berlin: 183–214.
(1971) 'Solon und die XII Tafeln', in *Studi in onore di E. Volterra* 3. Milan: 757–84.
(1988) *Römische Rechtsgeschichte* 1. Munich.
Wildberger, J. (2018) *The Stoics and the State*. Baden-Baden.
Wiles, D. (1991) *The Masks of Menander*. Cambridge.
Winkel, L.C. (1985) *Error iuris nocet*, tr. K.E. Mittring. Zutphen.
(2000–2001) 'Alcune osservazioni sulla classificazione delle obbligazioni e sui contratti nominati nel diritto romano', *Bulletino dell'istituto di diritto romano* 103–4: 51–66.
(2005) 'Quintus Mucius Scaevola once again', *Fundamina* 11: 425–33.
Wöhrle, G. and O. Hellmann (2011) 'Peripatos', in *Aristoteles Handbuch*, eds C. Rapp and C. Corcilius. Stuttgart: 405–9.
Wolf, J.G. (2015) 'Die XII Tafeln und Magna Graecia', in his *Recht im frühen Rom*. Berlin: 9–20.
Wolff, C. (2015) *L'éducation dans le monde romain*. Paris.
Wood, N. (1988) *Cicero's Social and Political Thought*. Berkeley.

Woolf, R. (2007) 'Particularism, promises, and persons in Cicero's *De officiis*', *Oxford Studies in Ancient Philosophy* 33: 317–46.
(2015) *Cicero. The Philosophy of a Roman Sceptic*. Abingdon.
Wootton, D. (2015) *The Invention of Science*. London.
Zanker, P. (1995) *The Mask of Socrates*, tr. A. Shapiro. Berkeley.
Zarecki, J. (2014) *Cicero's Ideal Statesman in Theory and Practice*. London.

Index locorum

This index contains all passages quoted or referred to. References in **bold** indicate passages translated into English.

General index